The First-Year Experience Monograph Series No. 5

Graduate Students in Transition

Assisting Students Through the First Year

Kenneth A. Tokuno, Editor

National Resource Center for The First-Year Experience® and Students in Transition
University of South Carolina, 2008

Cite as:

Tokuno, K. A. (Ed.). (2008). *Graduate students in transition: Assisting students through the first year* (Monograph No. 50). Columbia, SC: University of South Carolina, National Resource Center for The First-Year Experience and Students in Transition.

Sample chapter citation:

Rapp. K., & Golde, C. (2008). Transitions in context: An overview of U.S. graduate education. In K. A. Tokuno (Ed.), *Graduate students in transition: Assisting students through the first year* (Monograph No. 50, pp. 9-26). Columbia, SC: University of South Carolina, National Resource Center for The First-Year Experience and Students in Transition.

ISBN 978-1-889-271-61-3

Special thanks to Barbara F. Tobolowsky, Associate Director, for project management and editing; to Trish Willingham, Editor, Inge Kutt Lewis, Former Editor, Tracy L. Skipper, Editorial Projects Coordinator, and Dana Fish and Asheley Bice Schryer, Graduate Assistants, for copyediting and proofing; and to Erin Morris, Graphic Artist for design and layout.

Additional copies of this monograph may be obtained from the National Resource Center for The First-Year Experience and Students in Transition, University of South Carolina, 1728 College Street, Columbia, SC 29208. Telephone (803) 777-6229. Fax (803) 777-4699.

Library of Congress Cataloging-in-Publication Data

Graduate students in transition : assisting students through the first year / Kenneth A. Tokuno, editor.
p. cm. -- (First-year experience monograph series ; no. 50)
Includes bibliographical references.
ISBN 978-1-889271-61-3
1. Graduate students--United States. 2. Universities and colleges--United States--Graduate work. 3. Graduate students--Services for. 4. Graduate students--Counseling of. 5. Mentoring in education--United States. I. Tokuno, Kenneth A. (Kenneth Alan), 1947-
LB2371.4.G727 2008
378.1'55--dc22

2008014024

Contents

Preface

Student undergraduate attrition has been one of the most widely studied issues in higher education over the past 30 years. That this is the case is of little surprise. Evidence abounds that the earning of a college degree is important for individuals, as well as for institutions and society; and there are significant economic and social consequences for not doing so. Yet, data from the National Center for Educational Statistics tell us that on average more than 40% of all those who begin in a four-year institution fail to earn their degrees within six years. Little wonder then that an increasing number of books, articles, conferences, position papers, and state and federal reports have turned their attention to the question of what can be done to increase rates of college completion. Everyone now wants to know what works.

It is therefore quite surprising, given the importance of graduate education to a modern technological society that attrition among graduate students has until recently drawn so little attention. This is particularly striking among doctoral students where estimates of attrition are higher than for undergraduate students even though doctoral students, as a group, are more able and more committed to degree completion than are undergraduates. Fortunately, this is beginning to change as more researchers have turned their attention to master's and doctoral student attrition. Some, as do the authors here, are now asking what can be done to improve rates of graduate degree completion.

There are a number of challenges students have to meet to earn their graduate degree. None is more important than the challenge of transition, for all else depends on the student making a successful transition to graduate study and gaining competent membership in a program of study. As is the case for undergraduates, making this transition is more difficult for some students than for others, in particular those from minority backgrounds and from countries whose educational systems are quite different from ours.

Yet, while first-year programs to promote successful transition among undergraduates have long been a staple of institutional functioning, those programs have been relatively uncommon among graduate schools. This book aims to change this state of affairs.

After reviewing theories of transition and the available research on graduate student attrition and persistence, this monograph turns its attention to the important question of what can be done to reduce attrition during the first year. A range of possible strategies is discussed from graduate orientation programs to mentoring and learning communities that require students share the experience of learning together. In these and other chapters, the underlying message is clear, namely, that our capacity to decrease attrition requires institutions to change how they think about graduate education and to institute the kinds of changes at the graduate level that are already taking place at the undergraduate level. If institutions heed this message, graduate education will be the better for it.

Vincent Tinto
Syracuse University
August 2007

► Introduction ◄

Graduate Students in Transition: Assisting Students Through the First Year

Kenneth A. Tokuno

Graduate study is going to play an increasingly critical role in the future of our society. As technology and social complexity increase, the need for more sophistication in our work force will lead to a growing demand for workers with graduate educations. This need will undoubtedly make graduate programs the focus of national concern much as undergraduate education has been in recent years. With the increasing interest, it is likely that we will hear the same type of conversations about graduate education as we have heard about undergraduate study—questions about the value of graduate education given the costs, the need for accountability, and the steps programs are taking to ensure the success of their students. Those universities that take better care of their graduate students will be the ones who are more successful in addressing those concerns.

The history of formal education in the United States reveals a demand for higher credentials. As the 20th century began, it was sufficient to have completed elementary school to obtain a good job. By the start of World War II, the de facto requirement to start a sound career was a high school diploma. Not long after World War II, it became more common for employers to insist on a college degree for the better paying jobs available in what was becoming a service economy. As the 21st century begins, the trend continues. A bachelor's degree is no longer enough for better jobs in this age of information technology. The minimum requirement for many positions is increasingly a master's degree or some other form of postbaccalaureate training.

The demand for master's degrees is reflected in the steadily increasing enrollment at this level of graduate study (National Center for Education Statistics, 2006). During the 2004-2005 academic year, 574,618 master's degrees were awarded. This number has increased by more than 65% since 1990-1991. This rate of growth is about double that of bachelor's or doctoral degrees. As demand for master's degrees increases, the need for individuals with doctoral training to teach and advise master's students will also increase.

However, rather than a steady increase in the number of doctoral degrees conferred, there have been declines in the number of doctorates awarded in some recent years (for example, in 1998-1999 there were 1,933 fewer Ph.D.s awarded than in 1997-1998). While it is true that the overall number of doctoral degrees awarded continues to grow, it is at a much slower rate than master's degrees. In addition to the slower growth, there are also increased concerns that the attrition rate of doctoral students is untenably high at 40 - 50% (Denecke & Frasier,

2005). Holders of Ph.D.s are critical to the generation of new research and innovations in the public and private sectors. Other nations recognize this value and have become increasingly competitive for doctoral students (Yopp, 2003). These symptoms spark concern for the health of doctoral education in the United States.

Attrition concerns are not just at the doctoral level. Yet, efforts to identify the amount of attrition in master's degree programs nationally are rare, so we do not have a clear idea of the extent to which this is a problem for master's students. An informal, national survey of eight master's degree programs, by this author, found a one-year attrition rate of 20% among the more than 10,000 students enrolled—a very high percentage for what is usually a two-year program of study. If this statistic holds true beyond these eight programs, the loss of students at both levels of graduate education is unacceptable.

Clearly, much more is known about the problems of attrition and persistence for doctoral students than master's students as these issues are perceived as much more critical by the academy. In the past two years, the Council of Graduate Schools (CGS) has mounted a major effort, the "Ph.D. Completion Project," to study the problem. This is not the first such call to study the issues around doctoral persistence (e.g., Bowen & Rudenstine, 1992). However, none of the past efforts have considered the problem as one of transition to doctoral study, let alone examined the transition for both doctoral and master's students. A major thesis of this monograph is that attrition at all levels can be firmly addressed by focusing on the transition into graduate study.

The idea that graduate students might require some assistance in making the adjustment from undergraduate study or after a long absence from school has not been asked before. Skepticism of any such need is reflected in the belief that graduate students have already proven themselves to be successful students and, therefore, do not require additional support. Common questions that reflect this basic perception include: Is there really a problem of transition for new graduate students? Since graduate students are already familiar with the college environment, unlike first-year undergraduates, do they need transition assistance? Does their maturity make them more capable of handling change on their own? One of this monograph's goals is to begin to address these questions.

The decades of the 1980s and 1990s saw an impressive national effort to develop programs that help undergraduate students manage the changes confronting them upon entering college for the first time. Different campuses adopted different, yet generally successful, programs for easing these transitions. As complex as this was, the problem of developing programs for graduate students makes the undergraduate transition seem simple by comparison.

For undergraduates, the transition to college is made easier by the similarities across secondary school experiences and the fact that many first-year students start college immediately after high school. It is not the case for a large proportion of graduate students, who may enter graduate programs years after earning their bachelor's degrees. The intervening break creates diversity in terms of age and time away from academic work. Graduate students are also more diverse than undergraduates in terms of their marital status, career status, the kinds of support they will receive, country of origin, and their immediate educational objectives. The campuses in which the students find themselves also vary by discipline, degree level, and administrative structure serving the student, as well as the campus' mission, location, and size. These variables contribute to the diversity of the graduate student experience.

Additionally, programs differ depending on whether the student is in a professional program leading to licensure or certification or a traditional research-based academic program, and whether the program is traditionally offered or offered electronically and asynchronously. Today, many graduate students can complete much, if not most, of their study at a distance from the campus. This is not only due to what is popularly known as distance learning, but the more traditional need to do research in the field or wherever the information or data are. Finally, the element of time is a major consideration. Graduate students may be in the program for as little as one year or more than 10, may be enrolled continuously or have one or more breaks in their studies, and may need to extend study by conducting postdoctoral work.

How can there be any kind of national conversation on graduate student transition when the population that needs to be served is so diverse? To underscore this challenge, here is one more illustration of the complexity of graduate education. Different campuses have different methods for administering graduate programs. Some are centralized from admission to graduation. Some are decentralized to the point of having multiple offices handling graduate student issues depending not only on the discipline but also on the college in which the discipline is housed. Most have something between these extremes. Any approach to assisting graduate students in transition must consider the existing institutional structure and where the responsibility for various services and levels of service lie.

Furthermore, a major distinction needs to be made between the issues of transition for master's students versus doctoral students. The master's student faces a much shorter course of study, involving a lesser commitment of time and resources to earn an advanced degree. On the face of it, this might make the transition seem easier, but that same brevity creates a similarly brief period in which to become adjusted, and a false step early within such an abbreviated program might be fatal to the student's hopes. Many master's degree students are in professional programs resulting in licensing right after graduation, so the initial transition is also part of a professional socialization experience that must also be navigated successfully as they bridge to careers in social work, education, public administration, and numerous other professions.

No single national organization has approached the questions of graduate students' transitions in a comprehensive manner. As strongly as the CGS has advocated on behalf of doctoral students, these efforts look primarily at doctoral students at larger universities with more centralized graduate schools or divisions, which is just a fraction of the graduate student population. On the other hand, the major student services organizations, such as the National Association for Student Personnel Administrators (NASPA), do not make graduate student concerns a major priority. It is time to fill this gap and present a case for the transitional needs of graduate students.

Therefore, an important question to ask is: Who should read this monograph? It is possible that readers of this monograph will be anyone from a university president, who has a special interest in graduate students, to faculty, who are seeking better ways of assisting individual graduate students to become comfortable in their first year of graduate school. It may be read by the staff of a new graduate student orientation program wondering what can be done to assure that the aims of the orientation program persist beyond a brief introduction to the program and campus. It may be read by a dean of students, who is charged with making student support more inclusive of graduate students. The intent of this monograph is to help all such readers and anyone else who might be seeking ideas about how to help graduate students make the transition.

The monograph is divided into two major sections. The first section presents an overview of the current nature, issues, and theories regarding graduate students. The second section presents some ideas about how we can improve the transition into graduate school.

In the first chapter, Kim Rapp and Chris Golde present an overview of graduate education and graduate students in the first decade of the 21st century. They also show how diverse the graduate student population has become and discuss the myriad issues associated with the transition to graduate school. In chapter 2, I discuss relevant theories of transition, from both the viewpoint of developmental theories and theories about the impact of the college environment on students. In chapter 3, Joshua Alexander and Michelle Maher focus on the needs of master's students and share findings from a study about their needs. Chapters 4 and 5 focus on special populations: Miya Simpson considers the challenges facing graduate students of color and the programs that assist them, and then Maureen Snow Andrade presents information on the complex adjustments facing international graduate students.

The second section of this monograph offers a variety of strategies aimed at increasing persistence and reducing attrition by focusing on improving the graduate student experience in the critical first year of transition. Michael Poock's chapter explores the ways in which traditional orientation programs, so successful with undergraduates, have recently been expanded to help graduate students. In chapter 7, Jan Allen suggests a model for a transition course that uses the classroom as a location for providing important information about the graduate program, resources, and graduate-level survival skills. Richard Pratt and I begin chapter 8 by discussing the tradition of mentoring and then suggest how graduate programs can evolve into learning communities to improve the quality of mentoring and, in turn, the entire graduate experience. In chapter 9, Lydia Soleil focuses on another recent innovation, graduate student centers, which serve the specific needs of graduate students. In chapter 10, Leslie Sims looks at an array of graduate transition strategies from the point of admission to those that address long-term retention concerns. In the final chapter, I offer some recommendations culled from the monograph to help guide anyone hoping to create or improve existing programs that address the graduate student transition.

This monograph should be just the beginning of a change in the way graduate programs, graduate schools, and entire campuses see the graduate student experience. We hope that it generates research, stimulates program development, and—most important—increases the retention of graduate students. All of the authors represented here are grateful for the support and vision of the National Resource Center for The First-Year Experience and Students in Transition for enabling this work to be presented.

I would like to acknowledge the contributions of all of the authors with a special thanks to Vincent Tinto for writing a preface on short notice. I also want to thank my supervisor, Peter Garrod, dean of the Graduate Division of the University of Hawai'i at Manoa for his support for this work. Particular thanks goes to Barbara Tobolowsky, associate director of the National Resource Center, for her sustaining wisdom and perspective.

References

Bowen, W. G., & Rudenstine, N. L. (1992). *In pursuit of the Ph.D.* Princeton, NJ: Princeton University Press.

Denecke, D., & Frasier, H. (2005). Ph.D. completion project: Preliminary results from baseline data. *Council of Graduate Schools Communicator, 38*(9), 1-2, 7-8

National Center for Education Statistics. (2006). *Digest of education statistics,* Retrieved October 25, 2007, from http://nces.ed.gov/programs/digest/d06/tables/dt06_255.asp

Yopp, J. H. (2003). Changes in European higher education and their implications for U.S. graduate education. *Council of Graduate Schools Communicator, 36*(10), 2-5.

Overview of Graduate Student Education: Issues, Theories, and Specific Populations

Chapter One

Transitions in Context: An Overview of U.S. Graduate Education

Kim Rapp and Chris M. Golde

While this volume addresses what may be perceived as a common experience for new graduate students—the transition to graduate school—it is important to note that these students are a highly diverse, multi-dimensional group. Consequently, the challenges they face vary widely as a result of personal attributes such as age, race, gender, and other individual characteristics. In addition, the fields and disciplines students enter have their own cultures and expectations, which compound the variety. Then, the many degree types (e.g., M.A., M.B.A., Ph.D.) lead to different personal and professional goals as well. By providing a broad overview of these and other aspects of graduate education in the US, we seek to help the reader situate his or her students and programs in the landscape of graduate education and contextualize the information given in subsequent chapters.

Overview

The story of American graduate education as a whole is one of almost constantly increasing complexity and diversification. In the 19th century, the centers of scientific and scholarly development were found in Europe and, cumulatively, an estimated 10,000 Americans traveled to Germany for advanced study (Berelson, 1960). Today, nearly 150 years after the first doctorates were conferred in the United States, American institutions have become net importers, with nearly one third of all doctoral degrees granted each year going to aspiring scholars from other countries (Hoffer, Hess, Welch, & Williams, 2007). Similarly, master's and professional graduate programs (the education of lawyers, doctors, psychologists, and the like) have grown dramatically. Just in the last 30 years, the number of master's degrees awarded has risen from 316,602 per academic year to well over half a million (574,618). Similarly, professional degrees awarded in medicine doubled between 1950 and 1974, and in 2004 rose to 15,442 (Snyder, Tan, & Hoffman, 2006). One study estimates that within four years of graduation nearly 20% of all bachelor's degree recipients enroll in a master's degree program, and another 7% enter a professional degree program (Perna, 2004).

In the latter half of the 20th century, a more diverse graduate student body developed, prompted in part by the expansion of undergraduate education opportunities after World War II through the G.I. Bill (1944) and federal subsidies to graduate education through the National Defense Education Act (1958), the National Science Foundation, and the National Institutes of Health. Today, public universities subsidize the tuition of about half the doctoral degree recipients in the United States (National Academy of Sciences, 1995). This, together with the wide availability of student loans and tuition subsidies, has helped maintain relatively broad access to graduate education.

The presence of people with a wide variety of backgrounds and a range of reasons for enrolling in graduate school is considered by most to be a great strength of the U.S. postsecondary educational system. However, this diversity can also pose a challenge for faculty and administrators who seek to acculturate these students to the norms and expectations of graduate student life. Recognizing the diversity and variety at all levels of graduate education will help faculty, administrators, and students think more comprehensively about the graduate student experience and more critically about the role acculturation should (or should not) play in it. This, in turn, can help all groups work to facilitate students' transition from undergraduate or work life to graduate school. This chapter first discusses some of the frameworks for analyzing student transition, then describes the status of graduate education in the United States by looking broadly at graduate degrees, students, institutions, and programs. We conclude with suggestions of possible tools for assisting with transitions and, finally, pose questions for reflection and further research.

Why Study the Transition to Graduate School?

Regardless of the type of graduate program or field entered, the transition from undergraduate student or working adult to graduate student can be a difficult one. Psychologists often characterize transition (a short-term life change) as a loss, such as in the case of death, divorce, or job changes (Brammer, 1992). Student transitions to the graduate environment can also be experienced as a loss. In addition to the loss of social support networks experienced by students who leave their homes to take up residence at the graduate institution, new graduate students also experience a loss of identity and power. Students move from being upperclassmen or "adults" to once again becoming first-year students or novices. Many also feel that, in the new and often competitive educational atmosphere, they are intellectual imposters who should not have been admitted to graduate school (Clance & Imes, 1978). The task of managing such stresses and helping students develop effective coping skills often falls to campuses' personal counseling services. However, departments and programs also must claim responsibility for helping their "admits" make the transition through the first year of their programs.

Careful attention to the matter of how students make the transition to graduate school successfully (or not) is important to faculty and academic staff for at least two reasons. First, surprisingly high rates of student attrition have plagued graduate education for decades. One study estimates that at least 40% of students who begin a doctoral program fail to complete it (Golde, 2005). Denecke and Frasier (2005) found that attrition rates may be as high as 50% in some fields. By comparison, attrition rates are much lower in the professional schools: between 5% and 10% in law school (Wilder, 2003) and as low as 2% in medical school (Barzansky & Etzel, 2002). A number of factors are implicated in the high rates of doctoral student attrition, including the difficulty of funding doctoral studies, long time to degree, and an uncertain job market. Research recognizes the importance of the first year in predicting doctoral student persistence and, by extension, highlights the importance of the transition to the management of institutional resources, not the least of which are the money and time lost in high attrition (Golde, 2005; Lovitts, 2001).

Research on undergraduate education demonstrates that students are more likely to complete a bachelor's degree and be changed by the experience if they are well integrated into the academic and social life of their school (e.g., Tinto, 1993). This has also been shown to hold for doctoral degree completion, which is strongly correlated with the extent to which students are integrated into the academic community of their departments (Golde, 2005; Lovitts, 2001). The first year is critical for such integration.

Graduate education is quite different from undergraduate education in its expectations and pedagogical forms. As undergraduates, students are provided a clear list of requirements and expectations necessary for completion of their programs and their individual courses. These students are expected to acquire general knowledge and, in the case of traditionally aged students, mature into adulthood during the college years. Here, course completion is key. However, the "rules of the game" change considerably in graduate school. While courses must be completed, there are also specialized skills and attitudes that must be attained as well. In professional programs, students must demonstrate mastery both cognitively (acquiring knowledge) and in practice (learning skills). They are also expected to assimilate and demonstrate appropriate professional dispositions such as ethical conduct and empathy before completing their programs. Doctoral students should become independent scholars during their graduate school years, developing their own creative intellectual vision and becoming junior members of their disciplinary communities. In effect, once at the graduate level, students must move beyond just excelling academically: They must also assimilate disciplinary (and department) norms and cultures and learn departmental policies. To make this transition even more challenging, the students are usually expected to achieve these goals with little or no institutional guidance (Lovitts, 2001).

Making this transition takes time and can be an overwhelming experience. Undergraduate student orientation programs—many of which now provide information and support throughout the first year—recognize that facilitating transition into an unfamiliar system is, in large measure, about deliberately providing students with maps and tools. Certainly, for doctoral students, and perhaps for other graduate students as well, a similar level of attention to orient them to the informal and tacit norms and expectations of the program would go a long way towards demystifying a process that is often so "opaque that students are distracted from learning" (Golde & Dore, 2001, p. 29). When expectations are unclear, students waste considerable time, energy, and resources, and are at risk for attrition. (See chapter 6 for more information on orientation.)

The second reason to focus on the transition to graduate school follows from the fact that graduate and professional education is fundamentally about preparing students for careers that demand high-level cognitive skills. Many researchers and scholars of higher education view graduate and professional education through the lens of socialization, a theoretical perspective that emphasizes how an individual's beliefs and behaviors are shaped to conform with the norms of the group (in this case a profession or discipline) that the person is joining. Organizational theorists usually propose three stages of the socialization process. The first is the career pre-entry stage, referred to as a period of "anticipatory socialization" in which an individual begins taking on the values and behaviors of the career group even before joining as a member. The second stage, which constitutes formal training, is called "induction" and the third or final stage, "role continuance," is reached when the individual internalizes the new role, and becomes actively engaged with the profession (Corcoran & Clark, 1984, p. 133-5). One way to think of graduate training is as the anticipatory socialization stage of a career. For example, medical students begin to adopt the behaviors of physicians, and doctoral students begin to act like professors while still in their degree programs. Students who have unsuccessfully navigated the transition to graduate training risk not completing their degree programs or entering their professions inadequately socialized. Therefore, even if they do manage to persist to graduation, the students' delayed induction and role continuance may make them unreliable custodians of the field and, thus, affect the profession negatively.

U.S. Graduate Education

Before faculty and staff can provide appropriate supports to graduate students, it is important to understand the wide-ranging landscape of graduate education. This landscape varies in four major ways, in the diversity of graduate degrees, students, institutions, and programs. These different perspectives are of course interrelated, perhaps most clearly by a variety of overlapping purposes. Each of these features of the graduate education landscape has undergone important changes through time, including increased magnitude and complexity. These changes are worthy of exploration in and of themselves, but to keep with our goal of providing information to faculty and administrators seeking to facilitate graduate student transitions, we will focus on the situation at the start of the 21st century.

Degrees

American colleges and universities grant a rather bewildering array of post-baccalaureate degrees, ranging from the familiar (e.g., M.A., Ph.D., J.D., M.D., M.B.A.) to relatively specialized newcomers (e.g., Ed.S., Aud.D., D.A., M.P.H., M.A.T.). Graduate degrees are generally classified into three categories: master's, professional, and doctoral. In terms of the number of students enrolled annually, master's degrees are the largest category, followed by doctoral degrees, and then professional programs. Before looking at the numbers involved, we will discuss degree types.

Master's degrees. Generally one or two years in duration, master's degree programs rest between the baccalaureate and doctoral degrees and incorporate features of each. Like bachelor's degree programs, they are usually heavy on course work, and programmatic requirements and expectations can be summarized into a clear checklist of accomplishments. At the same time, the requirements for the degree in many programs also incorporate experiential or research components and culminate with a thesis or other capstone project, as do most doctoral programs.

Master's programs typically serve one of three purposes. For many students, particularly in the arts and sciences fields, it is a stepping stone to the doctorate. Some students deliberately start with a master's degree to confirm their interests and develop additional skills. Others intend to complete only the master's degree but become excited by the academic aspects of their programs and decide to continue studying towards the Ph.D. (Conrad, Haworth, & Millar, 1993; Katz, 2005). Some doctoral programs prefer that applicants have a master's degree in hand before admission, to provide evidence of accomplishment and promise. Other programs structure graduate studies so that "doctoral student" status is only conferred after master's degree requirements are completed.

The second purpose is to provide a professional credential that serves as the terminal degree destination for a particular field. Large proportions of master's students seeking a professional credential are in business, engineering, and education, but fields as diverse as fine arts, social work, and emerging technology and health fields also offer the terminal master's degree. The coursework in these programs is generally more practitioner-oriented and skill-based than research-oriented or theoretical.

The third purpose of master's degree programs is to enhance the professional development of individuals already working in a particular field. Teachers, for instance, are often encouraged to obtain a master's degree (either to enhance their teaching, increase their salary, or meet certification requirements). Many businesses, particularly those in technology and engineering, subsidize (or even coordinate) access to specialized advanced training for their employees through local universities.

Although the master's degree is quickly becoming the minimum degree requirement for mid-level positions in many industries, within the university itself, the degree is often viewed as "second-class," both in terms of prestige and quality (Conrad, Duren, & Haworth, 1998, p. 65). The existence of this institutional bias often means that master's students feel ignored by department faculty and discriminated against in the distribution of resources, particularly when weighed against the experiences of doctoral or professional school students. Inherently, master's students have fewer opportunities to become part of campus life or the departmental culture because of the relatively short period of time they are on campus compared to either undergraduates or doctoral students. This fact can add to the students' negative perceptions.

Nevertheless, the number and nature of master's degree programs continues to grow for two primary reasons: (a) financial pressures on institutions to increase tuition revenue and (b) political pressure to meet local needs. These programs are likely to be added without hiring additional tenure-line faculty, relying instead on existing faculty, adjuncts, and staff to run the new programs. The speed with which such programs are developed, and their almost inevitable association with "consumerist" trends, also feed into doubts about quality.

Given the diverse purposes and features of master's education, it is nearly impossible to generalize about the master's student experience. This, in turn, poses considerable challenges for those concerned with making the transition into graduate school easier for master's degree students. (See chapter 3 for insight into the master's student experience.)

Professional degrees. Professional degree programs typically prepare students to work in specialized, salaried occupations where entry and conduct are usually governed by accrediting bodies and where the professional is often required to put her or his training to use as an advocate on behalf of a client. Whereas professionals were once trained through workplace apprenticeships, today such preparation is the purview of colleges and universities. Admission into many of these programs is highly competitive and limited, which ensures some congruence between supply and demand.

Although fields such as nursing, engineering, public health, and architecture are widely considered professions, for the purposes of educational statistics the federal government (through the U.S. Department of Education National Center for Education Statistics or NCES) uses a more restrictive definition of 10 "first professional" fields. These include law; theology; medicine; and other health fields of chiropractic, dentistry, optometry, osteopathic medicine, pharmacy, podiatry, and veterinary medicine (Snyder et al., 2006). Law students comprise the bulk of this group (40%), followed by those in medicine (25%) and other health fields (25%); the remainder are in theology (10%; Choy, Cataldi, & Griffith, 2006). Most students enroll in these programs on a full-time basis, and do so soon after finishing their bachelor's degree. Professional degrees are credentials that often lead to lucrative and specialized work, although several additional years of training after academic study may be necessary before full employment begins. Professional programs are highly structured, and, for the most part, accredited and regulated by professional associations. Consequently, the student experience is relatively similar from one university to the next, and professional schools are often administered separately and autonomously from other campus departments/programs.

Customarily, the professional school's academic and student affairs staff, and even career placement staff, are specialized and assume responsibility for student transitions into and out of the programs. The transition into professional education is likely to be the most well thought out and formally organized of all types of graduate education. For example, in addition to acculturating students through coursework and rotations, medical school now usually starts with the formal White Coat Ceremony, in which new students receive a white laboratory coat and, in front of friends and family, recite the Hippocratic oath. This ritual marks the passage from layperson to physician and assists students in their transition from being undergraduate students to being students—and future practitioners—of medicine (Golde, 2006b).

Doctoral degrees. The research doctorate is the highest degree attainable, usually takes the most time, and on a per-student basis may require the most resources in higher education. Holding the doctorate is generally a requirement for teaching at the postsecondary level, although doctoral recipients also work in private industry, governmental, and nonprofit positions. The structure of doctoral programs varies a great deal both from campus to campus and among the disciplines, because the knowledge base and the ways in which knowledge is created and shared in each discipline are unique. The career paths of graduates may lead nearly exclusively to the academy, as in English, or to a broad range of careers, as in chemistry and education. On many other measures—scale of the enterprise, funding patterns, time necessary to complete the program, demographic diversity of students, scope and structure of a dissertation—there is considerable variation among the fields as well (Golde, 2006a).

Traditionally, the Ph.D. (Doctor of Philosophy) is the degree that represents successful completion of doctoral studies and represents the highest level of academic achievement. However, there are other doctorates as well. Most common is the Ed.D. (Doctor of Education), though a lengthy debate—one that shows no signs of resolution—has raged over the distinctions between it and the Ph.D. in education (see for example, Shulman, Golde, Bueschel, & Garabedian, 2006).[1] Additionally, the category of professional doctorates, of which the Psy.D. (Doctor of Psychology) is perhaps the most well known, continues to grow, particularly in health-related fields such as nursing and audiology.

Despite this proliferation, doctoral programs share several features and differ from other levels of education in ways that have particular importance for considering the transition into graduate studies. On average, doctoral studies require eight years of full-time study, though the time to degree is generally lower in the sciences and higher in the humanities fields (Hoffer et al., 2007). At the same time, an average of only one half of those who begin doctoral studies will complete the degree, with attrition rates lowest in the sciences and highest in the humanities (Golde, 2005). Because doctoral students learn to conduct high-quality research and to become independent scholars, doctoral study is usually an individualized, flexible, and open-ended educational experience. But "many students do not clearly understand what doctoral study entails, how the process works and how to navigate it effectively" (Golde & Dore, 2001, p. 28).

In most cases, doctoral study involves taking one to three years of coursework before conducting increasingly independent research, culminating in a written dissertation (either a research monograph or a collection of research papers). Most students are also expected to pass one or more examinations (either called qualifying or candidacy exams) around the midpoint of their programs. Because of their length and highly individual nature, doctoral programs require an enormous commitment from students, often without guarantee of future employment. More concretely, this length and complexity mean that students actually go through a series of transitions—into the doctoral program, from the coursework stage to the research stage, and finally into what is often an extended employment search process that often requires an additional two-to-four years be spent as a postdoctoral fellow—and each one can become a crisis point for attrition (Lovitts, 2005).

Distribution of degree types. According to the U.S. federal government, approximately 2.4 million students were enrolled in graduate or first professional degree programs during the 2003-2004 academic year (Choy et al., 2006), and 690,000 graduate and professional degrees were awarded. By comparison, in that same year, 14.7 million students were enrolled in undergraduate programs and 665,000 associate's degrees and 1.4 million bachelor's degrees were awarded (Snyder et al., 2006).

Sixty percent of graduate student enrollments are at the master's level, while first professional students account for 12%, doctoral 14%, and the remaining 14% includes students in certificate programs (such as in information technology, computer technology, or finance) or enrolled in individual courses without matriculating to a specific program (Figure 1; Choy et al., 2006). The long duration of doctoral programs and relatively high attrition rates among doctoral candidates help account for the fact that the number of doctoral students exceeds the number of first professional students on campus. In terms of degrees granted, however, master's degrees take center stage while doctorates are proportionally diminished (Figure 2).

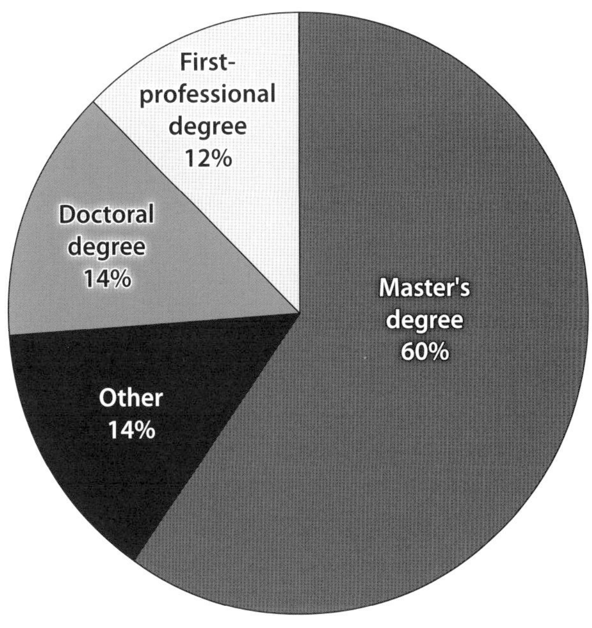

Figure 1. Enrolled graduate students by degree goal, 2003-2004. The category of "other" includes students taking graduate courses without being enrolled in a specific degree program and students enrolled in certificate programs (Choy, Cataldi, & Griffith, 2006).

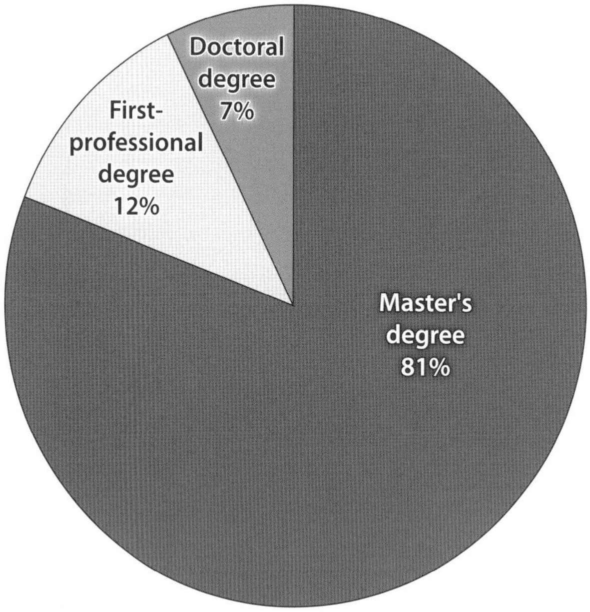

Figure 2. Graduate degrees granted, 2003-2004. Source: National Center for Education Statistics (NCES) Digest of Education Statistics Tables and Figures 2005, Table 246.

Students

Perhaps the most useful approach to understanding graduate school transitions is learning more about the students themselves. They enter graduate study to advance a wide range of personal and career goals, usually with some mixture of the quest for knowledge and understanding and the desire to acquire skills and expertise that translate into a job. In this section of this chapter, we will review the characteristics of graduate students and then focus on several aspects of their attendance patterns.

Demographics

In recent decades, like the undergraduate sectors of American higher education—where 61% of associate's degrees and 57% of bachelor's degrees are awarded to women (Snyder et al., 2006)—more women have been pursuing graduate education. However, gender composition varies a great deal by type of degree (Figure 3) and even more by area of study. Education, for example, is dominated by women at both the master's and doctoral levels. Conversely, engineering and physical sciences are male-dominated while medicine and the biological sciences are relatively balanced.

U.S. racial and ethnic minorities are underrepresented compared to the general population, while there are more international students among graduate students than among undergraduates. (See chapter 5 of this volume for a discussion of international graduate students in the U.S.) Native American students are nearly invisible in Figure 4, comprising less than 1% at any degree level—somewhat less than their representation in the general population (1.5% as reported on the 2000 U.S. Census). In fact, in 2004, only 131 doctorates were granted to

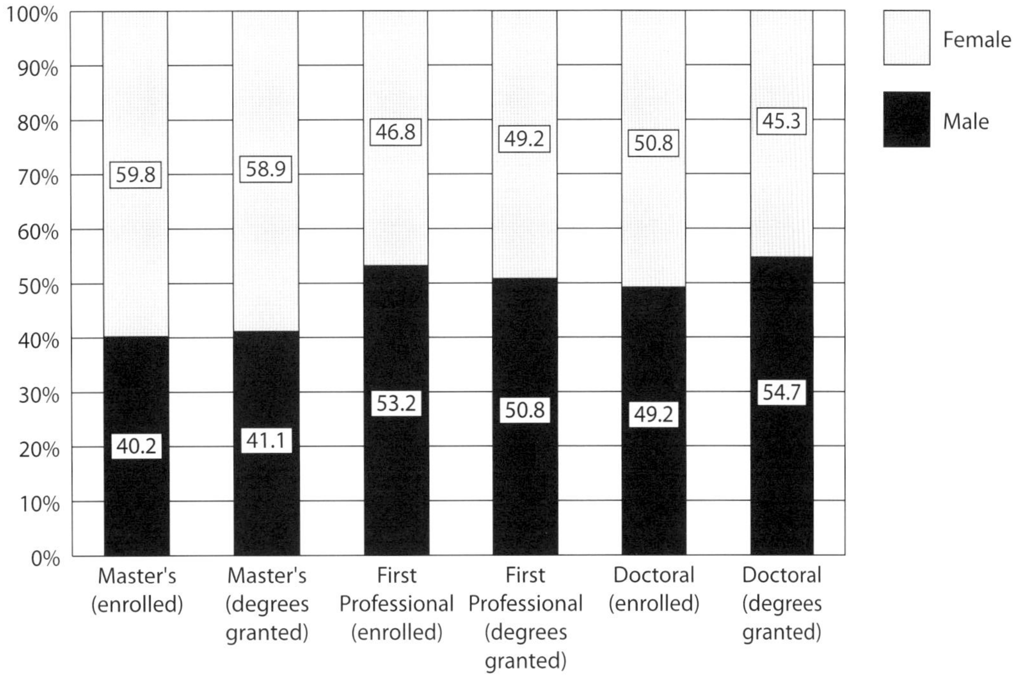

Figure 3. Gender of students by degree category, 2003-2004. Enrollment data from Choy, Cataldi, & Griffith, 2006. Degree data for master's and first professional from National Center for Education Statistics (NCES) Digest of Education Statistics Tables and Figures 2005 (Snyder et al., Table 246). Degree data for doctoral from Survey of Earned Doctorates (Hoffer et al., 2005).

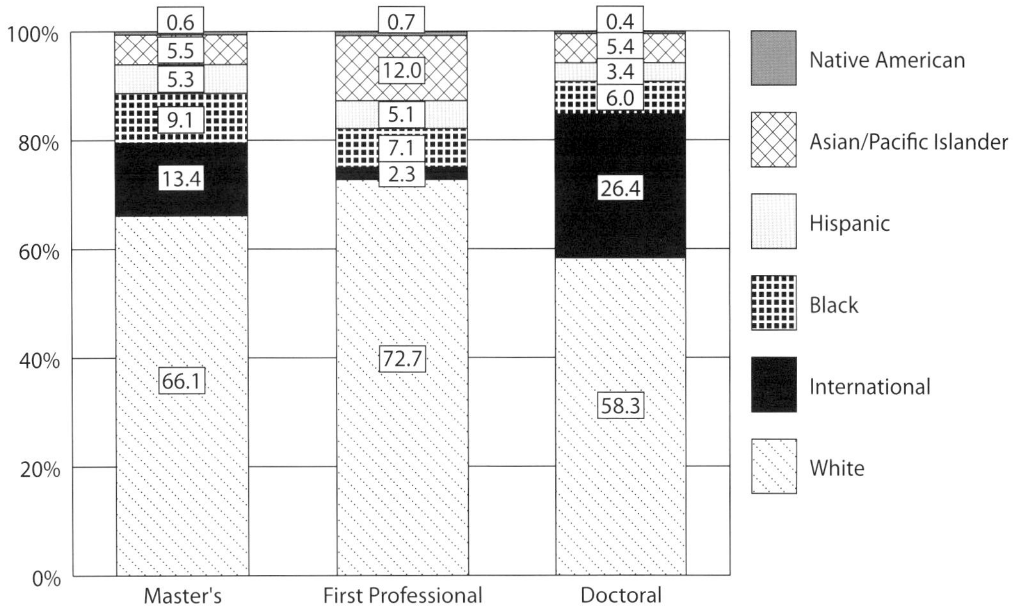

Figure 4. Race/ethnicity and national origin of enrolled students by degree level, 2003-2004. Source: National Center for Education Statistics (NCES) Digest of Education Statistics Tables and Figures 2005 (Snyder et al., 2006, Tables 264, 267, and 270).

Native Americans, one third of them in the field of education. Similarly, 40% of doctorates awarded to African Americans were in education (Hoffer et al., 2005). (For more information about graduate students of color, see chapter 4.)

Most universities assume that graduate students begin their education within a year or two of completing their bachelor's degree, but enrollment and age data belie this conventional wisdom. Twenty-five percent of master's students enroll three to six years after completing the bachelor's degree, and another 30% wait seven years or more. Students pursuing professional degrees tend to start more quickly; two thirds enroll within two years of completing their undergraduate programs. Doctoral students outside the field of education are distributed fairly evenly: About 20% enroll after less than a year; another 20% in one to two years; 30% in three to six years; and the remainder wait longer. In the field of education, however, two thirds of newly enrolled doctoral students are seven years or more beyond their baccalaureate (Choy et al., 2006). The average age for education doctoral recipients is about 42 years old, much older than in other fields (Hoffer et al., 2007). Thus, when planning programs and services to facilitate transition at the graduate level, institutions—and particularly education programs—must be sure to take into account the needs of older students, who are, among other things, more likely to be in partnered relationships and have dependent children. Faculty and staff working in graduate programs might also find it difficult to contend with the different world view and sense of educational purpose evinced by students who have considerable work experience and maturity.

Another measure of the diversity of the graduate student population is parental education. Doctoral recipients, not surprisingly, are much more likely to come from families that are highly educated. More than 25% have at least one parent with an advanced degree, and more than one third come from families in which both the mother and father have a college degree (Thurgood, Golladay, & Hill, 2006). Indeed, the level of parents' educational attainment is a strong predictor of post-baccalaureate enrollment overall (Perna, 2004). This may reflect the greater exposure to and, therefore, understanding of the graduate education enterprise, as well as the greater access to resources to facilitate entry into graduate education that students from highly educated families often possess. Students who do not possess this sort of "cultural capital" may well find the transition to graduate school more challenging.

Fields of Study

One truism of American graduate education is that the number of fields of study continues to grow. The master's level, in particular, is a site of experimentation for new inter- and multi-disciplinary programs and areas. The relative ease of starting a master's program allows universities to respond quickly to emerging intellectual and market needs. Some fields subsequently develop a sufficient theoretical base, set of research questions, and a critical mass of interest and faculty members to "mature" into doctoral-granting fields. In the last 30 years, computer science and neuroscience, aided by the intellectual, research, and career opportunities that accompanied the development of these fields, are two such cases.

Looking at field of study by degree level allows us to see the current distribution of student interest and trends. Among master's degrees granted in 2003-2004, 29% were awarded in education, 25% in business, 9% in engineering and computer science combined, 8% in health-related fields, and the remaining 29% in all other areas (Snyder et al., 2006). Within the professions, 48% were law degrees, 19% were in medicine (M.D.), 6% were theology degrees, and the remaining 27% were in other health professions (Snyder et al.). Doctoral recipients are typically categorized in seven groups in the annual Survey of Earned Doctorates (SED)[2]; the SED for 2005-2006 showed 21% in the life sciences, 16% each in physical sciences and engineering, 15% in the social sciences, 13% in education, 12% in the humanities, and 6% in other fields (Hoffer et al., 2007). As new programs develop, and students gravitate toward particular fields, college and university professionals must anticipate the expectations and challenges that accompany the transition into these courses of study.

Attendance Patterns

In addition to field of study, the distribution of students enrolled full-time versus part-time may have considerable impact on the transition to graduate school. Master's level students are least likely to attend full-time—only 29% do so. Nearly half (46%) attend part-time throughout the entire academic year, and the remaining 25% attend part-time but for only part of the year. Eighty-five percent of professional students enroll on a full-time basis, although theology students are the exception, mostly enrolling as part-time students. Doctoral students in the arts and sciences largely enroll as full-time students (62%), but those in education favor part-time enrollment (72.5%; Choy et al., 2006).

Just as part-time enrollment and commuting to campus are obstacles that are often cited as preventing undergraduate students from deriving all of the benefits of the college experience, graduate education may be less transformative when undertaken on a part-time basis. Part-time enrollment often prevents students from fully participating in the intellectual community of the department and university and can be a contributing factor in failing to integrate into academic life, thus contributing to attrition, especially in the first year (Lovitts, 2001). Planning for the successful transition of part-time students, then, must take into account both logistical and intellectual needs.

Institutions

American higher education is noteworthy in large measure because of the substantial number and diversity of institutions, and because there is relatively little (when compared to other countries) federal control and regulation of them. There are approximately 4,400 accredited colleges and universities in the United States, of which 40% to 50% offer post-baccalaureate degrees. U.S. postsecondary institutions can be broken down into five sectors (Figure 5). The associate's degree-granting institutions comprise 42% of the postsecondary universe, and the bachelor's degree-granting and specialized institutions[3] are small but numerous (Figure 6). Only about 20% of non-specialized institutions concentrate on providing graduate education. The master's degree-granting institutions, typically referred to as comprehensive colleges (most are either former state teachers colleges or baccalaureate institutions that have expanded their missions), comprise 15% of institutions and command 22% of total student enrollment. The doctoral degree-granting institutions make up only 6% of institutions, but they have significant enrollment—28% of all postsecondary students are enrolled at these universities (Carnegie Foundation for the Advancement of Teaching, 2005). Moreover, within this set of less than 300 doctoral degree-granting universities, influence is so concentrated that the 50 largest institutions award 50% of all doctorates in the U.S. (Hoffer et al., 2006).

The number of graduate students enrolled at a particular institution may both influence institutional culture and highlight tensions that surround twin goals of education such as research and teaching, or undergraduate and graduate training. However, other ways of "mapping" institutional variety may have a more direct bearing on questions of transition, including public versus private institutions; the geographic region in which institutions are located; rural versus urban setting; affiliation with a religious institution; and status as a Historically Black College or University.

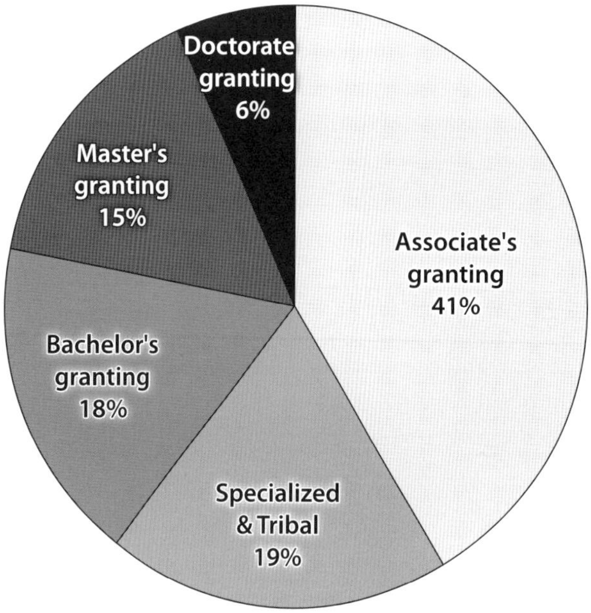

Figure 5. Institutions classified by institution type. Source: Carnegie Foundation for the Advancement of Teaching, Basic Classification Tables, 2005.

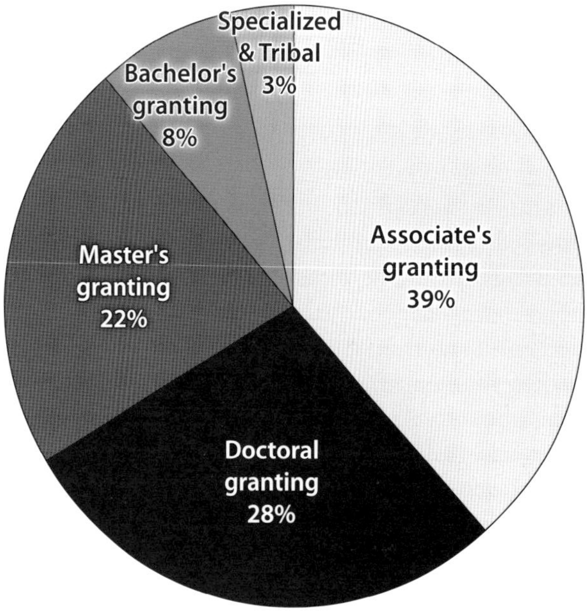

Figure 6. Total student enrollment at all degree levels by institution type. Source: Carnegie Foundation for the Advancement of Teaching, Basic Classification Tables, 2005.

Programs

There is a wide range of program options within each degree type. Unfortunately, there are scant concrete data available to provide a comprehensive record of program variety, but a sketch is possible. The need for continued professional development of working adults, the increasing financial austerity faced by colleges and universities, and the promise of learning technologies, coupled with trends of consumer culture and increasingly busy work and home lives, have fostered a wide variety of scheduling and program structures in graduate education. Scheduling options include the traditional full-time versus part-time enrollment, the now familiar evening and weekend programs, online choices that vary between completing all classes and work online and a mix of on-campus and online meetings, at-work programs that can also be online or on-site but are set up by the employer, and various combinations of these. Some universities also offer "co-terminal" or "fifth-year" degree programs in which students receive both the bachelor's and master's degrees simultaneously (typically in five years, fewer if the student enters with advanced placement credits). While such programs may seek to enable students to become specialists in their chosen field, research has shown that students themselves describe their "fifth-year" master's experience as "an extension of undergraduate education" (Conrad & Rapp, 2003, p. 29).

Programs can also be structured according to pedagogical practices and the learning needs of students. Conrad et al. (1993) have conducted the most comprehensive analysis of master's programs to date, arriving at four program types (i.e., ancillary, career advancement, apprenticeship, and community-centered) based on these and other factors. This classification of program types is important in our discussion of transition, as an understanding of these types may assist new master's students in becoming acculturated to their departments. For example, ancillary programs prepare master's students for doctoral work, but provide them with weak departmental and institutional support because the master's program is subordinate to the doctoral program. Students entering such a program must be prepared to be self-sufficient and, perhaps, to look to doctoral students for advice and mentorship. Career advancement programs are "client-centered" and prepare students for non-university work. Apprenticeship programs are usually academically oriented with strong mentorship—even for master's students—on the part of department faculty, whereas community-centered departments take a dialogic approach to teaching and learning in which faculty and students aim to benefit the broader community through their cooperative disciplinary or professional work (Conrad et al., 1993). Providing such clarity of purpose for individual departments can help graduate students manage their expectations and can help departments provide transparency in graduate recruitment materials. In other words, departments present an honest depiction of the social and academic atmosphere of the department, and thereby increase the ability of prospective students to more accurately determine "goodness-of-fit." This is not to say that one of the program types above, for example, is better than any of the others, but rather that an understanding of the reigning pedagogical culture of a department may increase an incoming student's chance of a successful transition to graduate school, particularly if he or she is deeply aware of his or her learning style and preferences.

The value of taking into account program type and its relationship to student needs can be further illustrated by examining the M.B.A. (Master of Business Administration) degree. Many business schools run three kinds of programs: (a) a traditional full-time M.B.A. program, (b) an evening part-time M.B.A. program, and (c) an executive M.B.A. (EMBA) program. Faculty may be shared between the programs, but the programs differ in at least three significant ways, each of which takes into consideration the needs generated by the students' lifestyles and circumstance. First, the schedules are different. Usually, the traditional M.B.A. program will meet regularly on campus during the day, the part-time program will offer evening and weekend courses; and the EMBA program will meet for a weekend or several days in a row on a monthly basis, most often on campus, but sometimes at another location. Second, the student demographics are different. Traditional day programs generally recruit early career professionals or those directly out of undergraduate school; evening programs are often designed for early- to mid-career professionals who work full-time; and executive programs are usually tailored to the needs of executives and senior managers with significant work experience and 10 or so years of experience in a management position. While the executive M.B.A. curriculum does include traditional coursework, its focus is generally on leadership development, and students draw on their own professional experience as well as that of their cohort. Finally, cost is a major factor in these programs. Although the degree granted to the students in each of these programs is usually the same (M.B.A.), the tuition is often substantially different, particularly for the selective and elite EMBA programs whose tuition costs are often covered by students' employers.

M.B.A. programs also highlight the ways program type can outweigh other factors in influencing the experience of transition. Many returning graduate students must contend with the double constraint of family and work, which impacts how fully and successfully they transition to graduate school. However, when "school" is relegated to one weekend a month, and its locus is not even necessarily on the campus or in the classroom, students' transitions may not be as difficult as in other more traditionally scheduled programs. Some M.B.A. programs tacitly assert that transitions, whether to a new identity or to new ways of organizing their time and work, may be unnecessary for students given their relatively high degree of "pre-socialization" in their chosen profession before matriculating.

Facilitating Transition Into the First Year of Graduate School

Focusing on the responsibility of graduate programs to provide for the socialization of the next generations of faculty members, doctors, lawyers, architects, social workers, and other professionals can highlight the importance of the transition into graduate school. Conversely, examining how graduate schools facilitate (or fail to facilitate) this transition can help identify "the gaps or discrepancies in the socialization process" (Austin, 2002, p. 97). But in both cases, analysis needs to be sensitive to the diversity of graduate programs and students. One university reported that communicating with students during the anticipatory socialization stage (after admission but before matriculation) and introducing them to the culture and requirements of the new graduate program fostered a sense of community among students and provided more realistic expectations of the departmental environment before they even arrived on campus (Taub & Komives, 1998). Such communication may be particularly useful for preparing students entering one- and two-year programs, where there may not be much time to internalize the norms of the department and field before graduation.

In other cases, strategies that have proven effective in one area can be productively applied to another after sufficient modification. Cohort-based programs, in which a class of students enroll in all of the same courses and proceed through the program together, are widely used to create community and provide peer support structures (Barnett & Muse, 1993). Though easier to coordinate in short, standardized programs, cohorts are gradually being adapted to doctoral programs in education (Barnett, Basom, Yerkes, & Norris, 2000). Cohort programs generally benefit institutions by targeting funds at a small set of courses and reducing scheduling problems (Barnett et al.), but as a pedagogic and socialization tool, the cohort structure can greatly benefit students as well. Specifically, effective cohorts may ease transition by providing a sense of belonging, a clear educational purpose, an opportunity to be recognized and valued for one's particular areas of academic strength and expertise, and a built-in support network of faculty and peers. Indeed, high completion rates are a noted outcome of cohort-based programs (Barnett et al.). But disadvantages have been noted as well. The emergence of personal conflicts and feelings of competitiveness among group members have been observed. Also, students who "stop out" of a cohort-based program often encounter difficulties when they attempt to rejoin and complete the program. The main disadvantages of the cohort structure appear, however, to be experienced by the faculty. These include increased workload due to advising obligations and friction between the instructors and demanding student blocs (Barnett et al.). (For more information on cohorts, mentoring, and learning communities, see chapter 8.)

The diversity or even fragmentation of graduate education can make departments inefficient loci of efforts to manage transition. While departments do hold multiple responsibilities, the academic, personal, and professional needs of students call for institution-wide approaches. Most universities do offer campus-wide resources to enhance the graduate experience, at least in terms of student life, through graduate student councils or associations, international centers, and other units. Through these resources, students have the opportunity to build a support network and get information about the university, local communities, and the institutional climate and resources (Terre, 2001).

The interdisciplinary, non-degree granting research program has also been identified as a possible setting in which doctoral students can build social and academic support networks, fostering connections outside of their major departments that can ease their transitions into graduate school and, ultimately, their professions (Rapp-Hanretta, 2005). Increasing graduate student participation in interdisciplinary academic communities as a way to promote student satisfaction and knowledge production is not a new concept (Hartnett & Katz, 1977). However, new research further suggests that such participation can also decrease doctoral student attrition rates (Rapp-Hanretta). Such programs may, therefore, also prove useful for facilitating graduate student transitions.

Conclusion

At this point in the study of higher education, we know much less about graduate students, their experiences, and the overall enterprise of graduate education than we do about undergraduate students and programs. There is still much to learn. Therefore, as we conduct the important work of helping students successfully make the transition to graduate school, we should consider several questions:

- ◇ How do graduate student transitions differ from undergraduate transitions?
- ◇ In what ways do the different structures of graduate programs, including duration of program, enrollment patterns, and curricular structures affect the transition into graduate school?
- ◇ In what ways do the different purposes of particular graduate programs affect the transition into graduate school?
- ◇ Who is responsible for facilitating graduate student transitions? What roles and responsibilities are played by students, faculty, and staff?

As we have tried to show in this chapter, graduate education in the United States is a complex, large, and diverse enterprise. Given this, it is impossible to provide a single roadmap that will help all graduate students navigate departmental and institutional cultures, policies, and procedures in order to arrive at a successful transition. The following chapters will provide a wide range of strategies and approaches to assist educators in developing appropriate supports that work for their unique graduate student population. By focusing concentrated attention on the transition to graduate school, this volume makes an important contribution to the field of higher education, and to the continued prominence of the U.S. as a leader in graduate education worldwide.

Notes

[1]The core of the debate is whether the two degrees are sufficiently distinct from one another. Ideally, the former prepares researchers and the latter, practitioners. As such, some argue that the degrees ought to be differently structured, with distinct requirements and assessments.

[2]The Survey of Earned Doctorates and the NCES Digest of Education Statistics show slightly different numbers of doctorates awarded each year. The SED is based on student self-reports at the time of graduation, and the NCES data come from reports from each university. For the 2003-4 academic year, the SED reports 42,155 doctorates awarded (Hoffer et al., 2005), and NCES lists 48,378 (Snyder et al., 2006).

[3]The Carnegie Foundation for the Advancement of Teaching defines Specialized Institutions as those that offer degrees ranging from the bachelor's to the doctorate, where at least 50% of the degrees awarded are in a single discipline. Examples of these institutions include: theological seminaries; medical schools; schools of engineering and technology; business schools; schools of art, music, and design; law schools; teachers colleges; and tribal colleges and universities.

References

Austin, A. E. (2002). Preparing the next generation of faculty: Graduate school as socialization to the academic career. *Journal of Higher Education, 73*(1), 94-122.

Barnett, B. G, Basom, M. R., Yerkes, D. M. & Norris, C. J. (2000). Cohorts in educational leadership programs: Benefits, difficulties, and the potential for developing school leaders. *Educational Administration Quarterly, 36,* 255-282.

Barnett, B. G. & Muse, I. D. (1993). Cohort groups in educational administration: Promises and challenges. *Journal of School Leadership, 3,* 400-415.

Barzansky, B., & Etzel, S. I. (2002). Educational programs in U.S. medical schools, 2001-2002. *JAMA, 288*(9), 1067-1072.

Berelson, B. (1960). *Graduate education in the United States*. New York: McGraw-Hill.

Brammer, L. M. (1992). *Coping with life transitions*. Ann Arbor, MI: ERIC Clearinghouse on Counseling and Personnel Services.

Carnegie Foundation for the Advancement of Teaching. (2005). *Basic classification tables, 2005*. Retrieved June 26, 2007, from http://www.carnegiefoundation.org/classifications/index.asp?key=805

Choy, S. P., Cataldi, E. F., & Griffith, J. (2006). *Student financing of graduate and first-professional education, 2003-04: Profiles of students in selected degree programs and part-time students* (No. NCES 2006-185). Washington, DC: U.S. Department of Education, National Center for Education Statistics.

Clance, P. R., & Imes S. A. (1978). The imposter phenomenon in high achieving women: Dynamics and therapeutic intervention. *Psychotherapy Theory, Research and Practice, 15*(3), 241-247.

Conrad, C. F., Duren, K. M., & Haworth, J. G. (1998). Students' perspectives on their master's degree experiences: Disturbing the conventional wisdom. In M. Anderson (Ed.), *The experience of being in graduate school: An exploration* (Vol. 101, pp. 65-76). San Francisco: Jossey-Bass.

Conrad, C. F., Haworth, J. G., & Millar, S. B. (1993). *A silent success: Master's education in the United States*. Baltimore, M.D.: Johns Hopkins University Press.

Conrad, C. F., & Rapp, K. (2003). A study of accounting education at nine universities and PricewaterhouseCoopers: A summary. In *Educating for the public trust: The PricewaterhouseCoopers position on accounting education* (pp. 11-39). New York: Pricewaterhouse Coopers LLP.

Corcoran, M., & Clark, S. M. (1984). Professional socialization and contemporary career attitudes of three faculty generations. *Research in Higher Education, 20*(2), 131-153.

Denecke, D., & Frasier, H. (2005). Ph.D. completion project: Preliminary results from baseline data. *Council of Graduate Schools Communicator, 38*(9), 1-2, 7-8.

Golde, C. M. (2005). The role of the department and discipline in doctoral student attrition: Lessons from four departments. *Journal of Higher Education, 76*(6), 669-700.

Golde, C. M. (2006a). Preparing stewards of the discipline. In C. M. Golde & G. E. Walker (Eds.), *Envisioning the future of doctoral education: Preparing stewards of the discipline*. Carnegie Essays on the Doctorate. San Francisco: Jossey-Bass.

Golde, C. M. (2006b). Preparing stewards of the discipline. *Carnegie Perspectives*. Retrieved September 3, 2007, from http://carnegiefoundation.org/perspectives/sub.asp?key=245&subkey=1811

Golde, C. M., & Dore, T. M. (2001). *At cross purposes: What the experiences of doctoral students reveal about doctoral education*. Philadelphia, PA: The Pew Charitable Trusts. Retrieved February 11, 2008, from http:// www.phd-survey.org

Hartnett R.T., & Katz, J. (1977). The education of graduate students. *The Journal of Higher Education 48*(6), 646-664.

Hoffer, T. B., Hess, M., Welch, V., & Williams, K. (2007). *Doctorate recipients from United States universities: Summary report 2006*. Chicago: National Opinion Research Center.

Hoffer, T. B., Welch, V., Webber, K., Williams, K., Lisek, B., Hess, M., et al. (2006). *Doctorate recipients from United States universities: Summary report 2005*. Chicago: National Opinion Research Center.

Hoffer, T. B., Welch, V., Williams, K., Hess, M., Webber, K., Lisek, B., Loew, D., & Guzman-Barron, I. (2005). *Doctorate recipients from United States universities: Summary report 2004*. Chicago: National Opinion Research Center.

Katz, P. M. (2005). *Retrieving the master's degree from the dustbin of history*. Washington, DC: American Historical Association.

Lovitts, B. E. (2001). *Leaving the ivory tower. The causes and consequences of departure from doctoral study*. New York: Rowman & Littlefield.

Lovitts, B. E. (2005). Being a good course-taker is not enough: A theoretical perspective on the transition to independent research. *Studies in Higher Education, 30*(2), 137-154.

National Academy of Sciences. (1995) *Reshaping the graduate education of scientists and engineers*. Washington, DC: National Academy Press.

Perna, L. W. (2004). Understanding the decision to enroll in graduate school: Sex and racial/ethnic group differences. *Journal of Higher Education, 75*(5) 487-527.

Rapp-Hanretta, K. (2005). *Persistence decisions of doctoral students affiliated with interdisciplinary programs: A case study*. Unpublished dissertation. University of Wisconsin – Madison.

Shulman, L. S., Golde, C. M., Bueschel, A. C., & Garabedian, K. J. (2006). Reclaiming education's doctorates: A critique and a proposal. *Educational Researcher, 35*(3) 25-32.

Snyder, T. D., Tan, A. G., & Hoffman, C. M. (2006). *Digest of education statistics 2005* (NCED 2006-030). Washington, DC: U.S. Department of Education. National Center for Education Statistics. Retrieved January 14, 2008, from http://nces.ed.gov/programs/digest/d05_tf.asp

Taub, D. J. & Komives, S. R. (1998). A comprehensive graduate orientation program: Practicing what we preach. *Journal of College Student Development, 39*(4), 394-98.

Terre, L. (2001). Making the transition to graduate school. *Eye on Psi Chi, 6*(1), 25-27.

Thurgood, L., Golladay, M. J., & Hill, S. T. (2006). *U.S. doctorates in the 20th century* (Special report). Washington, DC: National Science Foundation.

Tinto, V. (1993). *Leaving college: Rethinking the causes and cures of student attrition* (2nd ed.). Chicago: University of Chicago Press.

Wilder, G. Z. (2003). *The road to law school and beyond: Examining challenges to racial and ethnic diversity in the legal profession*. Newton, PA: Law School Admission Council.

Chapter Two

Theories Relating to the Transition Into Graduate Study

Kenneth A. Tokuno

The first year of graduate school is marked by major adjustments for the student. As the first chapter shows, graduate students in this first year come from a wide range of backgrounds and move into a wide range of fields. A serious question is, therefore, how do we shape programs that respond to the needs of such a diverse group? What do they have in common? An important answer to these questions comes to us from theory. Theories and models can help us understand what occurs with graduate students during that transitional first year, and the theories can guide our efforts to provide appropriate programs and supports for new graduate students.

Over the past 50 years, there have been cycles of scholarly activity on the graduate experience as concerns over the success of students at the highest levels of education have claimed national attention. Thus, there is a large body of research that attempts to account for attrition and persistence of graduate students, especially doctoral students. This activity has resulted in a few pertinent theories of student persistence to account for graduate enrollment patterns (Girves & Wemmerus, 1988; Tinto, 1993), but very few of them focus on the first year as a critical phase in graduate student development. This chapter will introduce some of the theories that show the most promise in understanding the transitional experiences of graduate students. It will also examine some broader theories of adult development.

Before beginning this exploration, it is important to question how readily theory can be applied to graduate students. Many theories were developed to help educators better understand the undergraduate experience. Although some of these may lend themselves to adaptation for understanding the graduate student experience, it must be understood that the two experiences are very different. First-year undergraduates, as diverse as they are, are still more homogenous than first-year graduate students. For instance, graduate students are more likely to be international students, married, and older than their undergraduate counterparts. Graduate students are also more mature and have been screened through a more selective process. Whereas undergraduate students share common core curricula and the pursuit of a bachelor's degree, the educational experiences of graduate students can be very different as they seek different degrees in a wider variety of settings. Graduate study is also more intense and focused, often involving a master-apprentice relationship with a faculty member that is rarely found among undergraduates and then with only the most advanced students. For all of these reasons, it is very difficult to apply theories of adjustment for undergraduates to graduate students.

A major source of variation among graduate students is whether they are pursuing a master's or a doctorate, which are extremely different experiences. Yet, the majority of research has focused on doctoral students. From the landmark work of Bowen and Rudenstine (1992) to work done by Nettles and Millet (2006), there is a comparatively large body of research and some efforts to propose models and theories on the doctoral educational experience (e.g., Baird, 1997; Tinto, 1993). In contrast, very little attention has been paid to master's students in the development of models or theories to explain the reasons for success or failure.

What is needed is a theory that explains why graduate students succeed, in general, regardless of level or type of program. Ideally for our purposes, this theory would contain a focus on the first year. The diversity across graduate programs by discipline, however, may defy any type of unifying theory. Indeed, as Tinto (personal communication, February 19, 2006) stated, "Such variation does not make for easy theory building." At the doctoral level alone, Nettles and Millet (2006) noted that the differences between the processes of obtaining a doctorate across different fields mandated separate analyses to determine which factors best predicted outcomes in a given field. Despite these obstacles, it is worth examining existing theories as they might contribute to a better understanding of the first-year experience of graduate students. Ideally, theory can inform practice and provide invaluable guidance to faculty and staff as they interact with students, which may lead to the students' persistence. Although some ideas are suggested as to how these theories might be applied to graduate students, readers should look to the original sources for a more detailed description of a theory to determine how best to apply it to specific student populations.

Some current theories focus on the socialization of students for their roles as faculty. Again, these target doctoral students, despite the fact that most doctoral students do not proceed into the professoriate (Nettles & Millet, 2006). This socialization points more toward the transition from graduate study into a career. Since this chapter examines the opposite transition—into, not out of, graduate school—and involves master's as well as doctoral students, it does not include theories of socialization for the professoriate.

Pascarella and Terenzini (1991) provide a useful framework for understanding how theory can be applied to transition issues for undergraduate students, which can easily be applied to graduate students. Their framework offers a helpful distinction among theories of student change, which will be employed here. One type of theory involves "developmental change" within individuals. Most of these theories suggest that students pass through a series of stages or along various dimensions. A second type of theory, termed "college impact" models by Pascarella and Terenzini, focuses on the environmental factors that influence college students.

This chapter is divided into three sections. The first section will examine several theories of developmental change to show how individuals are thought to change during the period of young adulthood, the time when most graduate students are actively pursuing advanced degrees. This will show the common issues that adults face in life as they transition into graduate school. The second section will consider college impact theories to see how the interaction between the student and the institution shapes the transition. The last section will consider "combined theories" that have incorporated both developmental change and college impact to provide integrated models, which seem to hold the most promise for showing how programs can be of value in assisting students through the transition.

Theories of Developmental Change

A strict interpretation of stage theories of development suggests that individuals progress through each stage in a set sequence, without skipping stages or returning to earlier ones. Usually, each stage involves the accomplishment of a task or resolution of some sort of conflict before one can advance to the next stage. Erik Erikson's (1950, 1959) ideas and those of his successors are called psychosocial theories since they consider the role of the individual within society as development takes place. Society must afford the appropriate opportunities for individuals to succeed and individuals must take responsibility for developing through each stage given the social opportunity. Such theories of development have almost no empirical support demonstrating a strict progression through stages. In fact, the research shows that people may move back and forth between stages (e.g., Marcia, 1976; Waterman, 1982). If this type of movement is possible, then we can suggest that the experience of graduate study can trigger developmental change for a person even if they have already resolved a developmental task or passed a certain stage, making these theories highly relevant for an understanding of the graduate student experience.

Erikson's States of Life Span Development

In his most important books, *Childhood and Society* (1950) and *Identity: Youth and Crisis* (1959), Erikson identified eight stages of life from birth to death and suggested that as a person experiences the challenges of each stage, he or she is propelled to the next stage in sequence. The successful navigation through each stage shapes the person's development in all of the succeeding stages. At each stage, a dichotomy lies between opposites, and the task is to find a balance.

This theory is perhaps most famous for the concept of the "identity crisis," which Erikson placed during adolescence. Empirical work on Erikson's theory (e.g., Marcia, 1966) indicates that college is actually the period in which identity is most likely to be formed, not during adolescence as Erikson theorized. At the stage of identity, the balance is between commitment to a stable sense of self and the opposing prospect of identity confusion. For identity development, it may be healthy to retain a certain balance of "confusion" to allow for some adjustments in one's life plans. According to Erikson, identity formation requires that the individual experiences a moratorium within which the identity crisis takes place. This "crisis" is not as dramatic as the word makes it seem, but rather a state in which the individual sorts through various choices in regard to such questions as "Who am I?" and "What am I to become?" For anyone who has been through graduate school, it is easy to see how such questions are relevant to the progress that a graduate student makes, as these are questions that some graduate students may ask of themselves daily.

The task of identity formation (as with all of Erikson's tasks) can only be successfully met if both the individual and society meet mutual obligations. Society should allow the individual in a state of moratorium a special suspended status with respect to fulfilling the normal adult obligations they might otherwise have upon having committed to a given identity. For identity to form properly, society and its institutions must also provide adequate choices, role models, and opportunities suited to the individual's abilities and interests. At the same time, the individual must take the initiative to investigate the choices and take advantage of the models and opportunities to commit to an identity eventually. The implications for graduate programs should be clear: As much as the individual student has a responsibility to learn and progress to the degree, the "society," which is the academic community, has an equal responsibility to provide the wherewithal for such development. It is equally clear that graduate study is much like the state of moratorium suggested by Erikson, albeit a late and an extended one, as graduate students often "suspend" careers and other major life events while focusing on their studies. To the extent that financial and social support allows them to enter into such a moratorium, they may be more successful as graduate students. Where conflict between ongoing social roles and the need to be a student arises, obstacles may occur. Other theories discussed below speak explicitly to this point.

Erikson's theory in itself does not readily lend itself to practical application, since the terms are not clearly defined and the strict interpretation of stages places the key stage of identity at an age far younger than most graduate students. The value of the theory as it is applied here can be seen in two ways: (a) It established the foundation for later theories, which built upon the need to consider the relationship between the individual (graduate student) and society (graduate schools), and (b) It spurred efforts to examine psychosocial development empirically, chiefly by James Marcia and his successors.

James Marcia's Empirical Study of Identity

Marcia (1966) operationally defined Erikson's ideas about identity and developed a set of four identity statuses, based on interviews with college students. These statuses are:

- *Moratorium.* A period of identity crisis—uncertainty, experimentation, and instability—in which the person questions his or her purpose and future.
- *Identity achievement.* This encompasses Erikson's original idea that a person would commit to an identity after having passed through a moratorium period.
- *Identity foreclosure.* In this status, individuals have formed an identity without going through a moratorium, which means that they accept an identity assigned to them by someone else.
- *Identity diffusion.* This status is similar to Erikson's suggestion that a failure to confront the task of identity successfully would lead to role confusion

The conclusion drawn from Marcia's work is that the most significant changes in identity formation occur during the traditional college years (Waterman, 1982). Marcia (1976) found that the statuses of identity achievement and moratorium were more likely to change than the other two statuses. Of course, it would be expected that the moratorium status would result in resolution to identity achievement or a retreat back to diffusion, but once achieved, it would seem that identity would be stable. Given that it is not, it is clear that the strict interpretation of identity as part of set sequence of stages is untenable. This being the case, it clearly has implications for graduate issues such as retention.

It is likely that graduate students who begin in a state of identity foreclosure may enter a moratorium, being subject to influences in the context of their graduate level work that lead them to question why they are in graduate school. If the individual decides that his or her choices were wrong, i.e., finds a new identity, the student is likely to leave. It is equally clear that a person who is in a state of identity achievement could also experience such a change; the only question has to do with the relative likelihood. Students who are in either the moratorium or diffused statuses may attempt to get into graduate school, but are likely to be doing so for the wrong reasons, i.e., they do not know what else to do.

Levinson's Life Structures

Levinson (1978) is better known for his elaboration of the male mid-life crisis, but his work also touches on earlier stages of adult development. Levinson's theory was developed using a small sample of 40 men, so there is some question as to whether the theory applies to women. Building on Erikson, Levinson suggested that development proceeds through the creation of "life structures" composed of the choices that a man makes around his family, career, hobbies, values, friendships, and life style. The stages of life involve the continual restructuring of these choices.

A youth in his 20s constructs his first life structure as he enters the adult world, involving what might be preliminary choices about careers, family, etc. A major transition, if it occurs, is around the age of 30 after which there is a "settling down" phase within the second life structure, marking the individual as a "full fledged adult" (Levinson, 1978, p. 141) who has made commitments to career and family. Both of these structures precede the mid-life crisis, which can result in further demolition and rebuilding.

It is within that first life structure that we would find the majority of graduate students, whether male or female. Levinson considers the life structure here as a provisional one in which the individual is a novice. The tasks are (a) to explore the possibilities of adult life while keeping options open and (b) to create the first life structure. While Levinson admits that these tasks are antithetical, he states that the individual must find a way to balance them. We see Erikson's influence in the dichotomy of this balancing act. In one direction, lies a lack of commitment, a rootlessness born of too much exploration; in the other, lies the danger of having failed to explore one's options due to a premature commitment to a life structure.

While many graduate students are within that first life structure, others have gone through the transition and decided to return to school for an advanced degree. As in the other developmental theories, the extent to which the student is committed, in this case to a life structure, is likely to go a long way in determining their persistence. If they are still exploring, they may fail to persist. The theory also predicts that older students are more likely to persist simply because they have "settled down."

Graduate students often seek to find the balance between their explorations and their needs for stability. Proponents of Levinson would argue that a student who is seeking more stability than graduate study can afford is likely to be at risk to leave. On the other hand, graduate students who have determined that an advanced degree is an integral part of their first life structure are more likely to stay. What the theory does not make clear is how to determine which students are at risk. It is also not clear how the theory pertains to women. For these reasons, this theory is not that helpful to the development of specific programs, but it does provide value in illustrating how the developmental concerns of individuals at this stage are multi-faceted and not simply psychosocial. In that sense, it sets the stage for the more complex integrated theories that will be explained below.

Chickering's Vectors of Adult Development

This theory is one of the more popular in higher education, since it speaks directly to issues involving college-age adults. It is not limited by age, so it is also attractive as a theory of possible application to graduate students. Working from Erikson's theory, Chickering (1969) identifies seven vectors that describe the development of college students. Chickering suggests that these vectors occur roughly in a sequence, although he does not insist that they constitute stages. He has suggested, though, that it would be well for institutions to try to move students along in this sequence.

The term *vector* indicates a movement toward a goal given by the name of each vector. This implies that there is a defined end point, which could be assumed to have been reached by the end of the undergraduate years. In a later work, Schlossberg, Lynch, & Chickering (1989) make it clear that this is not the case. Here, the authors address the concern of older students returning to undergraduate study. The focus here is clearly on transition, but the vectors remain the same, according to interviews conducted with adult learners. What changes for older students are the greater need to fill multiple roles, the wider range of individual differences, a wider variety of past experiences, more concern with practical application for their degrees, and a greater sense of self-determination rather than reliance on their professors. Many of these changes are consistent with what other theories of adult development would predict.

If the vectors remain the same for older students returning to undergraduate study, the same is likely to be true for graduate students, whether they are continuing directly after earning their bachelor's degrees or returning to do graduate study after being in the world of work for some years. A key difference between the older undergraduate students studied by Schlossberg et al. (1989) and graduate students is the level of study and the students' relationship to the institution. Looking at each of the vectors, however, it is possible to extrapolate how Chickering's ideas apply to the transition of graduate students:

1. *Developing competence.* For undergraduates, the development of competence includes physical/manual and interpersonal competence as well as intellectual competence. The demands of graduate study would indicate a quantitatively and qualitatively different focus on intellectual competence. This means that the demand to master content and to use various intellectual skills, such as analysis, synthesis, and application of knowledge is at a premium beyond what it was at the undergraduate level. This vector is unlikely to be a revelation because it is already central to the role of all graduate degree programs to provide the means for and evaluation of learning at the graduate level.
2. *Managing emotions.* Although graduate students should have learned much about managing their emotions (such as anger, depression, shame, and anxiety), it is likely that the intensity of graduate study could create new demands on such management, especially in the context of close one-to-one relationships with mentors. Administrators could encourage graduate departments and student services offices to be more aware of the extreme stresses facing graduate students and provide emotional support through the faculty or peer community. The idea of learning communities, as proposed in chapter 8, is one example of how this might be achieved.
3. *Moving through autonomy toward interdependence.* With research increasingly requiring collaboration, interdependence is a critical skill of graduate study for students in any area demanding scholarship. For all graduate fields, the opportunity to work cooperatively with other graduate students should be an important model for the types of work that may be required after completing the degree. Outside departments, any centralized offices that have responsibility for creating internships or other opportunities for graduate students need to be aware of the need for placing students in positions where they get practical experience in working with others.
4. *Developing mature interpersonal relationships.* Working closely with others in a graduate program while balancing the needs for intimacy with significant others is more likely to be a significant challenge for graduate students, who are more likely to be married or be in long-term relationships. While this may not be an area that can be addressed

programmatically, awareness of this vector should increase the sensitivity of program personnel to graduate students struggling with interpersonal relationships.

5. *Establishing identity.* By the time a person becomes a graduate student, such matters as comfort with one's appearance, a sense of self-esteem, and a placement of oneself into social and cultural contexts are generally resolved. It is likely, however, that the pressures of graduate study may cause some of these questions to resurface as was noted in the discussion of Levinson's and Erickson's theories.
6. *Developing purpose.* There will be continued pressure on graduate students to determine how they will employ themselves with a graduate degree. For doctoral students, this includes determining whether they will seek academic positions or not. While this may not be an issue that can be addressed in the context of the first-year transition, it may be helpful to beginning graduate students to know that the campus offers assistance with such issues as job placement once they are closer to degree completion. (Chapter 10 provides some good examples of relevant practices.)
7. *Developing integrity.* It is conceivable that many younger graduate students will arrive late to this final vector, meaning that the formation of personal values is still under way. It remains incumbent on graduate programs to teach such things as the ethical conduct of research and other professional standards to assist graduate students with their development in this area.

It should be evident from the above that there is much that graduate institutions and programs can do to foster movement along each of these vectors. What Chickering advocated for the successful development of undergraduates is no less true for graduates.

Katz's Theory of Development of the Mind

Joseph Katz (1976) offers the only developmental theory specific to graduate students. He suggests a loose progression through three developmental stages. At the first stage, upon entry into a graduate program, students are very insecure and must assimilate into the program. They may have matriculated with a sense of mastery, but this is immediately challenged by the volume of work they face. Students who successfully assimilate then move to the next stage around their second year in which they enter a socialization process of approaching equality with their professors. In their latter years, they move toward full identity as a peer scholar with the kind of autonomy granted to colleagues in academia.

Katz indicates that the student's success depends on the mutual efforts of the student and of the institution or program offering the degree. Unfortunately, Katz does not provide elaboration on the finer points of his theory, so application is difficult. His theory anticipates, however, the college impact theories described below. For that reason, the essence of his theory is readily integrated into practical applications for the first graduate year.

For Katz, the challenge of the first year is for the student to overcome the sense of insecurity created by the volume of work they have to master. The student must develop a broad knowledge base and gain the attention of professors while working collaboratively with other graduate students, actively engaging in exchanges at all levels. Programs cannot be expected to "take it easy" on the student, but orientation programs and other early sources of information could prepare students for the workload. Programs should provide strategies and mentoring to assist the student with the work. Eventually, as Katz states, the student will come to see that the load is not so bad, that is, assuming that the student persists to that point.

Perry's Scheme of Intellectual and Ethical Development

William Perry's (1970) work was based on interviews of male undergraduates at Harvard and focused largely on cognitive development as the student progressed. Like Chickering, this theory focuses on change during college and has implications for graduate students. Perry identified nine "positions" of intellectual and ethical development that can be clustered around four stages. The descriptions of the four stages below emphasize the process of intellectual development.

- *Dualism.* Students in this stage tend to see knowledge as dichotomous, i.e., there is either truth or untruth. The goal of learning is to find the truth, which converts into correct answers on exams. The faculty hold these truths, and it is up to the student to identify them. As the student moves forward and is freed from a simple true-false sense of knowledge, the dichotomies begin to splinter into "multiplicities."
- *Multiplicity.* Once the student has moved away from dualistic thinking, the newly acquired sense that knowledge is subjective leads to the sense of multiplicity—that there are multiple truths that are equally valid. For undergraduates, this can lead to a cynical view of the faculty and grading, which is seen as nothing more than the applied opinion of the faculty whose point of view should have no more weight than anyone else's.
- *Relativism.* At this stage, students advance from the idea of multiple truths to the understanding that a given opinion or idea may be valid within differing contexts or the relative perspectives with which knowledge can be viewed. Although students may be able to think critically and analytically, they may vacillate between points of view.
- *Commitment to Relativism.* Having moved through the earlier positions, the student now acts on their commitment to a given point of view or idea. The student is able to defend their perspective while considering other arguments in light of existing evidence. These students are more willing to learn the techniques for evaluating the quality of evidence underlying abstract ideas and research findings. Research on Perry's theory shows that it is rare for undergraduate students to be identified at this stage (e.g., Kurfiss, 1977). No research has been done on Perry's stages at the graduate level, so we can only speculate that it is likely that the challenges of graduate study would propel students to higher levels. It is equally probable that only those students who have reached these levels are suitable for graduate-level study.

As with other theories, there have been elaborations of Perry's work. Schommer (1994), for example, developed a three-dimensional model based on Perry's scheme. This work has resulted in empirical evidence showing that intellectual development seems to vary according to discipline (e.g., Paulsen & Wells, 1998). Elaborations of this research might show great promise in identifying whether graduate students are intellectually ready for graduate level work or not. Kitchener and King (1981) also elaborated Perry's ideas in their reflective judgment model. The chief value of this elaboration with respect to graduate students is that their model diverges from Perry's at the highest stages in which students come to employ inquiry-based evidence as the basis for objective reality. This level of development is important to success at the graduate level, since it underlies the types of methodological competence that graduate study requires.

An awareness of Perry's ideas holds value for those who are concerned with the transition of students into graduate-level work. Students who show signs of being intellectually unprepared for graduate school, even though their grades and test scores may qualify them for the pursuit of advanced degrees, are likely to be at risk if they cannot engage in the complexities of thought required by advanced study. A pedagogical issue is how to move new graduate students into the higher stages of Perry's scheme if they are not there at the point of matriculation. Programs concerned about promoting such development need to ask, "What experiences would serve that purpose?" Moreover, graduate programs must consider to what extent they will be able to help students develop along these lines and whether students who demonstrate lower levels of cognitive development should be discouraged from pursuing graduate work. There are no simple answers to either of these questions. While Perry's scheme does not give any direct answers to these questions, it provides another way to frame the question beyond more traditional methods of "screening" students within their first year, such as qualifying exams.

College Impact Models

In contrast to the theories of developmental change, college impact models are more sociological in nature. For many of these models, the students' initial contact with the college involves a socialization process whereby they learn the norms, roles, and values of their individual graduate programs. In general, these theories consider the interaction between the individual and the social environment of graduate school. For this reason and because these theories were developed specifically to explain graduate student attrition, the role of the institution is more apparent. An early theoretical effort was made by Girves and Wemmerus (1988), which set the stage for later theories. Among the existing theories of graduate student persistence and attrition, foremost is the model developed by Vincent Tinto (1993).

Tinto's Theory of Doctoral Persistence

Tinto used Durkheim's (1897/1951) seminal work on suicide to develop an explanatory model of why students leave college. He reasoned that a student's decision to leave college would parallel an individual's decision to "depart" society. Central to this decision-making process was the need for an individual to feel that he or she belonged to a community. For new students, this meant that they would need to make a successful transition from the familiar communities of their recent past to the new community represented in the campus. Each student comes to college with a number of individual qualities, such as the student's family background, skill level, commitment to college, and prior school experience. Tinto (1987) states that these qualities interact with the student's initial experience within both academic and social contexts of the institution to determine whether the transition to college is successful or not. If these experiences lead to the student's integrating in a positive way with the school, the student is more likely to stay. If the experience is negative, the student is more likely to leave.

As an appendix to his revised theory of undergraduate attrition, Tinto (1993) presented a theory of doctoral (not master's students) persistence shaped by his ideas on the integration of undergraduate students into the community of a college campus. Tinto recognized that the campus as a whole is not the actual community into which a doctoral student must integrate. The student must integrate into a specific graduate program. Nonetheless, he suggested that the basic processes are similar. The student must make a successful transition from an old to a new community by integrating with the people they meet upon entry into a graduate program. The difficulty in characterizing such communities lies in their diversity, where the nature of the community varies not by campus, but by departments within campuses.

Tinto identifies several conflicts facing the doctoral student trying to adjust to this level of study. Since graduate students are more likely to be employed full time or married, one complicating factor is the competing contexts of work and family. To the extent that these demands conflict with the demands of the academic community, greater difficulties may arise for the student. In addition, the existence of financial aid plays a major role, as those students who are supported will find it easier to integrate in comparison to those students who must rely on non-academic sources of income, which not only subtract time from the program but also draw them away from academic contacts and increase the potential for conflict. Resolution of this conflict will depend on the characteristics of the student and the institution. Similar conflicts may arise if the student perceives a need to integrate into broader, perhaps national, reference groups associated with their long-term careers. If these larger groups have norms that do not coincide with that of their specific academic programs, the student will need to choose which norms are more important. Any one of these conflicts could lead to the lack of integration that would result in the student's departure from the program.

Tinto (1993) discusses three stages in the movement of the doctoral student: (a) *transition*, which occurs in the first year and involves the student establishing membership in the academic and social communities of their doctoral program; (b) *candidacy*, which involves the acquisition of knowledge with a culmination in the comprehensive examinations; and (c) *dissertation*, which requires completion and defense of the dissertation.

The one that is of most interest here is the first stage, which parallels the transition from high school to college. The student must integrate both academically and socially with the primary community. This occurs via the establishment of personal contact with peers and faculty members. The key difference for doctoral students is that individuals reside within a program that usually consists of a small number of individuals; whereas, undergraduate students may focus on the campus as a whole.

During transition, the student must determine the degree to which the norms of this small community are consistent with his or her own attributes, goals, and interests. Since the smaller size of graduate communities is likely to result in greater idiosyncrasies, compared to an entire institution, the likelihood of a successful fit would seem to be much smaller. The perception of a poor fit is more likely to occur, hence the higher probability of departure.

Tinto's model (1993; Figure 1) begins by identifying the key background attributes of the student, such as race, gender, educational experience, and financial resources, as he or she enters doctoral study. These characteristics affect the student's commitment to the educational program, level of participation, and subsequent career goals. The students' initial involvement with their program is determined by their participation and the nature of their interactions with peers, faculty, and other individuals largely within the department as opposed to the entire campus. These interactions will shape the students' sense of belonging to the program. The resulting perception of being a member of their academic community has a great deal to do with the successful transition in the first year. Students who do not consider themselves members will have more trouble moving through the program than those who feel that they are a part of the community of scholars.

Tinto's model of doctoral persistence has not had the impact on research at the doctoral level that his college student attrition model has had at the undergraduate level. Adequate testing of Tinto's model would require longitudinal research, which is very expensive and fraught with methodological difficulties. None of this diminishes the importance of the ideas, however. Almost all other college impact models rely on the fundamental ideas he established in his seminal work on college student attrition.

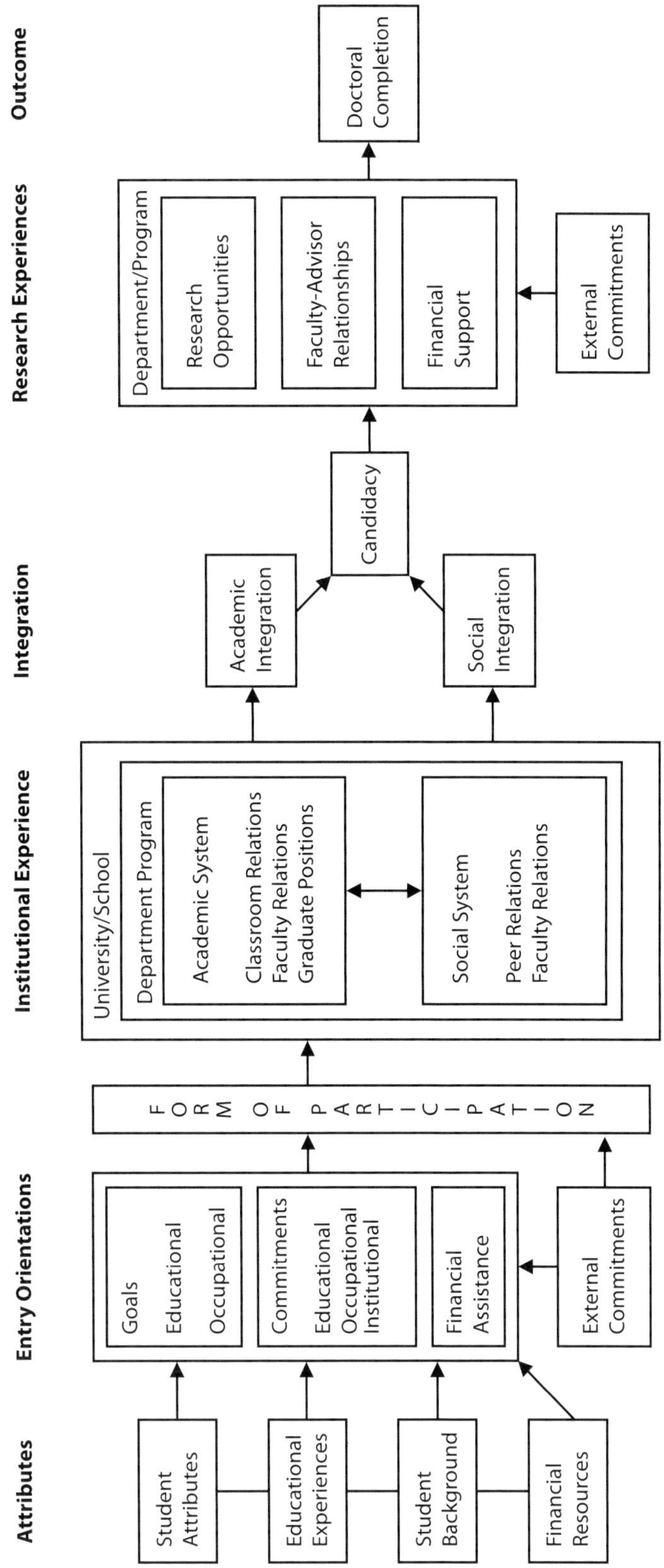

Figure 1. A longitudinal model of doctoral persistence. Copyright © 1993, University of Chicago Press. Used with permission.

Lovitts' Social Structural Theory of Departure

Lovitts' (2001) conducted interviews with doctoral students, faculty, and heads of graduate study within departments. Based on her findings and her understanding of social science theorists, such as Durkheim (1897/1951) and Tinto (1993), and social attribution theorists such as Ross (1977), Lovitts developed her own theory as to why doctoral students' rate of attrition is so high. She argued that programs focus too much on the qualities of the individual in explaining attrition and not enough on what can be done to improve completion rates by addressing program structure and procedures. While this chapter is not concerned with attrition, per se, and her theory does not include master's students, the ideas are of value in understanding the first-year transition.

Lovitts builds on Tinto's notion that students need to be integrated both academically and socially. Academic integration, which she calls task integration, occurs through the formal processes of working with faculty on courses and other tasks germane to the field of study. Socioemotional integration occurs informally during social gatherings and in casual interaction with faculty and fellow students. Lovitts believes that attrition stems from lack of integration, but that too much integration may result in departure as well. Namely, she claims that too much social integration may result in a graduate student "partying out" and that too much task integration may result in burning out.

To the concept of integration, Lovitts adds cognitive maps. Students create these maps as they gain information and use the maps to guide them through graduate study. The quality of these maps depends on how much good information students receive as they begin to integrate into the program. There are two kinds of maps: global and local. The global map is one constructed from formal information sources, such as the graduate student catalog that provides information on the requirements for degree completion (e.g., exams, courses, theses). Two types of local maps follow from integration: (a) the task map, which is derived from information gleaned at the department level, and (b) the social map, which can help guide the student through a knowledge of the relationships between faculty members, students, and staff. These maps are of interest since they should be formed during the first year of transition and are dependent on the accuracy and completeness of information available to the student, which is, in turn, dependent on how well they integrate. Students who do not become integrated will fail to develop good maps, which will then further hamper their later integration and might result in attrition.

Lovitts, in contrast to Tinto's three stages, posits four stages in the doctoral students path to the doctorate. A key addition is Stage 0, which she calls *prior and anticipatory socialization*. This occurs prior to admission as prospective applicants seek programs and campuses to which they will apply. Integration and the formation of cognitive maps begin here. If the information provided to prospective students is incomplete or misleading, it may lead the applicant to make a bad decision and apply to a program to which he or she is not well suited. Once the student applies, the process continues as he or she tries to get more information during this process to decide whether to attend.

Upon matriculation, Stage 1 of *entry and adjustment* begins and successful integration becomes critical. Lovitts affirms that programs can do more through a variety of methods, such as handbooks, orientation, and good advising to help students develop cognitive maps. In doing so, she speaks directly to the concerns of this chapter. These methods of early intervention are likely to reduce attrition. Programs that currently do so have more welcoming "cultures" and are thus more likely to have higher retention rates than programs that provide fewer opportunities for integration. Further, Lovitts argues that, from the beginning, programs should do more to make expectations explicit including (a) making clear the level of quality that graduate students are expected to produce in their work, (b) how their work is going to be judged, and (c) how they go about learning to become a professional.

Again, although this theory and her subsequent recommendations are in the context of doctoral education, Lovitts' ideas would readily apply to master's students, who would likely go through very similar processes in the initial stages of anticipatory socialization and entry.

Conrad, Haworth, and Millar's Decision-Situation Characterization of Master's Degree Programs

Conrad and his colleagues (Conrad, Haworth, & Millar, 1993) are the only ones to have developed a framework focusing exclusively on master's student success. Although it does not directly consider the issue of transition or matters of persistence and attrition, it has some value as a method for organizing research on these issues or developing programs to address them.

Based on interviews of a nationwide sample of master's students and other stakeholders (e.g., faculty, alumni, administrators, and employers), this model is organized around "decision-situations," which they define as the "types of circumstances in which stakeholders make decisions that influence how they and others experience their master's programs" (p. 43). Conrad et al. divide these decision-situations into three primary and two auxiliary categories. The primary decision-situations are those that they found most helpful in understanding the differences in master's student experiences of graduate school. These are (a) approach to teaching and learning, (b) program orientation, and (c) departmental support. The two auxiliary decision-situations are institutional support and student culture.

For each of these decision-situations, Conrad et al. describe various choices that are made by stakeholders. These stakeholders can be the program's faculty and administrators who determine the structures and approaches of their programs, or they can be the students who select among the different programs offered where they will attend. For example, within the "approach to teaching and learning," Conrad et al. identify three major types of approaches: (a) "didactic" involving the direct transmission of knowledge from teacher to student; (b) "facilitative" involving more direct learning experience done by the student, with the faculty member serving as a guide and the student an apprentice; and (c) "dialogical," where faculty and student engage in a mutual processing of discovery and understanding. Similar typologies are developed in the other four decision-situations.

Conrad and his colleagues use this taxonomy to identify the characteristics of quality master's experiences. This model could be viewed as a theory for the "ideal" master's level program, although there is no data showing whether such an idealized model improves the first-year experience for master's students. When and if a program is developed based on this theoretical model, it would be very important for an assessment of the program to show how effective it actually is.

Despite the fact that Conrad and his colleagues did not apply their model to an understanding of master's student persistence or attrition, it can be employed to better understand how the structure and approaches of master's degree programs can influence both persistence and attrition. Studies designed with this model in mind could identify the critical aspects of master's programs. For master's students, Tinto's requirement for a longitudinal design, employing Conrad et al's typology, would be much more feasible and has great potential to provide valuable insights into a degree level that is rapidly expanding in popularity.

Berkenkotter, Huckin, & Ackerman—Initiation Into Discourse Communities

Based on the idea that new graduate students are entering "discourse communities," Berkenkotter, Huckin, & Ackerman (1991) developed a model focusing on the transition to graduate study and on the linguistic dimension of academics. They begin with the premise that each discipline in higher education possesses a specialized literacy with its own rhetoric and language conventions. To become true scholars within that discipline, the student must master this literacy. It is an interesting variation on the idea of socialization into the discipline.

This model encompasses more than simply writing styles. Berkenkotter et al. (1991) expand the idea of the academic context into the idea of a "model of knowing" whereby the methodologies of the discipline are encoded in the language of that academic community. Not only must students become familiar with that language, but they must also be aware of the larger research community outside the campus, the media through which that community communicates, and the need for themselves to be initiated into the community through interaction with the faculty and peers.

Students first encounter discourse communities during their first term of course work, and they must begin to learn to use the language and writing conventions appropriate to their field. Berkenkotter et al. (1991) illustrate the process of initiation through papers written by a first-year graduate student in English at Carnegie Mellon over the course of the first year of graduate study. They argue that the progression of development in these papers provides clear evidence of students' movement toward the "specialist's perspective."

As intriguing as this model may be, there may be limitations for those disciplines where laboratory or studio work supersedes language as the primary mode for learning. The value of this theory is that it indicates that a goal of any program trying to improve retention should be to make graduate students aware of the larger discourse communities at the same time that they are engaging them in the language of their specific disciplines. Many programs may claim that the very nature of graduate study cannot help but stimulate this engagement, but as graduate study becomes more interdisciplinary and specialized, the ideas of Berkenkotter et al. become more critical. Programs need to keep the concept of linguistic integration firmly in mind as they greet new graduate students.

Kerlin's Theory of Women's Doctoral Persistence

Believing that narratives of women's experience in doctoral programs can provide useful insights, Kerlin (1997) undertook a study based on women's stories. She used those stories to construct her own framework to identify factors affecting women's progress in doctoral programs. Kerlin divides the factors into two groups: (a) personal and social factors (i.e., academic self-concept, age, gender, health, family status, financial status, and class/cultural identity) and (b) institutional factors (i.e., program status, department climate, department policies and practices, and advisor/advisee relationship).

Of particular interest is the discussion of the advisor/advisee relationship. Kerlin describes six styles:

1. *Uninvolved.* These advisors do not spend much time with their students, leaving them to fend for themselves.
2. *Laissez-faire.* Such advisors will meet with students, but they are reluctant to provide much constructive feedback.

3. *Negotiators*. These faculty will allow the student to take the lead but provide guidance as necessary.
4. *Proactive*. These advisors provide guidance similar to negotiators, but they will take more of a leadership role and use their power and authority to help students.
5. *Symbiotic*. Although this style involves being helpful, it also includes using the advisor's power to get something from the student.
6. *Autocratic*. This is a very authoritarian style in which the advisor seeks to form the student in his or her own image.

While Kerlin focuses on female graduate students, this taxonomy potentially has universal utility in providing a framework for understanding the range of relationships a student can have with an advisor. It is tempting to identify a "best practice" for advising from this taxonomy; however, Kerlin also points out that these styles may shift as the student matures and needs less guidance. It is also true that different styles of advisors will have different effects depending on the nature of the student or even the discipline. A mature, self-directed student working within a well-defined discipline may prefer an uninvolved advisor who leaves her alone to pursue her own work. A more dependent student in a rapidly changing discipline might be best assisted by an autocratic advisor, at least at the beginning. A focus on the advising styles is an over-simplification of this theory. Anyone who seeks to employ the above taxonomy would be well advised to read Kerlin's theory carefully to see how the advising relationships fit within the context of the other factors.

Combined Theories

The following theories combine elements of both college impact models and theories of developmental change. For that reason, they are presented here separately.

Lee and Roth's Application of Legitimate Peripheral Participation Theory

Lee and Roth (2003) employ the theory of "legitimate peripheral participation (LPP)" developed by Lave and Wenger (1991), which asserts that learning occurs within a broader social context of a "community of practice." For Lee and Roth that context consists of all of the scholars within the discipline who compose an academic community that crosses not only campus, but national boundaries. The original theory actually suggests that the best learning cannot occur in formal educational settings because it places students in a role that is effectively nonparticipatory. Lee and Roth suggest that graduate study fits the LPP model better than lower levels of education since students are in a role of apprenticeship similar to what Lave and Wenger describe for LPP. Graduate students enter on the periphery of the community and work their way toward the center, while making a contribution to the academic community even while they are learning from the more advanced members (faculty) of the community. The entire process is part of the discipline's ongoing and collective effort to grow as well as to more fully incorporate individual graduate students within it.

An interesting twist of this theory is that the relationship between individual graduate students and the academic community that they seek to join does not involve unilateral change only on the part of students. Rather, a student's effort to join the community results in a dialectical process in which the community, if only through changes in the mentors' perspectives, attitudes, and thoughts, is altered as well. Lee and Roth's (2003) belief that "Identity is something emerging from the struggle between the individual and the community…into which they are entering" has definite Eriksonian overtones. Erikson was quite clear that the accomplishment of identity was a mutual responsibility of the person and the society inhabited by that person.

Lee and Roth note that graduate students' participation may result in a deep emotional involvement in the discipline and their role within it. The more they become immersed in their identity as scholars, the greater the sense of loss upon failure to reach the final goal of becoming a full member of the community. While responsibility for success may belong to the individual, the academic community, in the form of not only the department to which the student belongs but the overarching community of that department's discipline, has an equal responsibility for assuring success. If the success of the discipline, as Lee and Roth suggest, depends on the success in retaining new members who can contribute to it, then all disciplines need to focus on graduate education to help assure that success. While how to achieve this is not clear, it is important to consider the dynamic relationship between the graduate student, the department, and the discipline.

Baird's Integrated Model

Leonard Baird (1993) combined the ideas of Tinto (1993), Katz (1976), and Berkenkotter et al. (1991) into an integrated model of graduate student success. Baird emphasizes two major influences on graduate students: (a) agents internal to programs (i.e., faculty and peers) and (b) external agents (e.g., employers, and family). The internal agents should help students understand their roles and develop the means for making progress. The external agents need to be supportive and not present obstacles to the student. In Baird's model, attrition is the result of a failure of the interaction between the students and these agents. For example, a lack of support from a spouse or a failure to develop good social relationships with one's peers would be more likely to lead to the student's failure. This chapter does not elaborate on Baird's work since the more detailed theory of Elaine Parent expands and improves upon it.

Parent's Rules, Roles, and Relationship

Parent (2003) focuses on three critical elements of Baird's work—(a) the intellectual, (b) social, and (c) personal/motivational factors—and nests these into Ford's (1992) Motivational Systems Theory. Ford has theorized that a person's motivation to continue toward a goal is a result of two factors: (a) what that person believes about his or her ability to attain a goal and (b) faith in the support that he or she is likely to receive from the relevant environment. Ford identified these as the source of "personal agency beliefs."

Parent extends Ford's theory to the need to develop competence through increased understanding of what graduate school will be like. First, when students are given more information, they are better situated to assess their own ability against the challenges faced in a graduate program. Ford would suggest that motivation is dependent on this assessment. Second, following Ford, students also need to know how much support they are likely to receive in order to proceed with the proper motivation. Thus, any increment in understanding by prospective graduate students will depend on how much information they possess about themselves, and the new task they are about to face. Parent posits that there are three R's for which students need an understanding of their graduate programs: rules, roles, and relationships. Later, Parent (2005) adds a fourth R: resources. Information about these four Rs is needed across three areas: (a) the discipline, (b) the academic department, and the (c) individual person. Each of these three areas intersects with all four of the Rs, within which an understanding must be gained, resulting in 12 intersections for which information is needed (i.e., information about rules, roles, relationships, and resources in the discipline, department, and individual).

To illustrate with one area: Within a *discipline*, students must learn the *rules* about conducting research. These methodological rules go beyond a simple understanding of the methods used in the discipline but include such things as understanding what are acceptable data and how to gather data as evidence, as well as the established and emerging paradigms in the field, and the structure of knowledge. The various *roles* that must be understood within a discipline could include membership in the various specializations of the discipline, becoming participating scholars by contributing knowledge, and membership within formal organizations at all levels of the organization. Third, students must come to understand the *relationships* between the various individuals and groups of the discipline within and beyond the students' department. These groups would include external agencies, other relevant areas of the university, and the various local and national groups comprising the discipline's audience. The student must identify and learn how to use the *resources* available to them and be provided the opportunity to find sources of information through the faculty, the literature, and the various organizations making up the students' environment.

The same is true for acquiring information about the department and the students' ways of working. Departments have their own rules, roles, relationships, and resources and the students' ways of working will evolve into the same four Rs as they make the transition through the first year. This last objective is very much a process of developing an identity as a scholar specific to the discipline. Not only does Parent's work echo Erikson, it is also supported by the theorizing and research that Lovitts (2001) has produced.

Parent's ideas have great appeal for the practical concerns surrounding the transition of the first-year student into graduate school. Programs that are concerned about attrition need to provide clear information about rules and the students' roles in relationship to the faculty. Of particular interest is what she has to say about the student's own role in self-understanding. According to Parent, while it is clear that graduate students bring a clear record of academic success with them, self doubt and loss of confidence would be an explanation for the high rate of attrition. Evocative of Erikson's (1950) argument that successful mastering of developmental tasks is the joint responsibility of the individual and society, Parent's structure provides a clear road map as to how the individual needs to work with and be assisted by the academic society to successfully negotiate the transition into graduate school.

Conclusion

In the late 1980s, a major movement occurred involving the transformation of the way undergraduates experienced their first year in college. There were three major types of programs involved in this movement, sometimes all of them occurring simultaneously on campuses. These three program types were: (a) learning communities, (b) first-year seminars, and (c) new student orientation. Although their histories differ, collectively, they have changed the landscape of undergraduate higher education and are all now firmly embedded as an important element in assisting first-year students in making the transition to college. Jean McGregor (personal communication, July 15, 2006) estimates that there are about 500 colleges with a learning community program. Although it is not the purpose of this chapter to go into detail on the value of these programs, there is sound evidence that they make a difference for undergraduates (Keup & Barefoot, 2005; Tokuno, 1993). These programs provide some validation to the theories regarding undergraduate retention and attrition.

While it is not the case that the undergraduate programs were developed on some kind of theory-based blueprint, it is encouraging that these programs are consistent with what such theories would predict. What does this mean for graduate students in transition? It would seem that theory is of use to guide the formation of programs to help students make the transition into graduate school. While there are sometimes vast differences in the graduate students experience across disciplines, a major commonality is the need of all graduate students to feel that they are part of a larger community of scholars. The kinds of programs, whether campus-wide or department-specific, that provide this kind of environmental support vary with theories of graduate student transition. Conrad et al. (1993), for example, provide models for master's-level programs that reach out to students and assist them in integrating into their disciplines within the relatively short time allocated for master's study. Berkenkotter et al. (1991) show the need for linguistic integration so that students can begin to speak and write the language of their fields. Lovitts speaks directly to the types of information that graduate students need and how programs should provide it. Parent (2005) brings these together with theories of individual development to demonstrate the types of information that students need from the onset to bridge the early path to successful induction as a scholar.

The decision to enter graduate school would seem to be one answer to the existential question, what do I do with my life? Erikson, Levinson, and other psychosocial-stage theorists lead us to the conclusion that new graduate students have claimed an identity or developed a first-life structure, and graduate school is a means for fulfilling their goals. Perry's theory suggests an additional extrapolation: If students who have advanced to the higher stages of intellectual development are aware of their abilities, then they would not only be interested in attending graduate school but would be successful when they got there.

Such explanations seemingly ignore economic factors (many people seek higher degrees for better paying jobs), purely academic factors (such as a deep and abiding interest in the subject matter of their discipline), and status factors (such as the esteem brought about by being able to place "PhD" after one's name). A theory that accounts for all of these factors would help explain why some students are able to persist while others depart.

The College Impact theorists, notably Tinto, do consider the attributes of individual students in determining their initial orientation to graduate study. From the perspective of the need to develop programs to assist students, however, the most careful integration of all considerations seems to be Parent's. Her consolidation of other theories may not take into account the initial motives of the student but certainly attends to the motivational needs of individual students and places them into the context of what programs can do to enhance the chances that first-year graduate students will earn their degrees. From a purely practical standpoint, then, her theory seems to be the most useful, even while it rests upon the ideas that came before her.

References

Baird, L. (1997). Completing the dissertation: Theory, research, and practice. In L. F. Goodchild, K. E. Green, E. Kluever, & R. C. Katz (Eds.), Vol. 25. *Rethinking the dissertation process: Tackling personal and institutional obstacles* (pp. 99-105). San Francisco: Jossey Bass.

Berkenkotter, C., Huckin, T. N., & Ackerman, J. (1991). Social context and socially constructed texts: The initiation of a graduate student into a writing research community. In C. Bazerman & J. Paradis (Eds.), *Textual dynamics of the professions: Historical and contemporary studies of writing in professional communities* (pp. 191-215). Madison, WI: University of Wisconsin Press.

Bowen, W. G., & Rudenstine, N. L. (1992). *In pursuit of the PhD.* Princeton, NJ: Princeton University Press.

Chickering, A. W. (1969). *Education and identity.* San Francisco: Jossey-Bass.

Conrad, C. F., Haworth, J. G., & Millar, S. B. (1993). *A silent success: Master's education in the United States.* Baltimore, MD: Johns Hopkins University Press.

Durkheim, E. (1951). *Suicide.* (J. A. Spaulding and G. Simpson, Trans.). Glencoe: The Free Press. (Original work published 1897).

Erikson, E. H. (1950). *Childhood and society.* New York: W. W. Norton & Co.

Erikson, E. H. (1959). *Identity: Youth and crisis.* New York: W. W. Norton & Co.

Ford, M. (1992). *Motivating humans: Goals, emotions and personal agency beliefs.* New York: Sage Press.

Girves, J. E., & Wemmerus, V. (1988). Developing models of graduate student progress. *Journal of Higher Education, 59*(2), 163-189.

Katz, J. (1976). Development of the mind. In J. Katz & R. T. Hartnett (Eds.), *Scholars in the making* (pp. 107-126). Cambridge, MA: Ballinger Publishing Company.

Kerlin, R. (1997). *Toward a theory of women's doctoral persistence.* Retrieved February 15, 2006, from http://kerlins.net/bobbi/research/diss/ch01.html

Keup, J. R., & Barefoot, B. O. (2005). Learning how to be a successful student: Exploring the impact of first-year seminars on student outcomes. *The Journal of The First-Year Experience & Students in Transition, 17*(1), 11-47.

Kitchener, K., & King, P. (1981). Reflective judgment: Concepts of justification and their relationship to age and education. *Journal of Applied Developmental Psychology, 2,* 89-116.

Kurfiss, J. (1977). Sequentiality and structure in a cognitive model of college student development. *Developmental Psychology, 13,* 565-71.

Lave, J., & Wenger, E. (1991) *Situated learning: Legitimate peripheral participation.* Cambridge: Cambridge University Press.

Lee, S., & Roth, W. (2003). Becoming and belonging: Learning qualitative research through legitimate peripheral participation. *Forum: Qualitative Social Research, 4*(2). Retrieved March 2, 2006, from http://www.qualitative research.net/fsq-texte/2-03/2-03leeroth-e.htm

Levinson, D. (1978). *The seasons of a man's life.* New York: Ballantine Books.

Lovitts, B. (2001). *Leaving the ivory tower.* Lanham, MD: Rowman & Littlefield Publishers.

Marcia, J. E. (1966). Development and validation of ego identity status. *Journal of Personality and Social Psychology, 3,* 551-558.

Marcia, J. E. (1976). Identity six years after: A follow-up study. *Journal of Youth and Adolescence. 5,* 145–160.

Nettles, M. T., & Millet, C. M. (2006). *Three magic letters: Getting to PhD.* Baltimore: Johns Hopkins University Press.

Parent, E. (2003). *A systems model for doctoral student development and retention.* Retrieved February 16, 2006 from, http://weber.ucsd.edu/~eparent/part1/Final_description_model.html

Parent, E. (2005). *The academic game: Psychological strategies for successfully completing the doctorate.* West Conshohocken, PA: Infinity Publishing.

Pascarella, E. T., & Terenzini, P. T. (1991). *How college affects students.* San Francisco: Jossey-Bass.

Paulsen, M. B., & Wells, C. T. (1998). Domain differences in the epistemological beliefs of college students. *Research in Higher Education, 39*(4), 365-384.

Perry, W. (1970). *Forms of intellectual and ethical development in the college years: A scheme.* New York: Holt, Rinehart, and Winston.

Ross, L. (1977). The intuitive psychologist and his shortcomings: Distortions in the attribution process. In L. Berkowitz (Ed.), *Advances in experimental social psychology* (Vol. 10, 174-224) New York: Academic Press.

Schlossberg, N. K., Lynch, A. Q., & Chickering, A. W. (1989). *Improving higher education environments for adults*. San Francisco: Jossey-Bass.

Schommer, M. (1994). An emerging conceptualization of epistemological beliefs and their role in learning. In R. Garner & P. Alexander (Eds.), *Beliefs about text and about text instruction* (pp. 25-39). Hillsdale, NJ: Erlbaum.

Tinto, V. (1987). *Leaving college: Rethinking the causes and cures of student attrition*. Chicago: University of Chicago Press.

Tinto, V. (1993). Toward a theory of doctoral persistence. In *Leaving college: Rethinking the causes and cures of student attrition* (2nd ed., pp. 230-243). Chicago: University of Chicago Press.

Tokuno, K. A. (1993) Long term and recent student outcomes of the freshman interest group program. *The Journal of the Freshman Year Experience, 5,* 7-28.

Waterman, A. (1982). Identity development from adolescence to adulthood: An extension of theory and a review of research. *Developmental Psychology, 18,* 327-341.

▲ Chapter Three ▲

Transitional Needs of Master's Students

Joshua Alexander and Michelle Maher

Institutions of higher education have developed various programs and services designed to acclimate students to their new campus environments and alleviate the pressures and anxieties they face throughout their transition. Although a significant focus has been placed on orienting and serving undergraduate students, graduate students are an often-neglected segment of the student population in terms of institutional support (Vlisides & Eddy, 1993). While the past two decades have seen increased interest in better understanding the doctoral student experience (Bowen & Rudenstine, 1992; Golde & Dore, 2001; Lovitts, 2001; Nettles & Millett, 2006), the plight of the master's student experience remains largely unexplored. This is unfortunate because in 2005, 574,618 students earned master's degrees, compared with 52,831 students who earned doctorates that same year (National Center for Education Statistics, 2006). Also, the rate of master's degree attainment has increased an average of 3% each year since 1987 (Brown, 2005). Thus, it is important for institutions of higher education to place more of their efforts on this frequently neglected population and create opportunities that will enable master's level students to find success throughout their transition to graduate school.

In this chapter, we identify the need for institutional transitional support at the master's level and recommend that it be comparable to that currently offered to assist undergraduate students as they adjust to their campus and program of study. We review existing literature on master's students' experiences, noting that limited research is available on the current state and scope of the needs and difficulties experienced by this student population. We then present a recent study that investigates the type and intensity of students' anxieties prior to and during their transition to their graduate programs. Our results indicated that a significant number of areas elicit anxieties and difficulties among study respondents. In particular, master's students participating in this study said the three greatest producers of anxiety and difficulty are (a) graduate-level academic demands, (b) balancing work and school, and (c) balancing finances.

The Need for Institutional Support at the Master's Level

Colleges and universities may fail to provide transitional services for the master's student population due to faulty assumptions. One assumption may be that master's students are familiar with available institutional services, since they have already completed an undergraduate degree (Rosenblatt & Christensen, 1993). However, another assumption is that because master's students are "mature, well-focused, goal oriented, and college graduates, they [are] capable of handling the responsibilities of graduate study without needing special services" (Polson, 2003, p. 59). These assumptions imply that all institutions operate along the same guidelines and principles and that an experience at one institution should prepare a student for any other collegiate experience. Also, such assumptions imply that only those who are immature and non-focused need assistance. Yet, any mature, well-focused, goal-oriented individual might need help in times of transition. Such generalizations cannot be made for any student population, especially when considering the range of institutions within the United States (e.g., private, public, single-gender, co-ed, religiously affiliated, nonprofit, for-profit).

Contrary to the above assumptions, researchers have found that many master's students are as anxious and confused about the transition to their new university as they were about the transition to their undergraduate studies (Rosenblatt & Christensen, 1993). Regardless of their age or maturity level, these students expressed the need for services to help them transition into a new situation (Baker, 1992; Rimmer, Lammert, & McClain, 1982). As such, institutions of higher education would benefit by recognizing the needs of master's students and addressing them during the first few months of matriculation (Vickio & Tack, 1989). Existing theories of graduate student persistence, such as Tinto's (1993) theory of doctoral persistence and Berkenkotter, Huckin, and Ackerman's (1991) model of transition into graduate study stress the importance of positive initial interactions with peers, faculty, and the larger academic community in the facilitation of student success. Additional information about these theories and others that detail the transition of graduate students to their graduate study can be found in chapter 2 in this volume.

Master's Students' Needs: Previous Research

Although they represent the majority of the graduate student population, we know substantively less about the needs of master's students than we do about their doctoral student counterparts. The limited research conducted on master's students has emphasized their goals (Globetti, Globetti, & Smith, 1991; Rimmer et al., 1982), their perspectives on their degree experiences (Conrad, Duren, & Haworth, 1998), their needs in adjusting to academics (Beeler, 1991), and the integral role advising plays in their experiences and success (Baird, 1995).

In an early example of this research, Rimmer et al. (1982) developed and administered a questionnaire that asked master's students to identify their needs at their universities. There were 82 respondents. The researchers concluded that

> [Master's degree] students have some special and perhaps unique needs that are not being met. In order to facilitate adjustment to and enrichment of the graduate school experience, student development professionals must become aware of these needs and make their fulfillment a commitment and priority. (p. 192)

Rimmer et al. found the greatest perceived needs included (a) departmental workshops on career planning, (b) professional development workshops, (c) a central location for information on social activities, (d) departmental orientation programs, and (e) a master's students newsletter. By providing each of these services, institutions of higher education would positively impact this student population and greatly improve their transition to graduate school.

More recently, Globetti et al. (1991) developed the Student Needs Assessment Survey out of concern that "unmet needs often frustrate career goals, while their satisfaction usually enhances personal and professional growth" (p. 42). The study, which was conducted at a southern public university and included responses from 122 graduate students, revealed that master's students incur a large amount of stress from finances, generated by both tuition costs and living expenses. They desire more support in the development of their speaking and writing skills, as well as resumé presentation. In addition, students desire more support from their university to handle the stresses and anxiety produced by the demands of their graduate program. The researchers reiterate that those concerned with the welfare of this student population will be increasingly challenged to meet these needs and others because not meeting the needs of these students will hinder their growth and development throughout their graduate experience.

Equally important to the needs of master's students are their perceptions of their educational experiences. Conrad et al. (1998) developed their research from perceived existing limitations on master's degree program literature, including minimal literature on students' experiences within their master's programs and little emphasis on the student perspective. They interviewed about 800 students, alumni, faculty, and administrators in 47 master's programs. Two themes emerged that were emphasized by master's students as important to their learning experiences: (a) their need for a community of learners and (b) their need for critical dialogue. A community of learners was defined as "the collegial and collaborative relationships among faculty and students... faculty and students [learn] from one another as 'co-learners'" (p. 66). Critical dialogue occurs when "faculty and students conjointly question existing knowledge, challenge key assumptions in their field, and develop and critically refine new understandings of knowledge and professional practice" (p. 67). These two elements engage students, enrich their experiences, and develop their appreciation for collaborative learning. The educational relationships built throughout the master's degree experience become powerful opportunities for professional development and encourage students to engage in their learning process. The research also illustrated the desire for more interactive and hands-on learning. These students value individual and peer leadership within learning. Conrad et al. also found that these students valued their experiences and the relationships they developed throughout their graduate studies.

The adjustment to academics and learning is also important to an educational experience. Beeler (1991) describes a four-stage framework for academic adjustment that is applicable to all full-time, first-year master's students. The adjustment begins with unconscious incompetence, where students have a "limited idea about what is to happen to them either in or outside of the classroom. Many of these individuals hold an inward, but subconscious, feeling of being academically under prepared to successfully handle advanced-level work" (p. 164). The second phase is conscious incompetence where students "are now aware of the deficits in dealing with some course topics... are reluctant to openly challenge professors' or peers' ideas" (p. 166). The third phase is unconscious competence where students "have an emerging academic competence but are largely unaware of it" (p. 166). The final phase is conscious competence where students "begin to openly display confidence in being able to perform with quality and feel competent in approaching future tasks" (p. 167).

Beeler recommends that those concerned with the welfare of this student population become familiar with these stages of academic adjustment and provide additional support outside the classroom to aid in each of these adjustment phases. Student affairs professionals, graduate program coordinators, faculty, and even graduate school representatives can help master's students develop their identity and achieve higher academic performance. They can do this by (a) designing programs that address academic concerns, (b) conducting research regarding academic stresses, (c) developing academic interventions, (d) making counseling available, and (e) educating the campus community on the academic needs of master's students.

Baird (1995) emphasizes the importance of the relationship between the faculty advisor and the master's student and how this relationship can positively or negatively impact the student's educational experience. Baird stresses the beginning phase of the master's degree career as the most important time for the student to adjust to the field of study and a time in which students need the most guidance. Challenges that students face within the first few semesters of their graduate program include (a) understanding the structure of the field, (b) becoming acquainted with the language and approach of the field, (c) becoming acquainted with the people and the emphasis of the program, (d) finding a group of peers, (e) finding an appropriate faculty sponsor, (f) obtaining sufficient financial assistance, and (g) dealing with the specifics of program and university requirements. The challenges that follow the first few semesters include (a) mastering the language and approach of the field, (b) identifying intellectual and professional interests, and (c) either choosing a thesis committee or preparing for comprehensive examinations. Baird emphasizes the importance of academic advisors playing an active role in supporting students during each of these challenges. Such support is an important investment in the collegiate experience of these students.

What is missing from our understanding of the experiences of these students is a current sense of the state and scope of master's students needs, campus services offered to address these needs, and student responses to those campus services. A more focused understanding of master's students will likely help create positive experiences for all students, regardless of their classification or status within the institution.

A New Effort to Understand Master's Students' Needs

In 2006, Alexander, the first author of this chapter, surveyed more than 200 master's-level students, investigating the anxieties they have prior to their entry into graduate programs and the difficulties they face during the transition into their graduate programs. The survey also examined the perceived impact of institutional and programmatic services offered to smooth the transitional process.

Alexander developed the Master's Degree Candidate Experiential Questionnaire for use in this study, based primarily on the findings of an earlier pilot study (Alexander, 2005). The questionnaire presented areas thought to produce anxieties before or difficulties during the transition to graduate school. Then, respondents were asked to rank each area using a four-point Likert scale. Areas included (a) adjusting to a classroom environment, (b) adjusting to graduate-level academic demands, (c) interacting with peers/colleagues in program of study, (d) interacting with faculty/staff and students in program of study, (e) adjusting to a new campus, (f) adjusting to university culture (e.g., campus trends and traditions), (g) living in a new city, (h) balancing work and school, (i) meeting familial commitments, (j) maintaining long distance and new relationships (e.g., friendships and romantic relationships), (k) finding a new religious/spiritual place for worship, and (l) fitting into program of study.

The questionnaire (which included some open-ended questions) was uploaded into Flashlight™ Online and was available for three months. Alexander identified a random sample of master's students from two large, public southeastern research institutions and then sent each student in this sample an e-mail describing the study's purpose and requesting their participation. A total of 3,996 e-mails were sent, and 203 students completed surveys, representing a 5% response rate. The respondents were primarily Caucasian (85.7%), women (79.3%), under the age of 30 (71%), single (64.5%), and did not attend the same university for graduate school as they did to receive their bachelor's degrees (76.4%). The students reported participating in eight different programs of study, ranging from engineering (2%) to education (24.6%).

Pretransition Anxieties and During Transition Difficulties

The ranked average anxiety and difficulty response means for all respondents are presented in Table 1. For analysis of this table, Alexander divided mean scores into 7 categories from "no anxieties/difficulties" (M = 0.00 - 0.99) to "extreme anxieties/difficulties" (M = 3.50 – 4.00). The anxieties and difficulties presented in the questionnaire elicited a variety of responses. All areas elicited some degree of anxiety or difficulty from respondents, ranging from none/minimal to moderate/extreme.

Table 1

Pretransition Anxieties and During Transition Difficulties Response Means (N = 203)

	Pretransition anxieties		**During transition difficulties**	
	n	*M*	*n*	*M*
Adjusting to a classroom environment	198	1.73	197	1.49
Adjusting to graduate-level academic demands	203	2.59	153	2.09
Interacting with peers/colleagues in program of study	203	2.09	124	1.70
Interacting with faculty/staff in program of study	203	2.17	203	1.61
Adjusting to a new campus	167	2.13	184	1.60
Adjusting to university culture (i.e., campus trends and traditions)	181	1.58	168	1.32
Adjusting to the demographics of students in program of study	192	1.61	165	1.42
Adjusting to the demographics of students in the university	184	1.49	197	1.38
Living in a new city	112	2.28	173	1.88
Adjusting to a new geographic culture	118	1.88	84	1.49
Balancing work and school	179	2.61	196	2.39
Meeting familial commitments	177	2.16	201	1.81
Maintaining long-distance friendships	170	1.82	200	1.66
Maintaining long-distance romantic relationships	80	2.33	186	2.10
Maintaining roommate relationships	79	1.68	112	1.60
Learning how to utilize campus services/resources	183	1.80	169	1.75
Finding a new religious/spiritual place for worship	90	1.52	83	1.35
Balancing finances	196	2.80	81	2.35
Fitting into your program of study	198	2.11	181	1.75
Other	22	3.00	20	2.20

Pretransition Anxieties

In reflecting on their greatest anxieties prior to their transition to graduate school, students noted that three areas elicited a moderate level of pretransition anxiety: (a) balancing finances, (b) balancing work and school, and (c) adjusting to graduate-level academic demands. Further down the scale, seven areas elicited a minimal/moderate level of pretransition anxiety, including (a) maintaining long-distance romantic relationships, (b) living in a new city, (c) interacting with faculty and staff, (d) meeting familial commitments, (e) adjusting to a new campus, (f) fitting into program of study, and (g) interacting with peers/colleagues.

During Transition Difficulties

Master's student respondents were also asked to reflect on perceived difficulties experienced as they engaged in their transition to their graduate school programs. In each area, students' mean response indicating the level of difficulty they *experienced* during their transition was lower than their mean response indicating the level of anxiety they *anticipated* prior to their transition. In addition, no area elicited greater than a response mean of 2.39 (moderate difficulty) on a 4.00-point scale. The areas that elicited the greatest level of transitional difficulty, student responses showed, were (a) balancing work and school, (b) balancing finances, (c) maintaining long-distance romantic relationships, and (d) adjusting to graduate-level academic demands.

Overall Perspective

The responses noted above confirm that while the level of anxiety or difficulty throughout their transition might vary by student, some master's students experience, a degree of anxiety and difficulty in all of the areas presented in the questionnaire. While all of these areas are important, three were rated the highest by the respondents: (a) adjusting to graduate-level academic demands, (b) balancing work and school, and (c) balancing finances. Based on past research, it can be concluded that these three areas are the greatest producers of anxiety and difficulty among this student population as supported by the findings of Baird (1995), Baker (1992), Beeler (1991), Globetti et al. (1991), and Polson (2003).

Institutional and Departmental Programs and Services

In the final two sections of the questionnaire, students assessed the effectiveness of institutional and departmental programs and services provided in response to their needs. Institutional programs and services included campus tours, graduate/professional student associations and federations, graduate student orientations, graduate student workshops, and online resources. Departmental programs and services included brown bag lunch discussions, departmental electronic mailing lists/program online resources, department orientations, faculty forums, and professional development workshops.

Table 2 presents the average means associated with the rank of each program and service assessed in this study, differentiating between institutional and departmental services. For analysis of this table, Alexander divided mean scores into two categories: Negative impact (M = 0.00 – 2.49), referring to scores that fell into the negative or extremely negative category, and positive impact (M = 2.50 – 4.00), referring to scores that fell into the positive or extremely positive category.

Table 2
Average Effect Means for Data Respondents (*N* = 203)

	Effect means	
Institutional program or service	***n***	***M***
Campus tour	41	2.95
Graduate student association/graduate & professional student federation	47	2.94
Graduate student orientation	90	3.04
Graduate student workshops	47	2.98
Online resources (e.g., student resource guide/graduate student FAQs)	116	2.97
	Effect means	
Department program or service	***n***	***M***
Brown bag lunch discussions	44	2.84
Department listservs/program online resources	150	3.13
Department orientation	155	3.12
Faculty forums	27	3.04
Professional development workshops	59	2.98

All programs and services elicited a positive effect on the students' transitional experience. The lowest response mean was associated with department brown bag lunches, rated 2.84, while the highest mean was associated with department orientations, rated 3.12. The respondents rated all of the programs and services with a positive rating, indicating that they all elicited a positive effect on average with the student transitional experience.

Conclusion

There is indeed a need for institutional support at the master's level, funneled through graduate school representatives, graduate program coordinators and faculty, and student affairs professionals. The support should be comparable to that currently offered to assist undergraduate students in their transition to their campuses and programs of study. Contrary to the faulty assumptions that master's students do not need this type or level of support, researchers have found that many master's students are just as anxious and confused about the transition to their new universities as they were about their transition to their undergraduate studies (Rosenblatt & Christensen, 1993).

Findings of our recent investigation undertaken to reveal the current concerns of master's students prior to and during their transition to graduate study suggest that key areas of concern are (a) adjusting to graduate-level academic demands, (b) balancing work and school, and (c) balancing finances. However, in the same study, master's students indicated that all programs or services offered by institutions of higher education were beneficial during the transition process—be they at the institutional level (e.g., graduate student associations/graduate and professional student federations, graduate student orientations, graduate student workshops) or at the department level (e.g., departmental electronic mailing lists/program online resources, department orientations, faculty forums).

When asked to provide advice to those who plan to enter graduate school, survey respondents' ideas could be grouped into seven themes as outlined below:

- ◇ *Be academically prepared.* One student sums up the experience "...be prepared for a different side of college. It's tough, and it's different from your undergraduate experience, but it is also rewarding."
- ◇ *Become familiar with resources.* Students encouraged others to "be proactive in seeking out information" and to "get to know your professors...knowing them will help you a great deal."
- ◇ *Make sure the school/region is a good personal fit.* One student encouraged others to "do a lot of research into campus culture to make sure you will fit with the people you are going to spend the next few years with."
- ◇ *Contact current students.* As one respondent advocated, "talk[ing] with current students in the program and ask[ing] what types of things they think you should know before entering the school."
- ◇ *Enroll at the right time in life for you.* "Do it immediately after you receive your undergrad degree. Don't want until family, marriage, job, and kids fill your plate," one student advised. Another student said "Work before you go back to graduate school; it gives you perspective."
- ◇ *Be prepared financially.* One student noted, "Having to work or worry about money is one more thing to worry about."
- ◇ *Be prepared to give up personal/free time.* One student noted, "Be prepared to give up your social life and learn to balance time very well." Another student advised "Kiss your weekend goodbye!"

We encourage readers who work with master's level students in various campus capacities to turn to those who are in the best position to share what services and programs they need—the students themselves. As Alexander found in his study with master's students, the transition to graduate school is fraught with challenges that exist beyond the first few weeks in a program. With more than a half a million students earning master's degrees each year, we must make a stronger commitment to offer appropriate transitional services to them and to the graduate student population as a whole if we hope to see more of them achieve their academic and career goals.

References

Alexander, J. (2005). *The graduate student transition: Experiences of an overlooked population.* Unpublished master's thesis, University of South Carolina, Columbia, SC.

Baird, L. L. (1995). Helping graduate students: A graduate advisor's view. In A. S. Pruitt-Logan & P. D. Isaac (Eds.), *Student services for the changing graduate student population* (New Directions for Student Services, No. 72, pp. 25-32). San Francisco: Jossey-Bass.

Baker, H. K. (1992). Service needs of traditional age and adult graduate students. *NASPA Journal, 30*(1), 20-29.

Beeler, K. D. (1991). Graduate student adjustment to academic life: A four-stage framework. *NASPA Journal, 28*(2), 163-171.

Berkenkotter, C., Huckin, T.N., & Ackerman, J. (1991). Social context and socially constructed texts: The initiation of a graduate student into a writing research community. In C. Bazerman & J. Paradis (Eds.), *Textual dynamics of the professions: Historical and contemporary studies of writing in professional communities* (pp. 191-215). Madison, WI: University of Wisconsin Press.

Bowen, W. G., & Rudenstine, N. L. (1992). *In pursuit of the Ph.D.* Princeton, NJ: Princeton University Press.

Brown, H. A. (2005). *Graduate enrollment and degrees: 1986 to 2005.* Washington, DC: Council of Graduate Schools, Office of Research and Information Services.

Conrad, C. F., Duren, K. M., & Haworth, J. G. (1998). Students' perspectives on their master's degree experiences: Disturbing the conventional wisdom. In M. S. Anderson (Ed.), *The experience of being in graduate school: An exploration* (New Directions for Higher Education, No. 101, pp. 65-76). San Francisco: Jossey-Bass.

Globetti, E., Globetti, G., & Smith, R. E. (1991). An assessment of goals and perceived needs of graduate students: Some implications. *The College Student Affairs Journal, 10*(3), 41-53.

Golde, C. M., & Dore, T. M. (2001). *At cross purposes: What the experiences of today's doctoral students reveal about doctoral education.* Philadelphia: Pew Charitable Trusts.

Lovitts, B. E. (2001). *Leaving the ivory tower: The causes and consequences of departure from doctoral study.* Landham: Rowman & Littlefield.

National Center for Education Statistics. (2006). *Doctor's degrees conferred by degree-granting institutions, by discipline division: Selected years, 1970–71 through 2004–05.* Retrieved September 2007, from http://nces.ed.gov/programs/digest/d06/tables/dt06_256.asp

Nettles, M. T., & Millett, C. M. (2006). *Three magic letters: Getting to Ph.D.* Johns Hopkins University Press.

Polson, C. J. (2003). Adult graduate students challenge institutions to change. In D. Kilgore & P. J. Rice (Eds.), *Meeting the special needs of adult students* (New Directions for Student Services, No. 102, pp. 59-68). San Francisco: Jossey-Bass.

Rimmer, S. M., Lammert, M., & McClain, P. (1982). An assessment of graduate student needs. *College Student Journal, 16,* 187-192.

Rosenblatt, H. S., & Christensen, C. (1993). "Welcome to the whole family:" A graduate student orientation. *College Student Journal, 27,* 502-505.

Tinto, V. (1993). *Leaving college: Rethinking the causes and cures of student attrition* (2nd ed.) Chicago: University of Chicago Press.

Vickio, C. J., & Tack, M. W. (1989). Orientation programming for graduate students: An institutional imperative. *NACADA Journal, 9*(2), 37-42.

Vlisides, D., & Eddy, J. (1993). Graduate student orientation models. *College Student Journal, 27,* 96-98.

Chapter Four

Graduate Students of Color: Unique Challenges

Miya T. Simpson

The limited research on the experiences of graduate students of color[1] reveals unique challenges in their transition into graduate study. Some of the factors found to affect the transition experience of graduate students of color include (a) their ability to integrate into the academic and social environment, (b) their feelings of isolation and marginalization, (c) the quality of the relationships with faculty and peers, (d) the presence of a critical mass in the program and on the campus, and (e) the availability of mentors and other support systems within the environment (Clewell, 1987; DeFour & Hirsch, 1990; Lewis, Ginsberg, & Davies, 2004; Smith & Davison, 1992). Culturally unaware and insensitive faculty, a lack of appreciation for diverse research perspectives, unfamiliarity with the nature of graduate education, and general dissatisfaction with the program may also influence graduate students' adjustment (Cuadraz, 1996; Gay, 2004; Vaughn, 1985).

Institutions have a responsibility to provide a supportive environment for graduate students of color that stimulates their growth as scholars, engages them in the university culture, and helps them achieve their goal of earning an advanced degree (Council of Graduate Schools, 2003b). Helping students of color negotiate the academic and social systems within the graduate program and university should be an institutional priority. An awareness of the environmental challenges that exist for ethnic minority graduate students and the factors that contribute to their adjustment and persistence is integral to easing their transition—only then is it possible to develop effective strategies and comprehensive programs to support graduate students of color and facilitate their successful transition into graduate school.

This chapter explores the transitional needs of graduate students of color. A brief review of the literature related to the experiences and transition of ethnic minority graduate students is provided, as well as an overview of best practices and programs aimed at helping students of color make the transition into the graduate environment. Finally, recommendations for designing programs and services that contribute to successful transition experiences and degree attainment are offered.

Graduate School Participation Among Students of Color

Of the approximately 2 million students enrolled in graduate school in 2005, the combined total for ethnic minority students was 377,300 students (*Chronicle of Higher Education,* 2007). African Americans accounted for the largest ethnic minority group (233,200 students) followed by Hispanic/Latino (130,700), and Native American (13,400) graduate students.

Though African American, Hispanic/Latino, and Native American students continue to be underrepresented in graduate education, the growing number of students from these groups enrolling in graduate school has been one of the most notable trends in graduate education over the past 19 years (Council of Graduate Schools, 2006). It is estimated that between 1986 and 2005, ethnic minority enrollment increased at an average annual rate of 4% to 6%, with Hispanic/Latino groups experiencing the greatest growth. Data reveal that most students of color continue to be concentrated in education programs (i.e., African Americans – 31%, Hispanic/Latinos – 31%, and Native Americans – 29%) and are least represented in the biological sciences, physical sciences, and engineering (i.e., accounting for 5% or less of all students enrolled across these fields).

While there have been steady increases in graduate enrollment over the last few decades, the risk of attrition remains high for students of color. Of the 52,631 doctoral and 574,618 master's degrees awarded in 2005, ethnic minority students earned an estimated 10% of doctorates and 15% of master's degrees (U. S. Census Bureau, 2008). Though students of color enter graduate programs with the aptitude, desire, and will to succeed, the non-academic challenges they may encounter by being one of few ethnic minority students in their program or on their campus may impede their adjustment to and progress within their graduate programs (Lewis et al., 2004; Nettles, 1990). Overcoming these potential barriers presents distinct challenges for graduate students of color as they attempt to successfully transition into the graduate environment.

Graduate School Experiences for Students of Color

Research on the experiences of graduate students of color reveals several factors that influence their transition. These include (a) the ability to integrate into the academic and social systems of the university, (b) feelings of marginalization and isolation, (c) the presence of a critical mass of peers and faculty of color, (d) access to faculty and peer relationships and mentoring opportunities, and (e) cultural stereotyping and discrimination. The extent to which these issues are present can have a profound impact on the experiences, socialization, and professional development of graduate students—all of which may influence their transition.

Academic and Social Integration

The degree of compatibility that exists between the student and the environment is crucial to the students' successful integration into the environment—the greater the compatibility the more likely it is that the student will persist. This compatibility can be explained in terms of academic and social integration (Ponce, 1988). *Academic integration* is defined as "the development of a strong affiliation with the college academic environment to include interactions of an academic nature with faculty, staff, and peers" (Nora & Cabrera, 1993, p. 235). Among ethnic minority students, academic integration may be influenced by variables such as the students' classroom experiences and satisfaction with the academic program and climate, as well as the interactions with and attitudes of faculty and peers (Allen, 1987; Cabrera, Nora, & Castaneda, 1993; Hurtado, Carter, & Spuler, 1996; Tinto, 1987). Students who find it difficult to integrate into the academic culture may be more likely to feel disconnected from the institution and consider dropping out.

Social integration is related to the students' informal or out-of-classroom experiences and is assessed through the students' personal and social success within the overall campus environment (Ponce, 1988). The notion of social integration has also been described as the development of a strong social affiliation with the collegiate environment and the informal social interactions that exist between the student and the faculty, staff, and peers in that environment (Nora & Cabrera, 1993) Finding a positive comfort level is of great importance to the adaptation and academic success of students of color and has an influence on their ability to adjust to and remain in graduate school (Turner, 1994). Encouraging students' involvement in activities that extend beyond the classroom such as informal discussion groups, research projects, student organizations and conferences, and other professional development opportunities are just a few examples of how social integration can occur.

Feelings of Marginalization and Isolation

Marginalization and isolation are major issues among graduate students of color, particularly those attending predominantly White institutions (Lewis et al., 2004; Gay, 2004; Nettles, 1990; Norton, 2000). Being the lone or one of a few students of color in a class or program can be intimidating, as their opinions and perspectives are all too often devalued or ignored. Feelings of marginalization can be particularly strong for women of color who report experiences of "multiple marginality," in which bias based on race, language, class, and/or gender occurs (Cuadraz, 1996; Rodriguez, Guido-DiBrito, Torres, & Talbot, 2000). Students of color, like everyone, desire to be acknowledged and affirmed, and the extent to which they feel included in or rejected by the graduate environment influences their ability to make a successful transition.

The marginalization and isolation encountered by students of color is intensified by the absence of culturally relevant content in the classroom and graduate curriculum, as ethnic and cultural differences are rarely taken into account in course materials, discussions, research, and pedagogy (Gay, 2004; Woods, 2001). The experiences and worldview that students of color bring to the academic environment not only offer opportunities for more varied and stimulating discourse but also advances diversity beyond the mere composition of the student body. Expanding the curriculum so that it is inclusive of different viewpoints, experiences, and interests contributes to a more enriched learning environment for all students and one in which ethnic minority students feel comfortable sharing their perspectives. However, care must be taken to ensure that when issues of race/ethnicity and diversity are raised, students of color are not perceived as representing or speaking on behalf of their entire ethnic group (Gay, 2004).

Presence of a critical mass. Having a critical mass of peers and faculty of color at the institution is one way to minimize the marginalization and isolation felt by ethnic minority graduate students and to foster a greater sense of community. For graduate students of color, an ideal community includes others who look like them, have similar needs and concerns, and can serve as mentors and provide support networks (Gay, 2004; Lewis et al., 2004). Without these, graduate students of color report feeling like they "stand out," and perceive greater scrutiny from faculty, peers, and others within the community (Cuadraz, 1996; Lewis et al, 2004).

The lack of a critical mass also presents fewer opportunities for graduate students of color to interact with others who can relate to their experiences as an ethnic minority and aid in their transition. A greater ethnic minority presence would afford students with role models and mentors who could help them cope with their experiences or advise them on navigating their graduate experience as a person of color. Aggressive and ongoing recruitment initiatives and hiring practices that attract individuals from underrepresented groups would increase the number of ethnic minority graduate students and faculty, thus creating the critical mass and sense of community necessary for students of color (Council of Graduate Schools, 2003b).

Faculty and peer relationships and mentoring opportunities. The frequency and quality of interactions that students of color have in the graduate school environment are important determinants of integration, success, and persistence (Nettles, 1990; Nora, 1987; Norton, 2000; Simpson, 2003). Positive relationships increase the likelihood that students will be satisfied with their experiences. Further, such interactions allow for the development of formal and informal socialization and mentoring opportunities. Mentoring creates opportunities for relationship building and helps students understand the values, norms, practices, and attitudes of the discipline and graduate culture (Crawford, Figert, Suarez-Balcazar, & Nyden, 1996; Johnson-Bailey, 2004; Laden, 1999). Supportive mentoring relationships contribute to a positive institutional climate (Council of Graduate Schools, 2003c; Richardson, Simmons, & de los Santos, 1987) and promote professional development among ethnic minority graduate students (Smith & Davison, 1992).

Faculty-student mentoring arrangements help students of color feel comfortable and supported in graduate school. The quality of the interaction with faculty can indicate to students that they are a valued part of the department and that they are developing into competent professionals (DeFour & Hirsch, 1990; Simpson, 2003). A close relationship with at least one faculty member can help to reduce feelings of alienation among ethnic minority graduate students and facilitate the student's transition into graduate study (Olson, 1988). Relationships with faculty advisors are especially important, because faculty advisors can provide opportunities for students to meet, interact, and form relationships with other professors within the student's field of study. Furthermore, they can help students of color understand the graduate and professional culture and negotiate the rules, both written and unwritten, that abound. Faculty also benefit from these relationships as they are able to get to know the student better and learn about their experiences not only as a graduate student but also as a person of color in that environment.

Peer-to-peer mentoring relationships are also valuable in helping graduate students of color in their transition. Peer mentors provide greatly needed support, encouragement, and motivation (Dorn & Papalewis, 1997; Smith & Davison, 1992). Strong relationships with peers may help students of color feel more of an attachment to their program and the institution. Further, these relationships offer social support for students of color as they grapple with the academic and personal difficulties encountered in the academic environment and may lead to long-lasting personal and professional relationships. For African American students in particular, research shows that the presence of and networking with African American peers is important for retention (Johnson-Bailey, 2004). Also, linking first-year students to more advanced students and alumni of color provides an opportunity for students to get candid advice about expectations and graduate student life, the campus climate, faculty, and navigating the graduate school landscape.

Cultural Stereotyping and Discrimination

The damaging stereotypes that may exist about African American, Hispanic/Latino, and Native American populations influence the way graduate students from these groups are perceived by faculty and peers within the academic environment as entrenched beliefs about minority group inferiority are often manifested in the behaviors and attitudes of certain faculty members (Rodriguez et al., 2000). As a result, incidents of racial stereotyping and discrimination are not uncommon for ethnic minority graduate students (Gay, 2004; Nettles, 1990). Students of color are very sensitive to the persistent doubt surrounding their intellectual capacity, the devaluation of their research interests and skills, and the expectations that their performance will be inferior to that of their White counterparts. This is especially true for students coming from historically Black colleges and universities and other minority-serving institutions who are overwhelmingly (and inaccurately) perceived as being underprepared for the rigors of graduate school. Unfortunately, the negative attitudes and expectations of faculty and peers can inhibit the minority students' academic success and prevent them from performing to their full potential. Therefore, it is imperative that institutions provide an inclusive learning environment where students of color and their perspectives (and those who encourage them) are recognized, appreciated, and supported and where those who engage in discriminatory and racist practices are held accountable.

Transition Programs for Students of Color

Formal and informal structures that aid in the transition and socialization of ethnic minority students are essential to improving retention and graduation rates among graduate students of color (Council of Graduate Schools, 2003b). The last two decades brought forth a considerable number of academic achievement, recruitment, and retention programs with the goal of increasing the number of students of color entering graduate school and earning advanced degrees. Programs that enhance preparedness and educational motivation, foster integration into the academic environment, and facilitate faculty and student interactions offer the greatest hope for increasing access to and persistence in graduate school among ethnic minority students (Frierson, Hargrove, & Lewis, 1994; Nnadozie, Ishiyama, & Chon, 2000).

Improving transition experiences for graduate students of color requires efforts at both the undergraduate and graduate level. Transition programs aimed at undergraduates can create a pipeline to graduate school by providing experiences that motivate and prepare them to pursue graduate study. These programs will be referred to as Graduate School Preparation Programs. Transition programs created to address the needs of enrolled graduate students provide support within the graduate environment and assist students in making progress toward the graduate degree. These programs will be referred to as Graduate School Support Programs. A description of successful programs in each category offers insight into the design, activities, and progress made in moving graduate students of color into and through graduate school. While programs may vary in structure, financial assistance available to students, and disciplinary focus, the following similarities exist: (a) an emphasis on enhancing the academic motivation, preparation, and success of underrepresented students; (b) participation in research, professional development and community-building activities; (c) mentoring and/or advising opportunities; and (d) social and academic support networks.

Graduate School Preparation Programs

The Ronald E. McNair Post-Baccalaureate Achievement Program (McNair Scholars Program) is one of six federal TRIO programs funded by the U.S. Department of Education. The program encourages and prepares high-achieving students from low-income, first-generation, and underrepresented backgrounds to enter and complete Ph.D. programs (U.S. Department of Education, 2005). Activities are designed to expose students to graduate education and help them develop skills that will lead to their entry into and success within graduate school. This includes providing information about graduate study and the application process, engaging students in scholarly research with university faculty, and developing research and presentation skills. McNair Scholars also have opportunities to interact with currently enrolled graduate students through panel discussions, campus programs, and national conferences. A profile of the McNair Scholars Program (U.S. Department of Education) shows that the percentage of undergraduate participants who enter graduate school, has grown steadily from 13% to 39% in less than four years. Approximately 40% of McNair participants who completed their bachelor's degrees in 2000-01 were accepted into a graduate program and of that number, 98% enrolled. A report also revealed that 16% of all participants had earned a master's degree and 4% (500 students) had earned a doctoral or other terminal degree (U. S. Department of Education).

The Summer Research Opportunity Program (SROP) was initiated in 1986 by Graduate Deans within the Committee of Institutional Cooperation (CIC), a consortium of 15 midwestern research universities that includes the "Big Ten." SROP is designed to encourage talented undergraduate students of color to pursue graduate study (ideally at CIC institutions) and careers in academia and to enhance diversity within the faculty ranks. The program involves three complementary components: (a) research internships, (b) campus-based workshops, and (c) a CIC-wide summer research conference. Each host campus offers weekly educational enrichment activities designed to expand students' views of graduate education and research, strengthen their technical skills, explore graduate admissions procedures and financial aid opportunities, and foster the development of a community of scholars.

More than 9,500 students from 493 colleges and universities in 50 states have participated in the SROP program. Of the 2,924 students successfully tracked beyond degree completion, over 75% have enrolled in or completed a graduate or professional degree. Of these, 204 have completed a Ph.D. and 645 have earned a master's degree (Zepeda, 2006).

The mission of the Meyerhoff Scholars Program at the University of Maryland – Baltimore County is to promote diversity in science, engineering, and math (SEM). The program targets high-achieving students interested in studying and pursuing careers in SEM fields and "successfully challenges notions about minority achievement while changing the perceptions and attitudes of the faculty, peers, and researchers with whom they interact" (UMBC, 2007). Originally intended to serve African American men, the program is now open to all U.S. citizens and permanent residents and is designed to create an environment of challenge and support for students, prior to college matriculation through graduation, and beyond. The comprehensive approach of the Meyerhoff Scholars Program increases students' engagement in their discipline and helps them make the transition into the academic environment. The four major objectives of the program include: (a) academic and social integration; (b) knowledge and skills development; (c) support and motivation; and (d) monitoring and advising. The program also offers merit based financial support from entry to graduation.

Since 1993, the UMBC Meyerhoff Scholars Program has graduated 557 students. Fifty-five alumni have earned a Ph.D. or M.D./Ph.D. and 189 are currently enrolled in a Ph.D. or M.D./Ph.D. program (UMBC, 2008).

Graduate Student Support Programs

The McKnight Doctoral Fellowship Program was established in 1984 to increase the number of African American and Hispanic faculty at colleges and universities in the state of Florida by increasing the pool of citizens with Ph.D. degrees qualified to teach at the university level. Up to 25 fellowships are awarded annually to study at one of the nine participating Florida universities. Fellowships consist of $17,000 per year for tuition, fees, and stipends. Annual renewal of the fellowship is contingent upon satisfactory performance and normal progress toward the

Ph.D. The program has increased the number of African Americans earning the Ph.D. in fields of study where they have not historically enrolled and completed degree programs. The retention rate for the program is estimated at 80%, with an average completion time of five years (Florida Education Fund, n.d.).

The Southern Regional Education Board's (SREB) Doctoral Scholars Program is part of a nationwide initiative to produce more Ph.D.s of color and encourage them to seek faculty positions. Since its founding in 1993, the Doctoral Scholars Program has supported more than 796 scholars attending 84 institutions in 29 states. Committed to providing "more than a check and a handshake," the program partners with states to encourage and enroll students in graduate school and provide academic and financial support to help them progress through their doctoral program and secure faculty positions (Norton, 2000, p. 7). SREB and participating states share resources as they work to expand their ethnic minority applicant pool and provide students with financial assistance for up to five years of graduate study. Students credit the program with reducing feelings of isolation and alienation within the graduate environment, creating a supportive network among faculty and peers, making doctoral degree attainment more affordable, providing access to mentors and professional socialization experiences, strengthening their research and teaching skills, and helping them persist to completion (Norton, 2000).

Each year, SREB hosts the Institute on Teaching and Mentoring, which focuses on mentoring and preparation for teaching and provides significant networking opportunities for students. This four-day conference has become the largest gathering of doctoral scholars of color in the country and draws national attention to the issue of faculty diversity (Southern Regional Education Board, n.d.). The conference provides a comfortable, supportive environment where minority scholars and faculty can share their experiences and discuss strategies for succeeding in graduate school and as a member of the professoriate. The Institute, along with the academic, financial, and professional development experiences the program provides, contributes to the success of the SREB Doctoral Scholars Program, which has a retention rate of approximately 89% and has served more than 400 graduates. In addition, 79% of all graduates are employed in an educational setting, with 97% working in a postsecondary setting (Abraham, 2008).

The Virginia Tech Minority Academic Opportunities Program (MAOP, 2006) encourages and supports underrepresented students to pursue and obtain academic degrees at all levels and is one of the few graduate school preparation programs with a focus on master's students. The MAOP promotes an academic success community founded upon the principles of self-help, mentoring, and peer support. Working collaboratively with academic departments, the program strives to enhance diversity within the campus environment; graduate education; and science, technology, engineering, and mathematics (STEM) disciplines. The program guides students through the academic pipeline and offers academic and financial support along the way. A primary component of the MAOP is the summer research experience that pairs students with faculty members to design and conduct a research project. Students also attend seminars related to graduate academic life and receive guidance and counseling on gaining admission to graduate school and preparing for the GRE. MAOP participants are also required to become involved in professional and career development activities and to engage in social support activities and organizations as a means of increasing faculty and peer interactions, establishing professional networks, identifying mentors, and building a network of support within and outside of the academic environment. Since its establishment in 1992, MAOP reports a graduation rate of 90% of its undergraduate students and an 88% retention and graduation rate among graduate participants.

The Meyerhoff Graduate Fellows Program at The University of Maryland-Baltimore County is modeled after the undergraduate training program and helps the university meet its commitment to increasing diversity and enhancing success for doctoral students on campus. The graduate component supports students in biomedical science and engineering through a summer bridge retreat, regular meetings to monitor students' progress, and discussions about students' experiences in their graduate programs. From 1996 to 2002, the number of Fellows increased from 2 to 31, representing a little less than half of the institution's Ph.D. students of color (Council of Graduate Schools, 2003a). The program is integrated with its undergraduate counterpart, the Meyerhoff Scholars Program, as well as the National Institute of Health (NIH) Minority Access to Research Careers and Undergraduate Student Training in Academic Research (MARC U*STAR) programs. The comprehensive support system provided by the university enhances success among graduate students of color and reduces feelings of isolation and alienation (Council of Graduate Schools, 2003a).

Recommendations

Improving experiences for students of color and easing their transition into the academic environment is more likely to occur in a caring and supportive environment where there is a true commitment to ensuring the success of all students (Council of Graduate Schools, 2003b). The existing literature, along with the successful graduate school preparation and support programs highlighted in this chapter offers insight into how institutions can address the needs and unique challenges of graduate students of color and enhance their transition to graduate school. Comprehensive approaches that take into account the roles of the institution, graduate school dean, faculty, and students are integral to creating a nurturing and supportive environment for ethnic minority students as are approaches that acknowledge, embrace, and value diversity. This chapter concludes with a discussion of specific recommendations for each segment of the graduate community.

Institutions

Institutional practices have a significant impact on transition experiences and persistence among students of color (CGS, 2003a; 2003b). Consequently, institutions should examine practices, policies, and programs to see if and how they affect the experiences of students of color. Findings may indicate the need for new, or changes to existing, strategies for recruitment, admissions, and advising; curriculum; research practices; and diversity training opportunities for faculty and students.

Institutions should also develop aggressive recruitment strategies that yield a significant number of students and faculty of color to establish a critical mass (Council of Graduate Schools, 2003a; 2003b). This might involve creating and/or partnering with pipeline programs that target promising underrepresented students and faculty, developing relationships with minority-serving institutions through research opportunities and faculty exchange programs, setting up campus visitation programs that allow students of color to interact with faculty and students in a graduate program of interest and get a feel for the campus, and establishing post-doctoral programs for recent Ph.D. recipients of color. It is critical that initiatives have adequate human and fiscal resources, as well as the commitment of the university leadership to move them forward.

In designing recruitment programs, it is extremely important that institutions realize that recruitment and retention go hand-in-hand. Simply attracting diverse students and faculty to the campus is not enough. Institutions must think beyond recruitment to envisioning the experiences individuals of color will have once they arrive on campus. Is the environment a welcoming and comfortable one? Will individuals of color feel valued on the campus and within their academic departments? Are there resources and support mechanisms in place to assist in their transition? Affirmative responses to these questions make retention more likely and will facilitate the individuals' integration into the academic and social fabric of the institution. A diverse and inclusive environment that supports and encourages all members, assists in their professional development, and offers a critical mass can minimize the feelings of isolation and marginalization experienced by students and faculty of color and ease their transition.

Ensuring a welcoming and supportive environment for students of color also calls for diversity within the curriculum and greater cultural competence and sensitivity among those within the academic environment. Institutions must acknowledge and address the need for effective cultural awareness training, particularly for faculty. It will also be necessary for institutions to provide the tools and resources that will enable faculty to teach and interact effectively with diverse students and design courses and materials that incorporate diverse experiences and perspectives.

Lastly, institutions must hold faculty and others within the academic environment accountable for the negative and discriminatory behaviors exhibited toward students of color. All too often emphasis is placed on changing student behaviors, particularily, teaching them to adapt to the environment instead of focusing efforts toward those who truly have the power to make a difference in improving the climate for students of color—faculty. Faculty who intentionally engage in behaviors that perpetuate isolation and marginalization of students of color should face punitive consequences. The consequences of such behavior would depend largely on institutional context but might include a written reprimand that becomes part of the faculty member's permanent record, mandatory diversity or sensitivity training, and restricted university support in securing internal or external funding. Such responses send a message that discriminatory behavior will not be tolerated. Conversely, institutions should reward the efforts of those leaders who promote a welcoming and inclusive environment for students of color.

Graduate School Deans

Graduate school deans have the influence and visibility to lead and support efforts that promote a more inclusive environment for students of color (Council of Graduate Schools, 2003a). More importantly, they have a responsibility to ensure that a diverse student body is recruited and that the academic and social climate is one that supports and encourages their transition and success. A common practice among graduate schools is to invite students to participate in structured campus visitation weekends and programs. These activities have become increasingly popular as a way for institutions to recruit talented and diverse students to their campuses and facilitate their entry into the graduate environment (Council of Graduate Schools, 2003a). The primary objective of most programs is to provide students an opportunity to experience the graduate program and department first-hand and become familiar with the campus and surrounding community. Through these visits, students of color can learn more about the graduate program and curriculum, interact with faculty and current students, obtain information about funding and student support, and get a feel for the academic environment. Armed with this information, students of color are able to make a more informed decision about their graduate school choice.

Structured orientation programs are also important and can serve as a means for welcoming new students of color to the campus, introducing them to key people within the university, and providing an overview of institutional and departmental policy and community resources. Orientation programs can help ease the students' transition by providing a supportive environment where they can get the information they need and meet and interact with graduate faculty and peers. During the orientation period, students of color could also be paired with a current graduate student who can act as a resource, guide, and campus connection assisting them in building relationships with others.

In addition to providing orientation programs, graduate school deans can be instrumental in creating other opportunities for social interaction among ethnic minority graduate students, faculty, and the academic community. Meet and greet sessions, open houses, informal brown bag discussions, and monthly seminars and lectures should be arranged to bring faculty and students together, inform students about the graduate school environment and culture they are entering, and aid in their transition and adjustment. Also, formal and informal mentoring programs would help to connect interested students with committed faculty and students who can serve as a resource and support system for them in the academic setting.

Finally, to ensure that graduate students of color make a successful transition and satisfactory academic progress, graduate school deans should provide leadership for implementing routine and consistent assessments of the campus and departmental climate for graduate students. Assigning a liaison to work with the faculty member or graduate program coordinator would allow for closer monitoring of each student; and, if necessary, appropriate notification and intervention strategies can be designed. Routine assessments would garner information on the experiences and treatment of ethnic minority (and other) graduate students and allow for any issues that exist to be identified and addressed in an appropriate and timely manner, as well as lead to opportunities for community building and socialization within the graduate environment.

Faculty

Relationships with faculty are critical for graduate students of color, both within and outside of the classroom. Faculty can facilitate academic interactions and reduce feelings of isolation among minority graduate students (Olson, 1988). Encouraging students of color to participate in classroom discussions and embracing the perspectives, ideas, and experiences they bring to the academic setting are paramount to making students feel comfortable and valued. Also, broadening the curriculum to reflect multiple racial and ethnic perspectives would lead to more stimulating and culturally relevant dialogue and a greater acceptance of diverse topics and approaches to research (Cuadraz, 1996; Gay, 2004).

Encouraging words and support from faculty foster a sense of belonging for students (Nora, 1987, Norton, 2000). Regular and supportive feedback, being accessible to students, showing a genuine interest in them in and out of the classroom, and offering support and encouragement are all effective ways to gain trust and insight into students' experiences and build meaningful, productive relationships. Acknowledging students' performance in the research setting, encouraging them to become involved in the academic environment, and helping students form relationships with students and faculty within the department are additional strategies for enhancing students' academic and social integration.

Faculty may want to pay closer attention to the interactions that occur outside the classroom, as students of color report few out-of-class interactions with faculty and too few opportunities to do so (Simpson, 2003). Encouraging and supporting students' involvement in research activities, providing publication and presentation opportunities, and facilitating social networking activities can contribute to students' professional development and ease their transition. Exclusion (intentional or unintentional) from professional development and other formal and informal networking opportunities can have a negative impact on graduate students of color (Johnson-Bailey, 2004; Simpson, 2003).

Students

Graduate students of color must not lose sight of the power they have in creating the conditions for their satisfaction and success. First, students have an obligation to do the necessary research and find out as much as they can about the institution and graduate environment they are entering. Students must not be afraid to ask essential questions (i.e., What is the racial/ethnic makeup of the department, academic college, and institution? What is the experience like for students of color at this institution? What are the retention and graduate rates for students of color?). In addition, they should not rely solely on the picture that the institution paints in brochures or during campus visits. Students of color need to identify students and faculty independent of those selected by the institution and talk with them about their experiences, as well as their perceptions of diversity and the institution's concern for students and faculty of color.

Students also need to be self-motivated, actively engaged in their learning process and willing to ask for help when needed. This last part might be difficult for many graduate students of color who may feel intimidated, lack the confidence to approach others for assistance, or have some concerns that doing so might suggest weakness or inferiority. It is imperative, however, that students work through these feelings and seek out information and resources that will help them achieve their academic goals.

It is also important for students of color to enter graduate school with some specific goals in mind regarding what they want to achieve academically, personally, and professionally and have an understanding of what needs to be done to achieve those goals. Along with this, students must make sure they have at least a general knowledge of the policies, procedures, and requirements that govern their academic program. Students should also maintain their own academic records and documentation so they can track their progress toward the degree (in addition to the system used by the department/institution).

Finally, students of color are advised to:

- Seek out and build their own community. This could be done through local church involvement, student and professional organizations, study teams, sports clubs, and other groups geared to their interests and goals.
- Keep an open mind, accept constructive feedback, and learn to discern it from criticism.
- Become informed about their rights as a student and member of the academic community, as well as the institutional policies and procedures for dealing with those who exhibit racist behaviors and attitudes. In the event that they encounter discriminatory behavior, students are not left to deal with it on their own; they can seek out the appropriate resources and individuals and follow the appropriate protocols to address the situation.
- Seek out champions who can offer support and advice on understanding and navigating the graduate school culture and system.

Conclusion

Graduate students of color are frequently confronted with many nonacademic challenges in the graduate environment that may impact their transition. If graduate schools are to enhance enrollment and satisfaction of ethnic minorities and create more inclusive environments for students from these groups, they must acknowledge and address the factors that interfere with their adjustment and impede progress. Programs and services both prior to and during graduate school are key to enhancing academic and social integration and to improving retention and graduation rates among students of color. As we have seen through the program descriptions presented in this chapter, comprehensive approaches that support students through the graduate school process, promote community building, facilitate meaningful faculty and student interactions, and respect the diverse experiences and perspectives students of color bring to the graduate environment are most effective in helping students of color transition into and persist through graduate school. Institutions that take these factors into account are poised to meet the unique needs of graduate students of color and facilitate their successful transition to graduate school.

Notes

[1]In this chapter, the terms, students of color, ethnic minority, and underrepresented groups are used interchangeably and include African Americans, Hispanics/Latinos, and Native Americans. Asian Americans are not included, because they are by some definitions not recognized as an underrepresented group in graduate education.

References

Abraham, A. (2008, February). *Achieving tenure and diversity: A decade, a difference…but still far to go*. Presented at the 2nd School of Education Student Association's annual conference, Blacksburg, VA.

Allen, W. R. (1987, May/June). Black colleges vs. White colleges. *Change, 19*(3), 28-34.

Cabrera, A. F., Nora, A., & Castaneda, M. B. (1993). College persistence: Structural equations modeling test of an integrated model of student retention. *Journal of Higher Education, 64,* 123-139.

The Chronicle of Higher Education. (2007). *The Chronicle of Higher Education Almanac*, 2006-2007 Retrieved August 29, 2007, from http://chronicle.com/weekly/almanac/2007/nation/0102002.htm

Clewell, B. C. (1987). *Retention of Black and Hispanic doctoral students, Part II: Retention of minority doctoral students: Institutional policies and practices*. (GRE Board Research Report No. 83-4R/ETS Research Report 87-10). Princeton, NJ: Educational Testing Service.

Council of Graduate Schools. (2003a). *Achieving an inclusive graduate community, Vol. 1*. Washington, DC: Author.

Council of Graduate Schools. (2003b). *Ensuring success, Vol. 3*. Washington, DC: Author.

Council of Graduate Schools. (2003c). *Recruiting for success, Vol. 2*. Schools: Washington, DC: Author.

Council of Graduate Schools. (2006). *Graduate enrollment and degrees: 1986 to 2005*.Washington, DC: Author, Office of Research and Information Services.

Crawford, I., Figert, A., Suarez-Balcazar, Y., & Nyden, P. (1996). The role of research participation for mentoring prospective minority graduate students. *Teaching Sociology, 24*, 256-263.

Cuadraz, G. H. (1996) Experiences of multiple marginality: A case study of Chicana "scholarship women." In C. Turner, M. Garcia, A. Nora, & L. Rendón. (Eds.), *Racial and ethnic diversity in higher education* (pp. 210 – 222). Needham Heights, MA: Simon and Schuster.

DeFour, D. C., & Hirsch, B. J. (1990). The adaptation of black graduate students: A social network approach. *American Journal of Community Psychology, 18*, 487-503.

Dorn, S., & Papalewis, R. (1997, March). *Improving doctoral student retention.* Paper presented at the Annual Meeting of the American Educational Research Association, Chicago, IL.

Florida Education Fund. (n.d.). *McKnight Doctoral Fellowship.* Retrieved February 26, 2008, from http://www.fefonline.org/mdf.html

Frierson, H. T., Hargrove, B. K., & Lewis, N. R. (1994). Black summer research students' perceptions related to research mentors' race and gender. *Journal of College Student Development, 35*(5), 475-480.

Gay, G. (2004). Navigating marginality en route to the professoriate: Graduate students of color learning and living in academia. *International Journal of Qualitative Studies in Education, 17*(2), 265-288.

Hrabowski, III, F. A. (2001). The Meyerhoff Scholars Program: Producing high achieving minority students in mathematics and science. *Notices of the AMS, 48*(1), 26-28.

Hurtado, S., Carter, D. F., & Spuler, A. (1996). Latino student transition to college: Assessing difficulties and factors in successful college adjustment. *Research in Higher Education, 37*(2), 135-157.

Johnson-Bailey, J. (2004). Hitting and climbing the proverbial wall: Participation and retention issues for Black graduate women. *Race Ethnicity and Education, 7*(4), 331-349.

Laden, B. V. (1999). Socializing and mentoring college students of color: The Puente Project as an exemplary celebratory socialization model. *Peabody Journal of Education, 74*(2), 55-74.

Lewis, C., Ginsberg, R. & Davies, T. (2004). The experiences of African American Ph.D. students at a predominantly White Carnegie-I research institution. *College Student Journal 28*(2), 231-245.

Minority Academic Opportunity Programs (MAOP). (2006). Retrieved August 29, 2007, from http://www.maop.vt.edu

Nettles, M. T. (1990). Success in doctoral programs: Experiences of minority and white students. *American Journal of Education*, 494-522.

Nnadozie, E., Ishiyama, & J., Chon, J. (2000, December). Undergraduate research internships: Student success in graduate school – A summary report. *Opportunity Outlook*, 9-11.

Nora, A. (1987). Determinants of retention among Chicano college students: A structural model. *Research in Higher Education, 26*(1), 31-58.

Nora, A. (2001). The depiction of significant others in Tinto's "Rites of Passage": A reconceptualization of the influence of family and community in the persistence process. *Journal of College Student Retention: Research, Theory and Practice, 3*(1), 41-56.

Nora, A., & Cabrera, A. F. (1993). Examining graduate education through structural modeling. In L. L. Baird (Ed.), *Increasing graduate student retention and degree attainment* (New Dimensions for Institutional Research No. 80, pp. 41-48). San Francisco: Jossey-Bass.

Norton, J. (2000). *More than a check and a handshake: The progress and promise of the SREB-State Doctoral Scholars Program.* Atlanta, GA: Southern Regional Education Board.

Olson, C. (1988). Recruiting and retaining minority graduate students: A systems perspective. *Journal of Negro Education, 57*(1), 31-42.

Ponce, F. Q. (1988). Minority student retention: A moral or legal imperative. In M. C. Terrell & D. J. Wright (Eds.), *From survival to success* (pp. 25-53). Washington, DC: National Association of Student Personnel Administrators.

Richardson, R. C., Jr., Simmons, H., & de los Santos, Jr., A. G. (1988, May-June). Graduating minority students: Lessons from ten success stories. *Change, 19*(3), 20-27.

Rodriguez, A. L., Guido-DiBrito, F., Torres, V., & Talbot, D. (2000). Latina college students: Issues and challenges for the 21st century. *NASPA Journal, 37*(3), pp. 511-527.

Simpson, M. T. (2003). *Exploring the academic and social transition experiences of ethnic minority graduate students.* (Unpublished Doctoral Dissertation, Virginia Polytechnic Institute and State University, 2003).

Smith, E. P., & Davison, II, W. S., (1992). Mentoring and the development of African American graduate students. *Journal of College Student Development, 33*, 531-539.

Southern Regional Education Board. (n.d.). *The SREB-State Doctoral Scholars Program.* Retrieved February 26, 2008, from http://www.sreb.org/programs/dsp/dspindex.asp

Tinto, V. (1987). *Leaving college: Rethinking the causes and cures of student attrition.* Chicago: University of Chicago Press.

Turner, C. S. V. (1994). Guests in someone else's house: Students of color. *The Review of Higher Education, 17*(4), 355-370.

University of Maryland Baltimore County (UMBC). (2007). *Meyerhoff scholars program.* Retrieved September 1, 2007, from http://www.umbc.edu/meyerhoff/20/numbers.php

University of Maryland Baltimore County (UMBC). (2008). *Meyerhoff scholarship program.* Retrieved March 6, 2008, from http://www.umbc.edu/meyerhoff

U. S. Census Bureau. (2008). *The 2008 statistical abstract: The national data book.* Retrieved March 4, 2008 from http://www.census.gov/compendia/statab/tables/08s0293.pdf

U. S. Department of Education. (2005). *A profile of the Ronald E. McNair Postbaccalaureate Achievement Program: 1997-1998 through 2001-2002.* Washington, DC: Office of Postsecondary Education, Federal TRIO Programs.

Vaughn, J. C. (1985). Minority students in graduate education. In B. L. R. Smith (Ed.), *The state of graduate education* (pp. 151-168). Washington, DC: The Brookings Institute.

Zepeda, Y. (2006). *CIC Summer Research Opportunities Program Overview.* Retrieved March 2, 2008 from Committee on Institutional Cooperation website: www.cic.uiuc.edu/groups/GraduateDeans/documents/SROPOverviewMay06.pdf

Chapter Five

International Graduate Students: Adjusting to Study in the United States

Maureen Snow Andrade

The first year of graduate school for international students can present transitional challenges beyond what domestic students may experience. Primary among these challenges are becoming accustomed to a different culture and education system and navigating these differences in a foreign language. International graduate students are a diverse group with varying needs based on their educational goals and individual backgrounds. Those who have completed undergraduate studies in the United States are more familiar with American higher education and culture than those who have not. Many speak English as a second language while others are native speakers of English. Their wide range of situations makes it difficult for institutions to know how to serve them.

This chapter provides a rationale for the importance of greater understanding of international graduate students' experiences and examines factors characterizing those experiences in their first year of study. The chapter next reviews theories relevant to international graduate student success with an emphasis on those related to cultural adjustment. The chapter ends by proposing institutional strategies to support student needs. For purposes of this discussion, international students are defined as those who are in the United States on student visas to pursue a university degree.

International Students in American Graduate Education

International students represent significant proportions of graduate enrollments. Nearly half of the 564,766 international students in the United States are enrolled in master's and doctoral programs (Institute of International Education, 2006). Of these, more than half are enrolled in Research I institutions (Brown, 2006b). Overall, international students represent 16% of the total graduate enrollment, 26% of the graduate enrollment at Research I institutions, 13% at doctorate-granting institutions, and 8% at master's-granting institutions. Business, engineering, social sciences, physical sciences, and life sciences attract 73% of international graduate students (Council of Graduate Schools, 2006b). Students from India, China, and Korea comprise

53% of the international graduate student enrollment with the Middle East accounting for an additional 5% (CGS, 2006b).

International students are the recipients of more than one quarter of all master's degrees awarded in the United States (National Center for Education Statistics, 2005b) and approximately 13% of all doctoral degrees (NCES, 2005a). Five-year completion figures show that international students finish doctoral programs at higher rates than domestic students—34% compared to 26%, yet time to degree completion is the same for both groups (i.e., 60% completion after 10 years; Denecke & Frasier, 2005). These figures demonstrate that only a small percentage of both groups complete doctoral degrees in a reasonable amount of time, indicating that all students encounter considerable difficulties on their path to degree. However, statistics fail to specify the kinds of struggles faced by either group or how their struggles may differ.

Typically, the two most significant areas of challenge for international graduate students—and what distinguishes their experience from those of most American students—are linguistic and cultural adjustment (Hechanova-Alampay, Beehr, Christiansen, & Van Horn, 2002; Lin & Yi, 1997; Mori, 2000; Murphy, Hawkes, & Law, 2002; Wan, 2001). Although some international students have achieved what are considered high levels of English proficiency in their own countries, their English skills may not be fully adequate for the academic rigor of graduate studies. Approaches to learning may also be unfamiliar, and cultural dissonance can affect daily life to the extent that concentration on educational goals is difficult. Given these factors, the success of international students is impressive, yet completion rates are discouragingly low, suggesting that more must be done at the institutional level to support international graduate students in their first year.

Providing the necessary support for international graduate students is especially important, as these students are critical to higher education in the United States. Financially, they contribute needed tuition dollars to institutions and, by paying for their living expenses, build local and state economies. Educationally, through their research efforts, international graduate students enhance the reputations of individual faculty, departments, and institutions (Jacobs, 2005; Trice, 2003). Culturally, they broaden the perspectives of classmates and professors by sharing their diverse backgrounds and worldviews. Some work in the United States after graduation, strengthening the competitiveness of American companies in the global marketplace (CGS, 2006b). Others assume faculty positions in the United States where they train the nation's future leaders in science, technology, engineering, mathematics, business administration, and economics—fields central to the economy (Jacobs). Politically, they are an investment in American foreign policy through their goodwill and support of American interests.

Although the United States is a leader in providing international graduate education, other countries are strategizing to attract the future elite of academia, politics, and business, causing concern (Brown, 2006a; CGS, 2006b; NAFSA, 2006). Additionally, the growth of higher education within India and China, the two largest sources of international graduate students for the United States, suggests the possibility of students staying in their home countries to pursue graduate studies (Brown, 2006a). International student enrollment declines from 2000-2004 may be evidence of these factors (CGS, 2006b). Increases in international graduate applications in the past two years are encouraging but do not fully compensate for previous declines (CGS, 2006a; 2006b). Given the significance of international students to American higher education, and the current arena of global competition, an in-depth understanding of these students is critical.

The Role of English Proficiency in Adjustment

The question of English language proficiency is particularly relevant to the first-year transition, as students need strong discipline-specific language skills to succeed in graduate level course work. However, international graduate students may have limited English proficiency. More than half of all international graduate and undergraduate students in the United States come from eight countries—India (13.5%), China (11.1%), Korea (10.4%), Japan (6.9%), Canada (5%), Taiwan (4.9%), Turkey (2.1%), and Germany (1.6%) (IIE, 2006). Students from China, Korea, and Japan are second-language English speakers. In countries where multiple languages are commonly used, such as India, the variety of English spoken differs significantly in vocabulary, syntax, and pronunciation from that used in the United States. Even students who are considered fluent and have met required English language proficiency measures have difficulties with the academic tasks required in graduate studies.

Listening and speaking tasks present unique difficulties for graduate students who are non-native English speakers. Because they may be hearing English spoken by native speakers for the first time, they may be unaccustomed to rapidity of speech, colloquialisms (Cheng, Miles, & Curtis, 2004; Lewthwaite, 1996), and native accents. This presents serious challenges in a typical classroom where students and professors freely exchange ideas. Comprehending and participating in class discussions is only one challenge related to English proficiency. Leading discussions on a research article, presenting at a professional conference, and group work are other common graduate school tasks that may intimidate international students who fear not being understood or making errors.

In addition, strong reading skills are required to comprehend academic materials such as journal articles. International graduate students report reading slowly and being overwhelmed with the amount of required reading (Cheng et al., 2004; Holmes, 2004). They not only have to understand abstract ideas but also analyze them, determine flaws in the author's reasoning or research, and synthesize ideas from multiple sources—tasks especially difficult when English is one's second language. Lack of proficient reading skills also affects writing abilities as writing assignments are typically based on information obtained from synthesizing and critiquing readings. The latter may be particularly difficult because of cultural traditions demanding respect for expert opinion and the written word (Holmes). Reluctance to critique an "expert's" work may result in papers that lack depth. Paraphrasing, another essential writing skill, requires an extensive vocabulary and the ability to vary grammatical structures while preserving meaning. Problems with grammatical accuracy and employing first-language discourse patterns due to unfamiliarity with those in English present additional writing challenges.

Outside the classroom, weak English language skills may also result in the inability to form new friendships. Although students may wish to improve their English by conversing with native speakers, they can find it difficult to meet and interact with their peers (Schutz & Richards, 2003). Consequently, international students may experience English-language related challenges in both their academic and personal lives.

The Role of Culture in Adjustment

Though international graduate students who speak English as a first language do not face the same linguistic challenges as nonnative speakers, they, like nonnative speakers, may be unfamiliar with American culture and the educational system. Evidence indicates that international graduate students find the first term of study in the United States particularly difficult (Hechanova-Alampay et al., 2002; Schutz & Richards, 2003). Understanding appropriate classroom modes of conduct and developing suitable learning strategies is critical to establishing patterns of success in the first year. The degree of difficulty varies, of course, depending on how similar the new culture and education system are to their own.

Students who have completed undergraduate degrees in the United States may not have the same level of adjustment difficulties as those new to the country. Though they still need to adapt to different levels of academic expectations, independence, and scholarship, their familiarity with American educational philosophy and culture may ease their transition. In contrast, international graduate students who are unfamiliar with the American education system and culture face a greater transition and may also lack social support, which exacerbates their challenges.

The Effects of Cultural Background on Academic Life

One of the most frequently mentioned characteristics of American-style education that represents a significant difference to many international graduate students is the interactive nature of the classroom. American classroom behaviors such as interrupting, commenting, asking questions, and volunteering answers seem "bold and immodest" (Holmes, 2004, p. 296) to international graduate students. They typically come from lecture-based systems where professors neither expect nor encourage differing views or discussion. Thus, they may be reluctant to participate and lack the skills for doing so.

Another major educational difference is that the undergraduate experiences of international graduate students may have been characterized by individual rather than collaborative learning styles (Schutz & Richards, 2003), poorly preparing them for their studies in the United States. Team building, collaborative research, and group projects are characteristic of graduate work. When group work is required, international graduate students may form teams with conationals, keeping themselves isolated from American students (Sarkodie-Mensah, 1998). Likewise, American graduate students may be reluctant to include international students (Parks & Raymond, 2004) because of communication difficulties due to cultural or language differences, perceptions that international students produce lower quality academic work, or preference for working with those of similar backgrounds. When this occurs, opportunities to improve English and intercultural communication skills are forfeited.

These new academic expectations also affect international teaching assistants. Their unfamiliarity with the education system sometimes makes it difficult for American undergraduates to accept them even though they have expertise in their disciplines (Mori, 2000). International graduate students who have positions as teaching assistants may begin these roles in their first year before becoming familiar with American educational approaches. Consequently, they may face student complaints about their accents, problems with miscommunication, and unfamiliar testing and grading practices (Lin & Yi, 1997). They may have difficulty understanding undergraduate behavior—talking, joking, whispering, and entering and exiting the classroom at will—which they view as disrespectful (Sarkodie-Mensah, 1998). These factors add to their stress and detract from their studies and well-being.

The Effects of Cultural Background on Social Life

In addition to academic adjustment, international graduate students new to the United States must contend with social adjustment in the first year. Overall, international graduate students have been found to have less social support than domestic students (Hechanova-Alampay et al., 2002) as cultural differences may affect their ability to establish a social support system. They may lack the skills for effective interaction within the American culture. Then, when they continue to follow the rules of their own culture, their actions may be misinterpreted (Chapdelaine & Alexitch, 2004).

Evidence suggests that when cultural differences are great, students have less interaction with individuals from the host country, perhaps due to high levels of discomfort. Yet, when students do interact with hosts, culture shock is less severe (Chapdelaine & Alexitch, 2004). The size of students' conational group decreases social interaction with hosts, possibly because it is easier to interact with conationals when the group is large. Being accompanied by partners and/or children similarly decreases social interaction with hosts. Greater levels of culture shock are experienced as the amount of social interaction with hosts decreases; if no interaction occurs, students are unlikely to learn appropriate cultural behaviors.

The idea that interaction with hosts is related to positive adjustment is significant; however, students often report lacking opportunities to interact. In some cases, students have few friends from the host country—either due to preference or lack of opportunity (Hechanova-Alampay et al., 2002). Views of friendship in the United States are also considered less permanent than in other countries; Americans seem friendly but may not be interested in closer friendships (Lacina, 2002; Mori, 2000). International graduate students may perceive that domestic students keep to themselves. They may also feel the time and effort to form friendships with Americans creates anxiety and detracts from study (Lewthwaite, 1996). Focus on educational goals at the expense of healthy, social interaction can cause international graduate students to "recoil into hard and impenetrable shells of isolation" (Sarkodie-Mensah, 1998, p. 219).

Students' integration into the new culture is sometimes slow or occurs minimally as they select how much of the culture they need or desire to understand, making only necessary adjustments for academic success, and pursuing deeper levels of cultural integration if time or inclination allows (Lewthwaite, 1996). Although interaction with hosts is important to adjustment, maintaining contact with conationals is also well-advised as students from the same cultures and linguistic background can provide needed emotional support, helping each other navigate the new culture. Students must find a balance between maintaining their own culture and adjusting to the new culture (Lin & Yi, 1997). Although students see value in their intercultural experiences, they may feel a tension about losing their own cultures (Lewthwaite, 1996). Regular contact with conationals can help alleviate this tension.

Insights From Theory

A number of theories related to adult development were introduced in chapter 2. Some of these may be adapted for understanding the international student experience. For example, the tasks described in Chickering's (1969) theory of psychosocial development may be complicated or intensified by the transition to a new culture and academic environment. Not only are international students *developing competence* (vector 1) in relation to graduate studies, but also American culture, a new educational system, and possibly, the English language. Their *emotions* (vector 2) may be difficult to manage due to feelings of isolation and anxiety about their unfamiliar surroundings. As noted earlier, collaboration is new to some international students, making the *interdependence* (vector 3) required for various types of scholarship in graduate school a challenge.

International graduate students are also negotiating a network of new and established *interpersonal relationships* (vector 4). They may be helping family adjust to the new culture and attempting to form new relationships with peers and professors, who will mentor them in their studies and new profession. These relationships may be made more difficult by cultural differences.

Due to differing social and cultural contexts, *identity* (vector 5) and self-esteem may be challenged. Students may feel they are losing their own culture as they adjust to American ways or may lack confidence as they navigate new social and educational systems. Because students are removed from their home countries, the connections needed to assist them in obtaining positions after degree completion may be challenging to establish or maintain, causing additional anxiety and complicating the *development of purpose* (vector 6). Finally, different customs related to academic honesty may challenge international graduate students' sense of *integrity* (vector 7), requiring behavior changes.

Other theories based on American students may also be relevant to international graduate students. Integrating into the graduate program, discipline, and a specific social/academic community—concepts identified by Tinto (1987) as important to doctoral student persistence—may be difficult for international graduate students due to contrasting cultural values, placing the student at risk of departure. Differing educational systems and cultural approaches to knowledge that clash with those represented in American graduate programs are one example. Conflicting views of friendship and cultural dissonance may negatively affect the sense of belonging Tinto believes necessary for persistence. Like the American graduate student, an international graduate student may also face the demands of work and family, but with significant differences. Linguistic and cultural challenges may contribute to work-related stress and affect the adjustment of family members. Financial challenges may be a burden as international graduate students have employment restrictions. Tinto argues that these factors potentially result in failure to integrate and greater likelihood of departure.

Taylor's (1994) cultural learning model explores the process of forming an intercultural identity. Although Taylor's model was not created for international graduate students, it provides insights into how an international graduate student might adjust in the first year. The model includes five stages as depicted in Figure 1. *Setting the stage* focuses on what the learner brings to the intercultural experience that contributes to readiness for learning. Prior events explain why individuals have chosen to live in a different culture and may account for their persistence. An international graduate student may be pursuing studies in the United States because of the quality of education and be determined to succeed. Previous positive intercultural experience and skills also contribute to readiness. *Cultural disequilibrium* is created by dissonance between the home and host cultures that results in stress and increased emotions, acting as a catalyst for intercultural learning. Disequilibrium, which may be intensified or muted by a variety of factors, happens continually but lessens over time as an individual becomes more culturally competent. An international graduate student may face stress when receiving a low grade on a paper due to lack of critical analysis, problems with grammatical accuracy, or the use of native-language discourse patterns. Based on this event, the student recognizes and gradually adapts to cultural differences in learning expectations.

Cognitive orientations refer to the degree of reflection toward critical learning incidents. A nonreflective approach entails little questioning of values or assumptions while a reflective orientation involves deeper awareness of the incident and its effects. In this orientation, learners attempt to make sense of the event causing disequilibrium, and are aware of their learning strategies, behavior changes, and emerging intercultural competence. The nonreflective approach is represented by an international graduate student who feels uncomfortable challenging the ideas of an author, but decides to adopt the behavior without much reflection simply because it is necessary to success. A reflective approach would be to analyze why critiquing an author causes feelings of discomfort, why Americans value it, determine reasons for or against adopting this academic behavior, and then act in ways appropriate to the new culture.

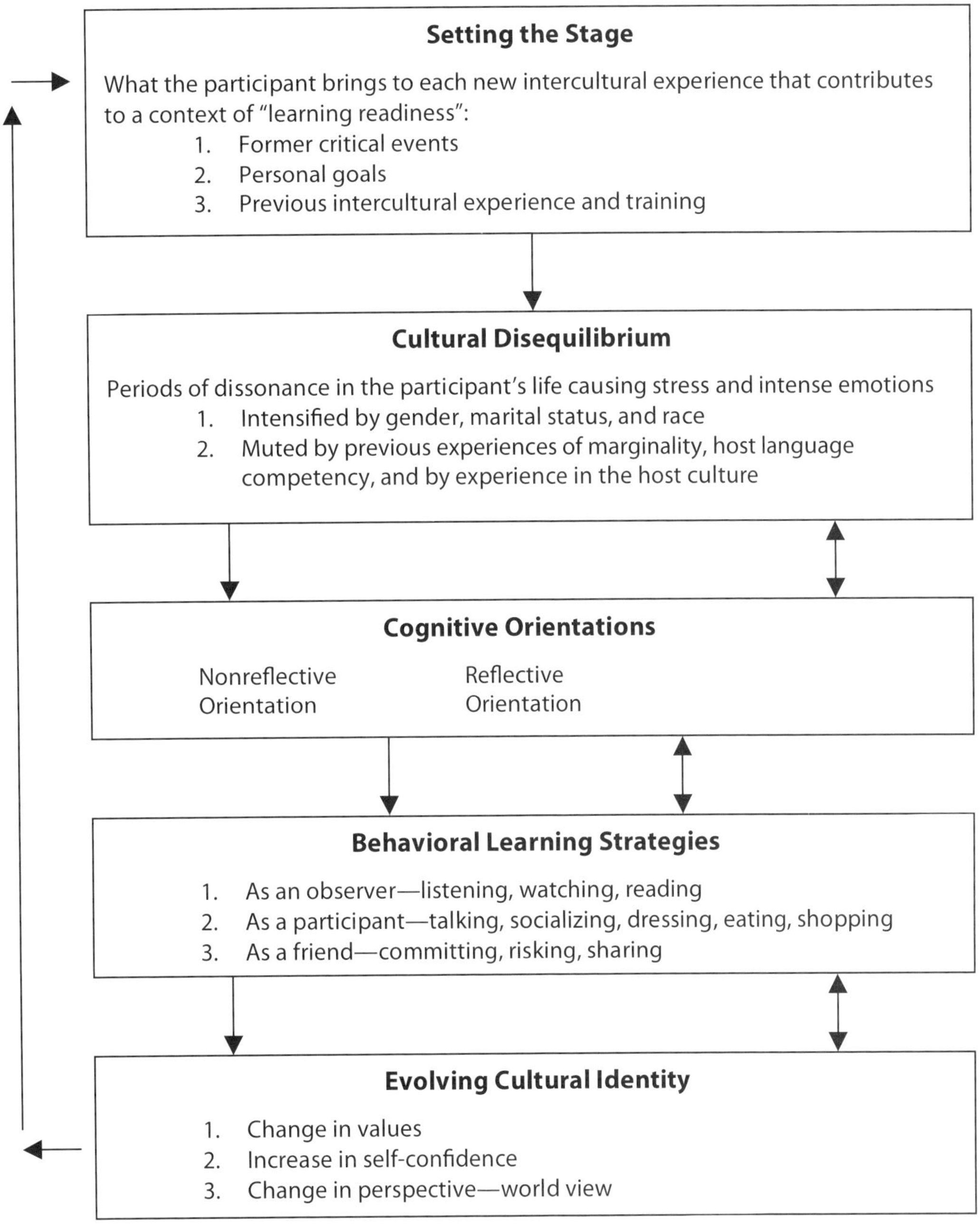

Figure 1. The process of learning to become interculturally competent (Taylor, 1994, p. 162). Used with permission.

Behavioral learning strategies are adapted by the learner to balance disequilibrium. These include observing, participating, and developing long-term relationships in the host culture. As international graduate students interact with classmates and professors in academic and social contexts, they are socialized into American culture and their professions. The deeper the level of their interactions (i.e., forming relationships v. simply observing), the more likely they are to balance disequilibrium. The final stage, *evolving intercultural identity*, does not require giving up one's own values, but reflects the ability to identify with different points of view. Individuals are not linked absolutely to one culture but are competent in the new culture and change their behavior accordingly. For example, an international graduate student may recognize American approaches to critical analysis, accept this approach, and follow it, but be able to use approaches appropriate in the home culture equally well in that setting.

A related, but less detailed, approach is Furnham and Bochner's (1986) Social Skills and Culture Learning Model, which emphasizes social interaction with hosts as central to adjustment. The model posits that the challenges of cultural adjustment result from lack of skills and knowledge necessary to function in the host culture. When international graduate students are not socialized into the new culture, they continue to rely on the behaviors and patterns of their home cultures. This creates conflict and culture shock. Situations that would not present a problem in the home culture—such as passive learning behaviors—become difficult in the new country because the student is operating by inappropriate cultural norms. The model essentially focuses on the disequilibrium aspect of Taylor's model, and points to the need to adopt the behavioral learning strategies explained by Taylor, specifically observing, participating, and making friends.

International graduate students are unlikely to progress toward intercultural understanding without training to help them reflect on their cultures and experiences. Developmental models such as those explored here can be tools for this purpose. Culture shock is a prerequisite to change and growth. Through trial and error, students test their new assumptions. The process ends in a change in their worldview and in the ability to meet the demands of the new culture. Individuals learn and grow from their cultural comparisons but do not need to forfeit their home culture. If students fail to recognize cultural differences, see them as threatening to their own ways of viewing the world, or ignore them, they not only miss opportunities for intercultural learning, but have difficulties adjusting due to misunderstandings. Recognizing and exploring differences and desiring to act in ways appropriate to the new culture are healthier approaches.

Bearing in mind that students' home cultures and educational systems vary, cultural adjustment theories may be more applicable to some subsets of international graduate students than others depending on the degree to which their primary cultures and educational backgrounds are similar. Additionally, international graduate students who have completed undergraduate degrees in the United States may have less of an adjustment to make than those new to American culture and education systems; however, one cannot assume this. Students may have been in the United States for lengthy periods of time and developed only minimal awareness of the impact of cultural differences, maintaining largely ethnocentric views. They may not have formed strategies moving them towards the formation of an intercultural identity.

Although no theory or model is comprehensive, particularly when individual differences and strategies for approaching cultural issues are considered, those described in this section provide insights into developmental processes and serve as a guide for creating programming to mitigate cultural adjustment challenges. These models not only have implications for international graduate students, but for American students, faculty, and staff who associate with and mentor them. Understanding intercultural communication issues and recognizing one's own behaviors is important to making a positive first-year transition. Social or cultural problems that detract from a student's academic focus create stress that may hinder success and result in attrition.

Institutional Strategies for Success

Challenges for international graduate students are significant, yet many manage to adjust to their new environment and succeed at their studies. How do they do it? Effort and individual strategies account for much success; faculty also contribute to helping students achieve their goals. The remainder of this chapter uses campus-specific examples to support recommendations for successful institutional efforts. It should be noted that information on programming for international graduate students is limited, either because institutions are not offering it or because they are not assessing their programs and reporting results. Several of the functioning programs highlighted are at English-speaking universities outside the United States, but address needs similar to those at American institutions. Given the diversity of international graduate students, one program will not be appropriate for all. The recommendations presented encompass the needs of various subsets of international graduate students.

English Skill Support

Although not all international graduate students speak English as a second language, a large percentage do. Even though these students have met admission standards for English language proficiency, the evidence from both faculty and students regarding challenges related to English is compelling (Cheng et al., 2004; Wu, Griffiths, Wisker, Waller, & Illes, 2001; Xu, 1991). Because standardized English proficiency measures may not provide a complete picture of students' abilities, some graduate programs require additional English language testing upon arrival. This may lead students to enroll in additional English language course work, writing workshops, or tutoring to improve their skills. The University of California Los Angeles, for example, requires all international graduate students who are nonnative English speakers to take a placement test that determines the need for enrollment in ESL courses unless they have had at least two years of study at an English-medium university in an English-speaking country (http://www.gdnet.ucla.edu/gasaa/admissions/ENGREQ.HTM). The University of Southern California has a similar requirement unless students have a bachelor's degree from a U.S. college or university (http://www.usc.edu/admission/graduate/international/proficiency/). Medical students at the University of Melbourne in Australia also undergo testing and are provided with English language support based on test results (Hawthorne, Minas, & Singh, 2004).

In some cases, international graduate students object to English skill requirements, particularly if they think their English is sufficient, the English course materials are not discipline-specific, or the additional courses are non-credit. This was the experience of the Masters in Business Administration program at Anglia Polytechnic University in the United Kingdom, which required CD-Rom-based English support (Wu et al., 2001). Students resisted the requirement and wanted to concentrate only on reading and assignments for their M.B.A. courses, which were made more difficult due to their weak English proficiency. Thus, English requirements must be communicated in a positive way, emphasizing the importance of English skills for academic success. Requirements should also be specific to disciplinary needs and part of degree requirements, where possible, to avoid lengthening time to degree completion.

One possible model for strengthening international graduate students' English skills involves the collaboration of disciplinary, English for Academic Purposes (EAP), and learning-skills experts to develop course support materials. These may include assistance with general academic vocabulary, discipline-specific vocabulary, pronunciation, written and spoken discourse patterns, presentation skills, and communication strategies, especially those enabling students to feel comfortable participating in class discussions. Research based in the Integrated Bridging

Program for international postgraduate students at the University of Adelaide in Australia found that peer modeling increased students' feelings of self-efficacy toward making a research seminar presentation (Adams, 2004). The findings suggest that even though peer presentations may be imperfect, they can be effective in teaching the needed English language speaking and presentation skills required for a research presentation, particularly in terms of building confidence. Another approach, at Ohio University, is to design CD-ROM-based support materials or online courses in oral communication (Kessler & Plakans, 2001). International graduate students may also benefit from support materials focused on more general skills such as reading speed improvement, reading strategies, and active learning.

International graduate students who are nonnative English speakers may require more help related to research and writing skills than their native-speaking counterparts. Content-based information literacy courses at Ohio University, featuring instruction in the use of research tools, allow students to do research in their own academic areas while developing their critical thinking and language skills (Bagnole & Miller, 2003). Class activities such as creating an annotated bibliography, discussing and analyzing readings, using information resources, designing search strategies, and teacher-student conferencing build English skills while developing critical thinking and research skills in the student's discipline. Writing tutorials focusing on paraphrasing, summarizing, and citation conventions are helpful, as well. Similarly, assistance with grammatical accuracy, citation conventions, and rhetorical patterns and genres is needed. This service can be offered through writing centers on campus, providing tutors are trained regarding how to address the specific types of writing challenges of nonnative English-speaking graduate students. Regardless of the specific focus, supplemental materials will be more valued and applicable when based on the content of the students' field. Collaborative efforts will ensure that academic content, language, and learning needs are integrated and adequately addressed. The model suggested here shares similarities with ESL content-based approaches (Brinton, Snow, & Wesche, 2003) in which English skill improvement occurs through the medium of discipline-specific materials. The materials developed could be delivered through one-on-one or small-group tutoring or be technologically based. As an alternative, discipline-based ESL courses could be offered as an elective or requirement providing time to graduation is considered.

International graduate students who plan to pursue careers in academia will benefit from programming that supports the development of their English language skills as English is the language of most academic journals and conferences. Overall, strengthening international graduate students' English skills in the first year will establish a strong foundation for success.

Cultural Support

The cultural adjustment models reviewed in the previous section may help international graduate students reflect on their experiences and understand that discomfort and frustration resulting from social and academic differences are a normal part of adjustment. Information regarding cultural adjustment can be shared with students in orientation sessions or handbooks. It may be most appropriately conveyed by cocultural peers (Mori, 2000; Smith, Chin, Inman, & Findling, 1999) in informal gatherings where cultural adjustment models are explained, and seasoned international graduate students relate their own experiences. Since adjustment is gradual, several sessions may need to be organized in the first year. First-year graduate students should have the opportunity to share their experiences in these sessions so that they can come to some understanding of them, gain insights from each other, and learn strategies for approaching differences. Individual support networks can also result from such programming.

Involvement with peers from students' home countries helps international graduate students maintain cultural connections and reinforce their cultural identity. Such ties can be promoted by institutions through culture clubs, which allow students from the same cultural or linguistic backgrounds to form associations. These clubs can also sponsor events on campus and in the community to increase intercultural understanding. Often times, American students or those from outside the specified country of the club join for purposes of intercultural learning, thereby providing additional opportunities for exchange. International student offices regularly sponsor intercultural learning events. Purdue University has an international education program in which students present information about their country and culture to local schools and civic organizations (http://www.iss.purdue.edu/Programs/). They also have an international festival that accomplishes the same goal on campus.

New York University offers an American Ways seminar with lectures on various aspects of American culture, and a United States Festival, a month-long celebration of American culture for foreign students and their families (http://www.nyu.edu/oiss/index.html). Purdue University has a Cultural Perspectives program in which international students are invited to meet every Friday evening to learn about American culture (http://www.iss.purdue.edu/Programs/). These events provide cultural support to international graduate students by contributing explanations and information that will increase their understanding of what they are observing and being exposed to in daily life.

Social Support

Social interaction plays a significant role in the first year and should involve making connections with home country peers and Americans. Forming support groups for a specific subgroup where both positive and troubling experiences can be shared in a safe environment is one possibility. Such a program is in place for Asian women who are international graduate and undergraduate students at Western Michigan University (Carr, Koyama, & Thiagarajan, 2003). Students meet weekly as a group with a facilitator. Discussion topics include cross-cultural communication, dating, friendship, discrimination, politics, academic issues, and so forth. International or graduate student offices or counseling centers can help students form these various networks and relationships through mentoring programs or facilitated discussion groups such as the one mentioned. Because international graduate students often lack time for social activities, preferring or needing to focus on their studies (Lewthwaite, 1996), programs must be carefully planned so that students see them as directly beneficial.

A solution to add-on programming is building cross-cultural interaction into the curriculum. The master's degree program in elementary education at New York University began a cultural sharing program in which international and domestic students were paired and participated in formal and informal activities to get better acquainted (Shigaki & Smith, 1997). They attended classes together, collaborated on assignments, met over coffee, visited each other's homes, and attended structured monthly meetings. As part of the course requirement, they kept a journal to record information about their relationship and growing cultural awareness. Benefits included increased empathy, strengthened knowledge of course content, better understanding of cultural traditions, and increased English competency for international students.

Although this program focused primarily on building cultural understanding, the results demonstrate that other positive effects occurred. Programs such as this could be developed for a variety of disciplines and needs such as content support and the exchange of practical tips necessary for graduate school success. Students enrolled in the same courses and/or programs can do much to sustain each other and share information in mutually beneficial ways. Similarly, students with related research interests could be paired to work on literature reviews and methodology issues. Although these support groups often form on their own, some engineering may be necessary to address the needs of international graduate students. The benefits are not one way. Cross-cultural partnerships can result in increased cultural understanding and the exchange of academic information pertinent to both American and international students. Prior to the development of partnerships, however, intercultural training, such as a discussion of the models introduced earlier, is advisable.

Programs that link international students with families in the community for purposes of cultural exchange and social involvement such as the International Friendship Program at Purdue University (http://www.iss.purdue.edu/Programs/), or those pairing international and American students such as the PALS program at the University of Texas at Austin (http://www.utexas.edu/international/) are fairly common. These programs can be of interest to international graduate students, but those offering a combination of academic and social support, and which are built into course curricula, might be more effective in addressing specific needs and recognizing the study demands of international graduate students.

Academic and Educational Systems Support

International graduate students not only need to learn about general academic practices and the American education system but also need to be socialized to their academic communities of practice. In some ways, learning the communication styles and audience expectations in a discipline is similar to learning a language. Students must acquire fluency in the language and culture of the discipline. All students need to learn how to be graduate students, but acquiring successful approaches to graduate study may be a greater challenge for international students who are often accustomed to far different educational practices.

Transitional programming to assist international graduate students into their first year of study must consider their unique backgrounds. To address this, the Integrated Bridging Program at the University of Adelaide, mentioned earlier, offers a course for international graduate students, which teaches skills for the research proposal genre (Cadman, 2002). The course is based on survey findings and interviews with research supervisors representing different disciplines who identified features they require in an international student research proposal. Supervisors had similar expectations such as well-defined research questions, locating the research in the literature, knowledge of current issues, appropriate methodology, and English accuracy. They also examined the academic capacity of the student—level of knowledge, personal approach and commitment to the project, and research competency—through the proposal. The course addresses the specific writing needs of second-language English speakers, which are different from those of native English speakers in terms of grammatical accuracy and familiarity with written discourse patterns and writing genres.

International graduate students may also have problems communicating with their advisor, because they may be accustomed to a more hierarchical relationship with faculty, leading students to feel unsupported when advisors provide only indirect or general advice (Scheyvens, Wild, & Overton, 2003). A compulsory course for international graduate students in engineering at Nanyang Technological University in Singapore addresses challenges related to learner autonomy and English language skills (McClure, 2001). The course helps students develop self-awareness as learners; manage reading, writing, and research tasks; become aware of the structure and genre of research writing; and gain confidence in oral skills so they are better able to communicate their research. A collaborative, student-centered approach is introduced to counteract passive learning styles but some structure is provided to help students feel comfortable. Students learn to analyze and critique research articles. They also complete writing tasks, such as composing an abstract in a group and presenting it to the class for feedback on language use. This course is an example of an integrated approach for strengthening language skills while developing culturally appropriate academic skills for graduate work.

Timing of Support

Some have suggested that orientation programming for international students consider four time periods: pre-departure, arrival, ongoing, and returning (Lin & Yi, 1997; Meyer, 2001; Tillman, 1990). For purposes of the first year, the first three phases are most applicable. Once again, transitional programming will differ depending on which subset of international students is being considered—those new to the country, those who have completed undergraduate studies in the United States, those who are nonnative English speakers, and so forth.

The pre-departure phase prepares students for their arrival with practical suggestions about what to bring, finances, immigration policies, housing, health care, campus directions, academic program information, and registration. Mentoring via e-mail prior to arrival is one way of helping new international graduate students connect with students who have already commenced their studies. They are able to ask questions related to the program, course work, faculty, and requirements and will already be familiar with someone in their program upon their arrival. Columbia University offers such a program—a peer advisor network consisting of continuing international graduate students from different disciplines whom new students can contact by e-mail prior to or after arrival (http://www.columbia.edu/cu/isso/incoming/). Web sites are another way of providing pre-arrival information such as the very thorough online multimedia guide at New York University, which features international students discussing immigration requirements, American higher education, campus facilities, faculty relationships, student life, and other pertinent topics (http://www.nyu.edu/oiss/index.html). Some universities sponsor on-site orientation in students' countries, such as the University of Southern California through its regional office in Hong Kong (http://www.usc.edu/dept/International_Offices/HongKong/.

Once on campus, at the arrival phase for orientation programming, students need assistance settling in and preparing for classes. They should be welcomed, introduced to campus resources and key people, and given factual information about the culture and the adjustment process. Continued mentoring, seminars, and workshops focused on educational, social, and cultural adjustment as well as physical and psychological well-being should be offered to provide ongoing support as students begin to encounter problems. At this stage, an understanding of cultural adjustment models may be of greatest need to help students understand how intercultural learning evolves over time.

Regardless of the structure and activities, orientation must focus on the unique content needed by international students and be presented appropriately. Introductions to services specifically for international students such as the international student office, international student advisor, immigration assistance, cross-cultural training, international and cultural student organizations, and ESL courses are essential. Information regarding tutoring and library services is also critical. Presentations and materials must be designed for the intended audience. If they are primarily nonnative English speakers, delivery must be adjusted accordingly. Programming should also include opportunities for social interactions. (See chapter 6 for more information on orientation programs.)

Faculty Training and Support

While international graduate students need to adjust to linguistic, cultural, and educational differences, faculty should develop "professional intercultural competency" (Feng, 2003, p. 138). By becoming more aware of students' backgrounds and how they perceive the classroom environment, faculty can make changes to accommodate international graduate students. This competency can be provided through training seminars or workshops at department or institutional levels, particularly for those unaccustomed to international graduate students. Faculty familiar with international graduate students likely have many solutions for meeting linguistic and cultural needs and can be used as a resource. Facilitation of faculty discussions on pedagogical issues related to accommodating students from diverse educational and linguistic backgrounds is a productive approach to supporting first-year international graduate students. A series of workshops might be developed and offered at the beginning of the academic year or over the course of the year. Follow-up discussions could be scheduled to allow faculty to share how ideas were incorporated or amended.

Workshops for faculty related to the needs of second language speakers may include reasons for their reluctance to participate in class discussions and pedagogical strategies to address this (i.e., allowing more time for students to process the flow of the discussion and form a response, facilitating class discussions to ensure equal participation, and requesting clarification from second-language students without embarrassing them). Teaching methods that aid second-language speakers to better comprehend the spoken language, such as providing handouts, explaining vocabulary, providing background information regarding unfamiliar allusions, and encouraging clarification questions would also be good topics for workshops. These teaching strategies not only benefit international graduate students, but all students as they adjust to the demands of graduate-level work and the expectations of their professors.

International students' writing may contain numerous grammatical errors, exhibit unfamiliarity with American discourse patterns, or be plagiarized due to English limitations or cultural practices, so professors must determine how to handle these issues. Workshop topics may focus on philosophies and strategies for approaching errors, how much diversity of linguistic form is acceptable, how to orient students to appropriate use of sources, and how to socialize students into their academic discourse communities. An understanding that organizational patterns in writing vary based on linguistic background may help clarify why students have difficulty with the conventions of academic writing in English.

Faculty training can focus on ways to be inclusive of cultural perspectives. This may include the use of internationally based course content when appropriate and culturally diverse teams for group projects as well as providing opportunities for international students to share their expertise. Faculty may also benefit from greater familiarity with students' cultures, learning styles, and interaction patterns.

Recognizing that faculty may have limited time or interest in furthering their knowledge in these areas, support programming must be based specifically on aspects perceived by faculty to be valuable and pertinent. The medical school at the University of Melbourne in Australia has recognized the need for its faculty to understand the cultural diversity of international students and be able to teach them effectively (Hawthorne et al., 2004). Rather than assuming faculty know how to teach diverse learners, the school is proactively providing information and training to faculty as part of the International Student Support Program. This support includes specific subject-based materials that consider students' linguistic and cultural needs, feedback on teaching, and training to increase skills for managing the learning problems of overseas students. For programs just beginning to consider such an approach, a needs analysis or survey determining faculty experiences with international graduate students and faculty interests and availability should precede any implementation of training. Also, training should be specifically related to the particular populations of international students with whom faculty work and the specific subject area of study.

Programming Approaches

While much of the information presented applies generally to international graduate students, the intention is not to convey that they all have the same requirements or experiences. Generalizations regarding international students and their experiences come at the risk of stereotyping. Their diversity underscores the need for institution- and discipline-specific solutions based on data concerning the perceptions of faculty and students regarding first-year challenges.

A variety of departments offer support services for international students. Among these are the international student office, student development center, ESL programs, international student organizations, library staff, academic departments, mental health units, tutoring services, and learning centers. Coordination among these entities can help institutions effectively and efficiently address student needs (Baron & Strout-Dapaz, 2001; Peterson, Briggs, Dreasher, Horner & Nelson, 1999; Sarkodie-Mensah, 1998) and develop or refine programs by combining resources (Tillman, 1990).

Some graduate schools have developed comprehensive programs to support growing international student populations. The International Student Support Program at the University of Melbourne, Australia medical school, mentioned earlier, is a unique example of outreach to address student-specific and profession-specific needs. The program enables the identification and monitoring of at-risk international students, provides individualized English language support and intercultural training, helps students adjust to unfamiliar pedagogical practices, and prepares faculty with needed information to address student challenges (Hawthorne et al., 2004). Students' English skills are assessed, and where needed, followed by small-group training focused on specific weaknesses. Communication skill needs are addressed within the context of the medical profession (e.g., patient-doctor communication) to ensure culturally appropriate and linguistically clear interactions. Pronunciation barriers are overcome with individual training of students whose English has been deemed incomprehensible by patients or clinicians. Support is provided for students having cultural or linguistic difficulties associated with the problem-based learning approach used in the curriculum and training provided for faculty to expand their skills in managing related issues.

Essentially, international students are given specific, individualized cultural and linguistic support in every aspect of their educational experience, and faculty are trained to respond appropriately to their needs. Students are constantly monitored to assess progress and identify problems. Few other programs reported on in the literature have addressed international student issues to this degree. As in this example, collaboration among support services and graduate programs enables institutions to provide pertinent and timely support in the first year so that students feel comfortable and have the skills needed for successful degree completion.

Conclusion

This chapter has provided a rationale for examining the first-year experiences of international graduate students, specifically their origins, numbers, fields of study, and contributions. It has also reviewed the challenges of international graduate students and made suggestions for programming. Awareness of students' linguistic and cultural adjustment issues is critical as is an understanding of how institutions can better support students. Although adjustment needs are greatest as students' commence their studies, adjustment occurs gradually and needs are ongoing. An important factor prior to program implementation is distinguishing among subsets of international students. Consideration must be given to variations in cultural, linguistic, and educational backgrounds.

International graduate students come to the United States to gain an education and expand their horizons. American students and faculty also benefit from their associations with international graduate students. "The American way of life owes its success and vitality to our historical ability to harness the best in knowledge and ideas, not only those that are home grown, but also those that come from outside our borders" (NAFSA, 2006, p. 11). To continue in this tradition, institutions of higher education must engage in learning more about the international graduate student experience, establish innovative and creative strategies to address needs, and establish patterns of success in the first year of graduate study.

References

Adams, K. (2004). Modelling success: Enhancing international postgraduate research students' self-efficacy for research seminar presentations. *Higher Education Research & Development, 23*(2), 115-130.

Bagnole, J. W., & Miller, J. W. (2003). An interactive information literacy course for international students: A practical blueprint for ESL learners. *TESL-EJ, 6*(4). Retrieved December 16, 2006, from http://tesl-ej.org/ej24/a1.html

Baron, S., & Strout-Dapaz, A., (2001). Communicating with and empowering international students with a library skills set. *Reference Services Review, 29*(4), 314-326.

Brinton, D. M., Snow, M. A., & Wesche, M. (2003). *Content-based second language instruction.* Ann Arbor, MI: The University of Michigan Press.

Brown, H. A. (2006a). Data sources: 2006 international applications. *Communicator, 39*(4), 3-4.

Brown, H. A. (2006b). *Graduate enrollment and degrees: 1986 to 2005.* Council of Graduate Schools. Retrieved November 23, 2006, from http://www.cgsnet.org/portals/0/pdf/R_GED2005.pdf

Cadman, K. (2002). English for academic possibilities: The research proposal as a contested site in postgraduate genre pedagogy. *Journal of English for Academic Purposes, 1*(2), 85-104.

Carr, J. L., Koyama, M., & Thiagarajan, M. (2003). A women's support group for Asian international students. *Journal of American College Health, 52*(3), 131-134.

Chapdelaine, R. F., & Alexitch, L. R. (2004). Social skills difficulty: Model of culture shock for international graduate students. *Journal of College Student Development, 45*(2), 167-184.

Cheng, L., Myles, J., & Curtis, A. (2004). Targeting language support for non-native English-speaking graduate students at a Canadian university. *TESL Canada Journal, 21*(2), 50-71.

Chickering, A. W. (1969). *Education and identity.* San Francisco: Jossey-Bass.

Council of Graduate Schools (CGS). (2006a, March). *Findings from 2006 CGS international graduate admissions survey phase 1: Applications.* Retrieved July 4, 2006, from http://www.cgsnet.org/portals/0/pdf/R_intlapps06_1.pdf

Council of Graduate Schools (CGS). (2006b, October 23). *Findings from the 2006 CGS international graduate admissions survey phase III: Admissions and enrollment.* Retrieved November 23, 2006, from http://www.cgsnet.org/portals/0/pdf/R_Intlenrl06_III.pdf

Denecke, D. D., & Frasier, H. S. (2005). Ph.D. completion project: Preliminary results from baseline data. *Communicator, 38*(9), 1-4.

Feng, A. (2003). Intercultural competency for TESOL professionals. *Reflections on English Language Teaching, 2,* 138-172.

Furnham, A., & Bochner, S. (1986). *Culture shock.* New York: Methuen & Co.

Hawthorne, L., Minas, I. H., & Singh, B. (2004). A case study in the globalization of medical education: Assisting overseas-born students at the University of Melbourne. *Medical Teacher, 26*(2), 150-159.

Hechanova-Alampay, R., Beehr, T. A., Christiansen, N. D., & Van Horn, R. K. (2002). Adjustment and strain among domestic and international student sojourners. *School Psychology International, 23*(4), 458-474.

Holmes, P. (2004). Negotiating differences in learning and intercultural communication: Ethnic Chinese students in a New Zealand university. *Business Communication Quarterly, 67*(3), 294-307.

Institute of International Education (IIE). (2006). *International students by academic level.* Retrieved November 23, 2006, from http://opendoors.iienetwork.org/?p=89206

Jacobs, B. (2005). The tangible contributions of international graduate students: An alternative approach and some evidence from the University of Rochester. *Communicator, 38*(4), 1-3.

Kessler, G. & Plakans, L. (2001). Incorporating ESOL learners' feedback and usability testing in instructor-developed CALL materials. *TESOL Journal, 10*(1), 15-20.

Lacina, J. G. (2002). Preparing international students for a successful social experience in higher education. In B. W. Speck & B. H. Carmical (Eds.), *Internationalizing higher education: Building vital programs on campuses* (New Directions for Higher Education No. 117, pp. 21-27). San Francisco: Jossey-Bass.

Lewthwaite, M. (1996). A study of international students' perspectives on cross-cultural adaptation. *International Journal for the Advancement of Counselling, 19*(2), 267-185.

Lin, J. G., & Yi, J. K. (1997). Asian international students' adjustment: Issues and program suggestions. *College Student Journal, 31*(4), 473-479.

McClure, J. (2001). Developing language skills and learner autonomy in international postgraduates. *ELT Journal, 55*(2), 142-148.

Meyer, J. D. (2001). A conceptual framework for comprehensive international student orientation programs. *International Education, 31*(1), 56-78.

Mori, S. (2000). Addressing the mental health concerns of international students. *Journal of Counseling & Development, 78,* 137-144.

Murphy, C., Hawkes, L., & Law, J. (2002). How international students can benefit from a web-based college orientation. In B. W. Speck & B. H. Carmical (Eds.), *Internationalizing higher education: Building vital programs on campuses* (New Directions for Higher Education No. 117, pp. 37-43). San Francisco: Jossey-Bass.

NAFSA Association of International Educators. (2006, June). *Restoring U.S. competitiveness for international students and scholars.* Retrieved July 4, 2006, from http://www.nafsa.org/_/Document/_/restoring_u.s.pdf

National Center for Educational Statistics (NCES). (2005a). *Digest of education statistics tables and figures. Doctor's degrees conferred by degree-granting institutions by racial/ethnic group and sex of students: 1976-77 through 2003-04*. Retrieved December 16, 2006, from http://nces.ed.gov/programs/digest/d05/tables/dt05_267.asp

National Center for Educational Statistics (NCES). (2005b). *Digest of education statistics tables and figures. Master's degrees conferred by degree-granting institutions by racial/ethnic group and sex of students: 1976-77 through 2003-04*. Retrieved December 16, 2006, from http://nces.ed.gov/programs/digest/d05/lt3.asp#19

Parks, S., & Raymond, P. M. (2004). Strategy use by nonnative-English-speaking students in an MBA program: Not business as usual! *The Modern Language Journal, 88*(3), 374-389.

Peterson, D. M., Briggs, P., Dreasher, L., Horner, D. D., & Nelson, T. (1999). Contributions of international students and programs to campus diversity. In J. C. Dalton (Ed.), *Beyond borders: How international developments are changing student affairs practice* (New Directions for Student Services No. 86, pp. 67-77). San Francisco: Jossey-Bass.

Sarkodie-Mensah, K. (1998). International students in the U.S.: Trends, cultural adjustments, and solutions for a better experience. *International Library Education, 39*(3), 214-222.

Scheyvens, R., Wild, K., & Overton, J. (2003). International students pursuing postgraduate study in geography: Impediments to their learning experiences. *Journal of Geography in Higher Education, 27*(3), 309-323.

Schutz, A., & Richards, M. (2003). International students' experience of graduate study in Canada. *Journal of the International Society for Teacher Education, 7*(1), 10-23.

Shigaki, I. S., & Smith, S. A. (1997). A cultural sharing model: American buddies for international students. *International Education, 27,* 5-21.

Smith, T. B., Chin, L., Inman, A. G., & Findling, J. H. (1999). An outreach support group for international students. *Journal of College Counseling, 2*(2), 188-190.

Taylor, E. W. (1994). Intercultural competency: A transformative learning process. *Adult Education Quarterly, 44,* 154-174.

Tillman, M. J. (1990). Effective support services for international students (New Directions for Community Colleges No. 70, pp. 87-98). San Francisco: Jossey-Bass.

Tinto, V. (1987). *Leaving college: Rethinking the causes and cures of student attrition*. Chicago: University of Chicago Press.

Trice, A. G. (2003). Faculty perceptions of graduate international students: The benefits and challenges. *Journal of Studies in International Education, 7*(4), 379-403.

Wan, G. (2001). The learning experience of Chinese students in American universities: A cross-cultural perspective. *College Student Journal, 35*(1), 28-44.

Wimberley, D. W., McCloud, D. G., & Flinn, W. L. (1992). Predicting success of Indonesian graduate students in the United States. *Comparative Education Review, 36*(4), 487-508.

Wu, S., Griffiths, S., Wisker, G., Waller, S., & Illes, K. (2001). The learning experience of postgraduate students: Matching methods to aims. *Innovations in Education and Teaching International, 38*(3), 292-308.

Xu, M. (1991). The impact of English-language proficiency on international graduate students' perceived academic difficulty. *Research in Higher Education, 32*(5), 557-570.

Strategies, Initiatives, and Innovations

Chapter Six

Orientation Programs for Graduate Students

Michael C. Poock

Orientation programs for incoming undergraduate students have long been a tradition at colleges and universities, but they have only recently been implemented for graduate students. Yet, research indicates that orientation lessens the anxiety of making the transition to graduate school, increases the opportunity for developing social networks, reduces attrition, and increases satisfaction (Boyle & Boice, 1998; Buchanan, 1989; Isaac, 1993; Miller, Miles, & Dyer, 2001; Phillips, Daubman & Wilmoth, 1986; Rosenblatt & Christiansen, 1993)—much as it does for undergraduates. Given that as many as one third of new doctoral students stop out during their first year (Golde, 1998) and that 40% to 50% of all graduate students never make it to graduation (Denecke & Frasier, 2005; Golde, 2005), orientation programs can play a critical role in graduate students' persistence. Practically, they are also in the interest of departmental faculty and staff, because they fund these students, rely on their services, and invest much time and energy in the admissions process.

Orientation is rooted in socialization theory. As Rapp and Golde describe in chapter 1, graduate students face a dual socialization process, since they are "simultaneously directly socialized into the role of graduate student and are given preparatory socialization into the profession" (Golde, 1998, p. 56). Students are socialized into the campus culture through campus-wide activities where they have the opportunity to develop social networks outside their academic department, learn the cultural norms associated with being a graduate student within the larger academic community, and have the opportunity to learn about various aspects of their new environment. In addition, students are socialized into the profession via their academic departments. Students learn norms of the profession, skills associated with teaching and/or research, and expectations in the academic apprenticeship process.

This chapter addresses graduate student orientation by, first, providing a background on orientation. Second, a brief discussion is offered on relevant socialization theories, their application, and related research findings. Finally, this chapter concludes with recommendations for the improvement of orientation programs for graduate students.

The Purpose and Goals of Graduate Orientation

Orientation programs for undergraduate students have existed (in some form) for several decades. In many cases, orientation programs in the United States are about as old as colleges themselves (Ward-Roof & Hatch, 2003). The focus of these programs has been to assist traditional-aged undergraduate students with the transition from high school to college. For most of these students, attendance at college is the first time they have been away from home for any extended period. Although the curricular choices were initially limited (unlike the vast number of majors and course selections students enjoy today), faculty acknowledged that there were transitional issues associated with entering a new environment (Ward-Roof & Hatch). Today, these transitional issues range from the operational (e.g., how to register for classes and where to find classroom buildings) to the emotional (e.g., anxiety, loneliness, and homesickness) (Boyle & Boice, 1998). College administrators implemented orientation programs to assist entering first-year students with these transition issues.

Graduate students, on the other hand, have generally been viewed by faculty and administrators as self-sufficient, with few of the adjustment issues associated with the undergraduate transition (Meloni, 1986). Unlike their undergraduate counterparts, graduate students are older and have succeeded in achieving their undergraduate degree. Some may be married, have children, and or have been employed full time during or after their baccalaureate experience. Therefore, when they return for graduate work, they may be viewed as competent in handling the operational issues involved in attending a new campus (Antony, 2002; Perna & Hudgins, 1996).

However, faculty and administrators came to realize that "many graduate students when first entering their respective programs are just as confused and anxious as they were as new undergraduates" (Rosenblatt & Christensen, 1993, p. 503). Given the human and fiscal resources colleges and universities invest in graduate students, any effort to increase retention can be viewed as cost-effective. Indeed, not only do orientation programs allay anxiety (Vlisides & Eddy, 1993) and reduce attrition (Boyle & Boice, 1998; Buchanan, 1989; Isaac, 1993), but they are also essential to a graduate student's successful academic career (Turner & Thompson, 1993).

Though orientations may vary by campus, a common definition of orientation was offered by Upcraft and Farnsworth (1984). That is, orientation is "any effort on the part of the institution to help entering students make the transition from their previous environment to the collegiate environment and enhance their success" (p. 27). Although this definition is accurate, it is very broad and could include a wide range of efforts. It is also slanted toward undergraduate students. Therefore, for purposes of this chapter, orientation is defined as academic and cocurricular activities and programs that address transitional issues of immediate interest to new graduate students, generally offered by a central administrative unit on campus (e.g., Graduate School) and/or individual academic units (e.g., Department of History) and held prior to the beginning of their first classes. This translates into both campus- or school-wide programs in conjunction with activities by academic departments. In many cases, a day-long orientation program is coordinated by a school within the university that may also include either weekly or monthly events at some point during the academic year. This type of orientation may also include programs by academic departments that complement activities organized by the larger school unit.

Orientation programs for graduate students should achieve two major goals: (a) facilitating the transition to the campus environment and (b) facilitating the transition into their profession (Boyle & Boice, 1998; Golde, 1998; Tinto, 1993). Indeed, this latter element—transitioning into one's discipline—and the socialization process that accompanies it is what separates orientation programs for graduate students from programs for undergraduates.

Socialization of Graduate Students

Over the years, numerous theories have been offered on the socialization of graduate students (Baird, 1990; Corcoran & Clark, 1984; Gansemer-Topf, Ross, & Johnson, 2006; Weidman & Stein, 1990). For example, in 1990, Baird asked the simple question, "If socialization occurs in graduate school, how does it happen?" He responded by identifying four devices in the socialization process: (a) a rigorous admissions process to ensure that students are committed to the profession; (b) sequestration or isolation from much of the rest of campus, both physically and temporally; (c) apprenticeship, or what many consider the primary element in the socialization process; and (d) an emphasis on student groups by admitting students in cohorts and having them work in and solve problems as a group to help develop norms, reinforce commitment to the field, and provide a means of social support.

Unlike Baird's work, which focuses on socialization into the profession, the model of socialization offered by Stein and Weidman (1989; Weidman & Stein, 1990) can be applied to socialization to the institution as well as the profession, thus having practical application for staff who plan either campus-wide or departmental orientation activities. Stein and Weidman's model of socialization has four stages. In the *anticipatory* stage students enter programs with personal beliefs and values, which they dismiss in favor of a more realistic view of the profession and their abilities to fulfill a future role. In the *formal* stage, students are involved in structured experiences involving knowledgeable colleagues and faculty. From here students move to the *informal* stage where they learn about expectations that are not formally stated, including flexibilities in the ways in which their role expectations are achieved. Finally, in the *personal* stage, individual values become interconnected with those of the profession.

Weidman, Twale, and Stein (2001) offer a framework for the socialization of graduate students that extends the work of Stein and Weidman (1989; Weidman & Stein, 1990). While Stein and Weidman argued that the relationship between student and environment is somewhat fluid, Weidman, Twale, and Stein suggest an even greater dynamic socialization process where "identification with and commitment to professional roles are complex, continuous, and developmental" (p. 37).

As Figure 1 illustrates, this model has at its center both institutional culture (i.e., academic programs, peer culture) and socialization process (i.e., interaction, integration, and learning). It is this core portion of the model where department faculty have the greatest influence over what is commonly thought of as the socialization process.

Surrounding the core are external or personal influences. These include the student perspective upon entering the program; identity and commitment of the novice practitioners; influence by professional communities related to the academic discipline; and a student's personal communities, comprised of family, friends, and employers.

The authors illustrate their figure with dotted lines to indicate the permeable nature of these forces on the core socialization process. These are not discrete elements but rather are complementary and indeed dependent upon each other. In short, socialization is not static operating in a vacuum; rather, it influences—and is influenced by—the various forces related to the student, the discipline, and the academic program.

This theory has practical applications for orientation programs that address socialization into the profession (primarily) and campus community (secondarily). Indeed, the nucleus of this model addresses the students' involvement with the university, including knowledge acquisition, integrating norms, and understanding climate. Orientation programs at both the departmental and campus-wide level can address the core elements of this theory.

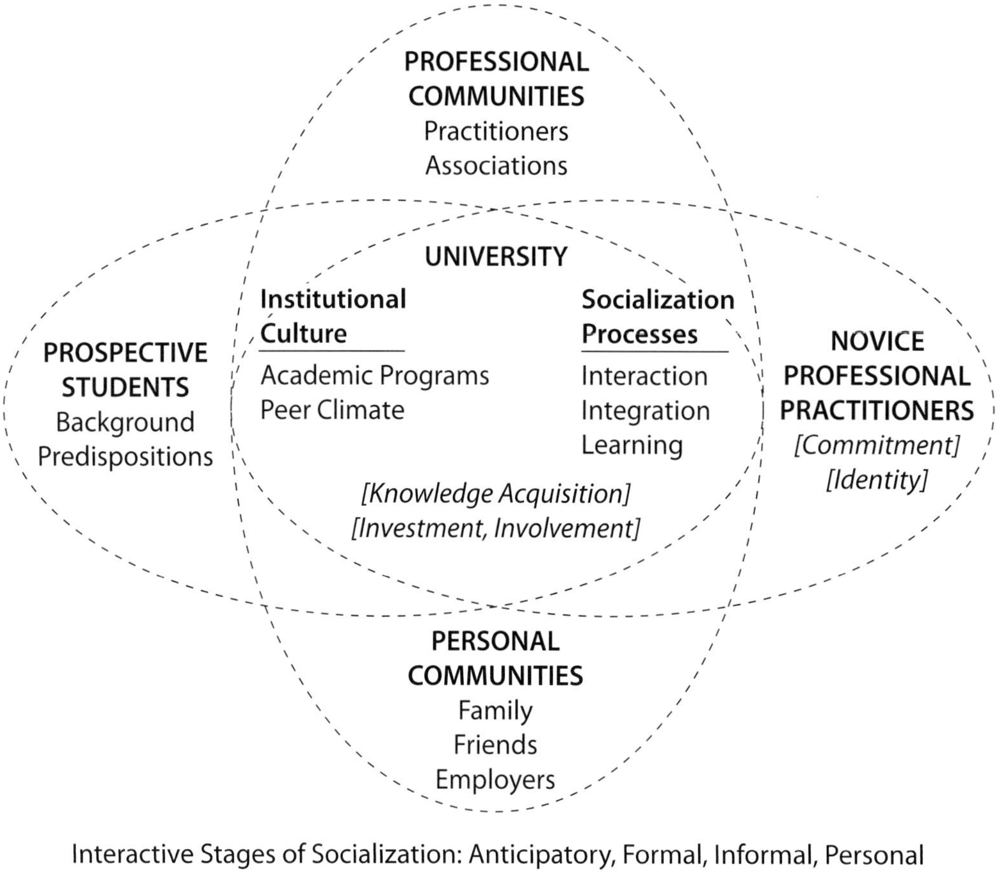

Figure 1. Conceptualizing graduate and professional student socialization (Weidman, Twale, & Stein, 2001, p. 37). Reprinted with permission.

Institutional Orientations on Campus-Wide and Departmental Levels

If socialization is the theoretical underpinning of a successful graduate student career, then its operational form begins with orientation programs. Consequently, because socialization for graduate students is a dual process—into the institution and the discipline—orientation programs, too, are best offered on an institutional (or campus-wide) basis and by specific academic departments. Below are applications of graduate orientation programs, based on research, for both the campus-wide and departmental levels.

Campus-wide Orientation Programs

There have been several studies addressing graduate student orientation at the campus-wide level. In 1989, Buchanan surveyed almost 300 graduate students at Oklahoma State University asking, among other items, the quality of orientation. Her findings included the perception that even though improvements were needed, orientation was important to graduate students. Barker, Felstehausen, Couch, and Henry (1997) surveyed more than 400 students at Texas Tech

University and discovered that the majority of the 454 respondents thought the orientation program they experienced was beneficial. Additionally, the respondents stated that using the format of a workshop, which allowed students to rotate among rooms and attend sessions that best fit their needs, was the desired format. The findings by Barker et al. are consistent with Vlisides and Eddy (1993), who studied campus-wide orientation models at various research universities. While the programs varied in focus and scope, they were effective at assisting the students' transition to graduate study.

In 2002, Poock queried more than 200 graduate students at the University of North Carolina at Chapel Hill to compare orientation needs and methods of delivery (i.e., campus-wide vs. departmental). The author found that information on university services was best met through a campus-wide orientation program while social and academic needs were best met by activities offered by academic departments. Two years later, Poock (2004b) shared the results from a national survey on graduate student orientation practices, finding that orientation programs for graduate students tend to be offered exclusively in the fall term and typically use a simple format where students remain in a room while speakers rotate in and out.

Based on the results of these studies, as well as others (McDavis, Molden & Wilson, 1989; Miller et al., 2001; Vlisides & Eddy, 1993), it is clear that orientation programs provide a valuable service in assisting students in their transition to a new academic campus. At the campus-wide level, there are economies of scale that make such orientation programs worthwhile. Students who are new to a campus clearly have many non-academic, social, and personal issues including obtaining health insurance and parking permits, establishing e-mail accounts, learning about career services and other assistance available to students. These interests tend to be best addressed through a campus-wide orientation. Perhaps one of the primary social benefits of a campus-wide orientation program is the opportunity to meet other graduate students in greater numbers. Unlike undergraduate students who take courses in a number of academic departments, graduate students tend to have a social network limited to fellow students within one department. Given the time demands on graduate students, there is often little time or opportunity to meet students in other disciplines. The campus-wide orientation offers students the chance to meet students from across campus, which can offer unique benefits for some students. For instance, because many graduate students are older and have children, the campus-wide orientation affords the student-parent a way to meet other students in a similar situation who can share babysitting and other child-care duties. Also, non-majority students (i.e., students of color; gay/lesbian/bisexual/transgender, GLBT, students; or international students) are afforded the opportunity to meet larger numbers of like students than those just in their (smaller) academic department. Indeed, research suggests that this is a primary reason why African American graduate students have a greater preference for campus-wide orientations than do White students. African American graduate students tend to be few in number on campus, and campus-wide orientation is an effective method of meeting other African Americans (Poock, 2002).

Because isolation is an inherent condition of graduate study (Baird, 1990), one can only imagine the magnification of those feelings for students who are arriving in the United States for the first time. As a result, many universities have orientation programs specifically designed for international students (e.g., Columbia University, the University of North Carolina at Chapel Hill). While these were often optional in the past and directed toward the role of graduate teaching assistants, such activities are increasingly important for international students due to new federal mandates (i.e., Patriot Act) for individuals holding student visas; failure to comply with such mandates can have severe implications for these students. It is quite common for international students to begin their orientation many days prior to any campus-wide or departmental efforts, and this orientation may last many days and overlap with institutional or departmental activities. Indeed, if there is a challenge for academic departments it is finding time to include international students that does not conflict with their international orientation.

Departmental Orientation Programs

Departmental orientation programs should be viewed not as separate and distinct, but rather as complementary to the campus-wide events. Indeed, Boyle and Boice (1998) studied best practices for transition and found that "the departments that excel at enculturating graduate students supplemented the [campus-wide] orientation with a departmentally sponsored orientation" (p. 88).

As with campus-wide orientations, researchers have studied discipline-specific orientation programs. Taub and Komives (1998) studied orientation in the College Student Personnel program at the University of Maryland and identified five departmental goals: (a) offer students the opportunity to assess the academic program and institution, (b) provide students with essential information, (c) personalize the orientation, (d) develop a community among graduate students, and (e) facilitate the transition to graduate school.

A few years later, Miller et al. (2001) analyzed a doctoral orientation seminar at an anonymous institution. The authors determined that the orientation was quite effective at assisting students in the social and academic transition to doctoral study. Unlike the findings provided by research on campus-wide orientation programs, departmental activities appear to be specifically focused on academic issues (Poock, 2002). These include advising, selecting an advisor, registering for classes, funding issues, and learning expectations of being a graduate student. When compared to campus-wide orientations, departmental efforts are more highly valued by most incoming graduate students (Poock, 2002). This is not surprising when one considers that applicants to undergraduate institutions apply to an institution; prospective graduate students apply to a specific academic program, although the operational aspects may be centralized.

Due to the number of graduate students holding teaching assistant (TA) positions, many universities have orientation programs specifically for new TAs that are in addition to the general campus-wide or departmental orientations. At the University of Tennessee, for example, new TAs experience a teaching orientation through the Graduate School. Many academic departments also offer teaching orientations generally directed by departmental faculty. Centralized TA training tends to focus on method while departments tend to focus on content. That is, the centralized process instructs TAs on pedagogical techniques, and departments instruct the TAs on the specific subject matter to be covered in the undergraduate courses to be taught.

Considerations for Other Special Populations

Part-Time and Distance Education Students

There are many unique groups of students within the larger graduate population. A few of those special populations are discussed in chapters 4 and 5, focusing on the substantive needs of students of color and international students respectively. However, a growing number of graduate students are part-time and/or distance education students, and these micro-populations have unique structural needs. These students spend limited or no time on campus, may have full-time, non-academic obligations, or may live and work in locations that are geographically distant from campus. Thus, attending on-campus orientation programs is problematic due to temporal and/or geographic constraints.

Baird notes that students who are not enrolled full-time on campus face the challenge of "finding time and energy to meet the demands of several competing roles" (1990, p. 384), balancing their academic demands with their professional obligations and personal commitments (e.g., being a spouse and/or parent). Moreover, Baird suggests that part-time students may feel greater isolation within the academic department and perceive themselves to be at a disadvantage when seeking advice and direction from professors. Poock (2002) reports that advisement issues were significantly more important for part-time students than for full-time students. In addition, he found other differences between these two student populations. In his research, full-time students viewed teaching and research assistant benefits, when and how payment occurs, and housing significantly more important than did their part-time counterparts.

Delayed-Entry Students

As noted in chapter 1, the notion that students begin graduate study immediately upon completing their baccalaureate degree is a misconception. Indeed, fewer than half of all master's students continue on to graduate school without interruption. The data are similar for doctoral students, with the exception of those entering the field of education (Choy, Cataldi, & Griffith, 2006).

Those graduate students who do choose to continue their education uninterrupted are likely to be familiar with operational issues (e.g., registration, opening an e-mail account) and services available to students (e.g., health care, psychological counseling, student activities). However, for the bulk of the entering graduate students, it has been several years since they were undergraduates. In the field of education, for example, the span of time between graduating with an undergraduate degree and entering a doctoral program can be substantial. In fact, the average doctoral recipient in the field of education is more than 43 years of age (Hoffer et al., 2006). Clearly, students who enter graduate study after a long absence from college may likely face an operational landscape (e.g., registration, student services) that is either unfamiliar and/or long forgotten. It is important that orientation planners consider the specific needs of their graduate students population.

Recommendations for Best Practices Based on Research

This section offers recommendations for best practices for faculty and administrators who plan campus-wide and departmental activities.

Campus-Wide Orientation

The orientation needs of graduate students clearly may vary among institutions. The type of institution, number of enrolled graduate students, and campus culture may all affect what campus leaders choose to address during orientation. Moreover, some campuses have no centralized graduate school, thus making a campus-wide orientation operationally problematic. However, many recommendations apply to any institution offering campus-wide orientations.

Notify new students of orientation early. Given the logistical demands of relocating to a new environment, students are best served by orientation information that is provided several months prior the start of their first semester. This practice is generally in place at most institutions (Poock, 2004a), although there is variation in how the information is distributed. Whether accompanying an admissions letter or sent under separate cover, allowing students to plan ahead for their orientation is critical to its success. Orientation programs should be organized intentionally with the understanding that demands on the time of incoming students can be substantial. Therefore, campus-wide orientation programs should take into account students' obligation with departmental orientation, and other planned activities.

Provide information on student services. Orientation can be viewed as a division of labor, with campus-wide orientation providing non-academic information. Most colleges and universities have a wide array of services available to students, graduate and undergraduate alike. Whether it is health insurance, social organizations, or psychological services to name a few, incoming students need to know what services are offered and that they are available to graduate students. Perhaps the most effective means of providing this information is the student services information fair, something currently offered at the University of North Carolina at Chapel Hill and the University of Georgia. In this format, students have the opportunity to visit numerous booths in a large room, gather information on services and activities, and talk with representatives staffing the booths. This type of event allows the student to obtain printed material, and most importantly, talk with the representatives in a relaxed and central location. In short, rather than requiring students to search the campus for offices and services of interest to them, the offices and services come to the students during orientation at the information fair.

Foster social interaction. One of the greatest benefits of a campus-wide orientation is the opportunity to meet other students. Once classes begin, this opportunity rapidly diminishes. Those who plan campus-wide orientations can foster social interaction in two effective ways. First, they can offer social activities (e.g., receptions, dinners, and tours). Second, the information offered during orientation can be provided in a manner that facilitates social interaction. The most common structure of campus-wide orientation activities takes place in a room where speakers come and go but students are chair-bound (Poock, 2004a). While this may facilitate interaction with students on one's immediate right or left, a more effective method may be reversing the structure, with students moving from room to room with speakers in their respective rooms (Barker et al., 1997). This approach would enable students to interact with a far greater number of colleagues while still obtaining important information provided by the speakers.

Address the needs of special populations. There is no greater opportunity to introduce non-majority students to each other than at campus-wide orientation activities. Offering social activities sponsored by specific offices or student groups would enable students to meet other new students as well as currently enrolled students. For example, a social reception sponsored by the campus office that advocates for GLBT students would enable these students as well as students with interests in GLBT issues, to meet, interact, and learn about relevant issues on campus. Similar receptions could be sponsored by offices that address the needs of African American students, women, and students with children.

Part-time and/or distance-education students. At first glance, it may appear that a campus-wide orientation may be a logical way to address the isolation and other issues facing part-time students. However, given that a part-time student's time on campus is severely limited, every hour spent at a campus-wide orientation means less time attending departmental activities. Thus, addressing the socialization and orientation needs of part-time students appears to be the purview of academic departments. While there is no one solution, it would appear that offering some orientation activities during times that are not traditional work hours (e.g., on weekends or evenings during the work week), introducing the students to other part-time students, and suggesting that faculty and staff offer some office hours during non-traditional times would be effective means of addressing the needs of this population. Distance-education students, who may take anywhere from 50% to 100% of their classes online, can benefit from the points noted above. The master's in business administration fellows program at Johns Hopkins University (n.d.) is a blended-delivery model distance education program. Although students live and work throughout the country (and indeed the world), they still meet face-to-face at the beginning of the program for orientation-related activities (and periodically throughout the program). The director of the program indicates this face-to-face orientation is essential for students' success in the program (R. G. Milter, personal communication, February 9, 2007). Clearly, even part-time and distance-education students can benefit from orientation programs.

Involve students in planning. Students who have recently completed their first year of graduate study should be included in planning, because they may be in the best position to inform administrators of students' needs and assess the effectiveness of the previous year's orientation program. Additionally, it is not uncommon for the graduate student government on campus to be involved in some aspect of the campus-wide orientation, even if it is simply being represented at an information fair. Because this group represents all the graduate students on campus, they would be an excellent resource for obtaining orientation feedback and planning for the following year. Therefore, the president of the graduate student government (or his/her representative) should be included on the committee that plans and implements the campus-wide orientation. This would provide the professional staff with easy access to students and their views about what the effectiveness of previous orientation processes.

Departmental Orientation

Although academic departments vary greatly by disciplines, numbers of graduate students, and resources, they all have the common challenge of assisting new students in the enculturation process. Toward that end, several recommendations are offered regarding departmental orientation activities.

Partner with campus-wide activities. Coordinated planning between campus-wide and department efforts is essential for students' orientation experiences to be successful. In short, this means allowing time in the departmental agenda for students to attend the campus-wide orientation and encouraging them to do so. This would have the added value of ensuring that information discussed in the department activities is not duplicated in the campus-wide activities (or vice versa). Because students' time is valuable, duplicating information could easily be viewed as "a waste of time."

Foster social interaction. The primary focus of the campus-wide orientation is to provide non-academic information and foster social interaction, but these are important objectives of departmental activities as well. Student isolation is a concern for both majority and non-majority students, and any effort faculty and staff can make to further facilitate student interactions is beneficial (e.g., departmental social hour, intramural sports, cookout). These events should not be limited to the new students in the program because involvement with returning students and departmental faculty and staff facilitates incoming students' connection with the new environment that will be their universe for possibly many years.

Build a sense of community. It is important for faculty and staff to develop a sense of community within the department. While this is beneficial to all students, it tends to be of particular interest to women (Ellis, 2001; Kurtz-Costes, Helmke, & Ulku-Steiner, 2006). Community means establishing trust, offering a non-competitive environment, and, in general, feeling part of a greater whole. Building community starts with departmental orientation activities that foster social interaction but extends throughout students' academic careers in the program. Clearly, this can include social activities offered throughout the year but it can also entail admitting students in cohorts, requiring academic assignments, and problem solving based on group work (Baird, 1990). These recommendations reinforce social support, commitment to the discipline, and facilitate the establishment of professional norms that are an inherent element of the socialization process.

Strategically address academic information. Incoming students clearly need to know a great deal of academic information (e.g., choosing an advisor, selecting a thesis or dissertation committee, grading policies). However, faculty and staff can triage the information they provide based upon the needs of the students. That is, make sure the information discussed is of immediate interest to students; discussing information that may be valuable once students reach their second semester may not be the best use of time during orientation. The most pressing academic issues for new students include how and when to register for classes, the courses they should be taking the first term, and—for RAs and TAs—expectations of the assistantship and how and when they get paid. Providing this information early in orientation, rather than incorporating it within myriad other academic policies and procedures, has a two-fold impact: (a) it provides the students with the information they most eagerly desire, and (b) it helps alleviate anxiety by addressing the unknown.

Take the necessary time. Orientation need not be rushed. Research suggests that students are quite willing to arrive on campus several days prior to the start of classes to participate in orientation activities (Poock 2004a, 2004b). This means that when it comes to meeting the needs of students, as noted above, faculty have several days in which to partner with campus-wide activities, foster social interaction, build a sense of community, strategically address academic information, and address the needs of part-time students. But as noted above, incoming graduate students can face great demands on their time than their undergraduate counterparts. From locating a place to live and establishing child care, to attending campus-wide and departmental orientation programs, faculty and staff organizing orientation activities should be cognizant that students have demands external to the department. Of course, coordinating departmental activities with those offered campus-wide is essential. If students are to benefit from both departmental and campus-wide activities, those efforts should be planned in conjunction with each other and not in competition.

Model Orientation Programs

This section presents models of orientation programs offered at three different institutions. In many ways these three programs are representative of programs throughout institutions of higher education. And while these are offered as models, one should not infer that they are the only exemplary graduate orientation programs. The first model is offered by the graduate school at a public research institution; the second model is offered at a private institution that does not have a centralized graduate school, and thus, orientation is offered by a school within the university. The third model is offered at a master's level institution that has residential and commuter students.

Campus-Wide Orientation at a Large Public Institution

The University of North Carolina at Chapel Hill informs all admitted students at the time of acceptance about the campus-wide orientation program. This one-day program is presented prior to the start of classes in the fall. Most admitted students pursue their degrees full-time, and thus orientation is geared toward this population.

The date for the one-day session is selected approximately a year in advance, providing academic departments ample notice to organize their activities around the graduate school's efforts.

The morning session entails three repeating workshops on issues of interest to new students: (a) a roundtable discussion with current graduate students, (b) a session on how to obtain in-state residency for tuition purposes, and (c) a session on how to obtain external funding and other sources of financial aid. These one-hour sessions are repeated twice, providing students the opportunity to attend the workshops in the order they choose. A student service information fair follows the workshop. Students gather in a large hall and visit booths with representatives from approximately 40 offices/organizations on campus (e.g., student organizations, health insurance, student legal services, child care). Following lunch, students can tour the campus and local community. The day ends with a large social event.

Though the actual orientation is a one-day activity, the staff in the graduate school offer monthly activities throughout the academic year including social and recreational activities within the geographical area; sessions for students with an interest in African American, Native American, or international issues; and sources of funding for the following academic year.

School Orientation at a Private Institution

Columbia University has no centralized graduate school, and each school organizes its own orientation in conjunction with programs offered by departments within the school. This example focuses on the Graduate School of Arts and Sciences, which informs all new students of a school-wide orientation program shortly after they are admitted. As with the previous example, most admitted students pursue their degrees full-time, and orientation is organized accordingly.

Unlike other institutions, this school has two orientation tracks. While substantively similar in content, one track is for doctoral students and the other track is for master's students. This orientation starts with a welcome by the president and dean of the school, information about the structure of the day, and reference materials (e.g., relevant office phone numbers, student handbook). This is followed by smaller, interactive sessions similar to the student service information fair noted above. Again, grouped as doctoral or master's students, these sessions cover a variety of points of interest for new graduate students, including but not limited to health services, libraries, and career services. The day ends with a social event for new students and faculty.

Following this day-long program of activities are continuing orientation activities throughout the next month. These events include a comprehensive library orientation, social events that include shopping trips, tours of the local area, a harbor cruise, a welcome reception for students of color, and a barbeque with the dean of the school.

Campus-wide Orientation at a Master's Institution

Drury University informs all applicants of its orientation for new graduate students. Unlike other institutions, all applicants are invited to orientation about two weeks prior to admissions notices being mailed. Following this general notice, all admitted applicants are sent a formal invitation to the graduate orientation.

Held two days prior to the start of classes, graduate orientation is a one-day event divided into two tracks. The first track is a general session held for all newly admitted individuals; that is, undergraduate, graduate, and continuing education students. It is during this orientation that financial aid opportunities are discussed and representatives from different offices speak about what services they offer. This event concludes with a campus tour.

The second track is specifically for all graduate students (except M.B.A. students who participate in a separate event), which begins with departmental faculty and staff introducing themselves to the new students and is followed by general information on academic policies and deadlines. It is during this track that graduate students are told how to obtain a parking permit and student identification card, how to register for classes, and how to contact faculty and staff.

The college has a large number of distance-education students who pursue their degrees either at an off-campus location and/or via online instruction. They are invited to all orientation events, but they are also provided the substantive information (e.g., how to register for classes, academic policies, how to obtain a student identification card) through a detailed e-mail message. This somewhat impersonal approach is supplemented with a more hands-on approach as staff in the graduate dean's office personally contact each new student (via telephone) to welcome them and respond to questions.

Conclusion and Recommendations

Grounded in socialization theory, graduate orientation facilitates a dual enculturation process, initiating students into the academic department and the broader academic community on campus. Individuals who organize campus-wide orientation activities for graduate students play an important role in providing students the opportunity to meet their nonacademic needs. Departmental faculty and staff also play a critical role in the initiation of students into the campus culture and profession with the departmental orientation.

In conclusion, here are three specific recommendations to improve the orientation experience for graduate students. First, divisions of student affairs should take a greater role in graduate student orientation. As Poock (2004b) notes, most orientation programs are coordinated and funded by faculty/staff in either a centralized graduate school or by an academic college when there is no centralized graduate school. Vice presidents for student affairs or staff in their division typically play a minimal role in graduate orientation. It is not unreasonable, therefore, for incoming graduate students to feel that, at worst, campus-wide student services are reserved solely for undergraduates or, at best, graduate students are not the primary constituent group for student affairs. This author has experienced countless encounters with graduate students who did not realize that student services were available to all students, undergraduate and graduate alike. Greater involvement in orientation by divisions of student affairs could be quite effective at encouraging graduate students to take advantage of those services.

Second, graduate orientation can be expanded throughout the academic year. Although some topics need to be addressed prior to beginning of class for new students (Poock, 2002), there are other issues that only become important later in a graduate student's first year. In other words, offering ongoing, year-long orientation activities can address the needs of students that crop up throughout the year. Examples of such activities may include instate residency at public institutions, how to obtain financial aid/fellowships/grants for the following year, social and recreational activities in the geographical area, employment opportunities for spouses/partner, what to expect in the following years (especially for doctoral students), research resources in the library, and summer employment opportunities for students.

Third, orientation should be the first step in the professional development of master's and doctoral students. The vast majority of master's programs are career-related (e.g., M.B.A., M.Ed., M.P.T.). And many doctoral students seek nonacademic employment upon graduation (Fisher & Zigmond, 1998), and those who do pursue academia are likely to encounter "a new and rapidly changing set of conditions and values defining the enterprise" (LaPidus, 1998, p. 96). In short, the landscape of graduate education is changing, and the needs of graduate students extend beyond orientation toward more comprehensive professional development. Many voices are supporting this call, including the Council of Graduate Schools, American Association of Colleges and Universities, National Academy of Sciences, and numerous academic associations (Poock, 2001). And while orientation, by itself, is important to graduate students it is just one piece of a larger professional development initiative.

References

Antony, J. S. (2002). Reexamining doctoral student socialization and professional development: Moving beyond congruence and assimilation orientation. In J. C. Smart & W.G. Tierney (Eds.), *Higher education: Handbook of theory and research* (Vol. XVII, pp. 349-380). New York: Agathon Press.

Baird, L. L. (1990). The melancholy of anatomy: The personal and professional development of graduate and professional school students. In J. C. Smart (Ed.), *Higher education: Handbook of theory and research* (Vol. VI, pp. 361-392). New York: Agathon Press.

Barker, S., Felstehausen, G., Couch, S., & Henry, J. (1997). Orientation programs for older and delayed-entry graduate students. *NASPA Journal, 35*(1), 57-68.

Boyle, P., & Boice, B. (1998). Best practices for enculturation: Collegiality, mentoring, and structure. In M. S. Anderson (Ed.), *The experience of being in graduate school: An exploration* (New Directions for Higher Education, No. 101, pp. 87-94). San Francisco: Jossey-Bass.

Buchanan, D. A. (1989). *A study of graduate student perceptions of the Oklahoma State University environment.* (ERIC Document Reproduction Service No. ED 330 284)

Choy, S. P., Cataldi, E. F., & Griffith, J. (2006). *Student financing of graduate and first-professional education, 2003-04: Profiles of students in selected degree programs and part-time students* (No. NCES 2006-185). Washington, DC: U.S. Department of Education, National Center for Education Statistics.

Corcoran, M. & Clark, S. M. (1984). Professional socialization and contemporary career attitudes of three faculty generations. *Research in Higher Education, 20*(2), 131-153.

Denecke, D., & Frasier, H. (2005). Ph.D. completion project: Preliminary results from baseline data. *Communicator, 38*(9), 1-2, 7-8.

Ellis, E. M. (2001). The impact of race and gender on graduate school socialization, satisfaction with doctoral study, and commitment to degree completion. *Western Journal of Black Studies, 25*(1), 30-45.

Fischer, B. A., & Zigmond, M. J. (1998). Survival skills for graduate school and beyond. In M. S. Anderson (Ed.) *The experience of being in graduate school: An exploration* (New Directions for Higher Education, No. 100, pp. 29-40). San Francisco: Jossey-Bass.

Gansemer-Topf, A. M., Ross, L. E., & Johnson, R. M. (2006). Graduate and professional student development and student affairs. In M. J. Guentzel, & B. E. Nesheim, B. E. (Eds.), *Supporting graduate and professional students: The role of student affairs* (New Directions for Student Services, No. 115, pp. 19-30). San Francisco: Jossey-Bass.

Golde, C. M. (1998). Beginning graduate school: Explaining first-year doctoral attrition. In M. S. Anderson (Ed.), *The experience of being in graduate school: An exploration* (New Directions for Higher Education, No. 101, pp. 55-64). San Francisco: Jossey-Bass.

Golde, C. M. (2005). The role of the department in doctoral student attrition: Lessons from four departments. *Journal of Higher Education, 76*(6), 669-700.

Hoffer, T. B., Welch, V., Webber, K., Williams, K., Lisek, B., Hess, M., et al. (2006). *Doctorate recipients from United States universities: Summary report 2005*. Chicago: National Opinion Research Center.

Isaac, P. D. (1993). Measuring graduate student retention. In L. L. Baird (Ed.), *Increasing graduate student retention and degree attainment* (New Directions for Institutional Research, No. 80, pp. 13-25). San Francisco: Jossey-Bass.

Johns Hopkins University. (n.d.). *Johns Hopkins M.B.A. Fellows Program*. Retrieved March 21, 2007, from http://olms.cte.jhu.edu/olms/output/page.php?id=3590

Kurtz-Costes, B., Helmke, L. A., & Ulku-Steiner, B. (2006). Gender and doctoral studies: The perceptions of Ph.D. students in an American university. *Gender & Education, 18*(2), 137-155.

LaPidus, J. B. (1998). If we want things to stay as they are, things will have to change. In M. S. Anderson (Ed.), *The experience of being in graduate school: An exploration* (New Directions for Higher Education, No. 100, pp. 95-102). San Francisco: Jossey-Bass.

McDavis, R. J., Molden, I. T., & Wilson, S. R. (1989). Summer programs: A method for retaining Black graduate students. *Journal of College Student Development, 30*(3), 272-274.

Meloni, C. F. (1986). *Adjustment problems of foreign students in U.S. colleges and universities. Q&A*. ERIC Clearinghouse on Languages and Linguistics, Washington, DC. (ERIC Document Reproduction Services No. ED 276 296)

Miller, M. T., Miles, A. S., & Dyer, B. G. (2001). Graduate student orientation through a professional seminar: A case study of doctoral students, 1997-2000. *Journal of College Orientation and Transition, 8*(2), 22-31.

Perna, L. W., & Hudgins, C. (1996). *The graduate assistantship: Facilitator of graduate students' professional socialization*. Paper presented at the Annual Meeting of the Association for the Study of Higher Education, Memphis, TN. (ERIC Document Reproduction Service No. ED 402 822)

Phillips, M. S., Daubman, K. A., & Wilmoth, D. (1986). A graduate student orientation program. *Journal of College Student Personnel, 27*(3), 280-281.

Poock, M. C. (2001). A model for integrating professional development in graduate education. *College Student Journal, 35*(3), 345-352.

Poock, M. C. (2002). Graduate student orientation: Assessing needs and methods of delivery. *Journal of College Student Development, 43*(2), 231-245.

Poock, M. C. (2004a). Graduate student orientation: Applying CAS Standards to national practices. *College and University Journal, 80*(2), 19-26.

Poock, M. C. (2004b). Graduate student orientation: Results from a national survey. *NASPA Journal, 41*(3), 470-486.

Rosenblatt, H. S., & Christensen, C. (1993). "Welcome to the whole family": A graduate student orientation. *College Student Journal, 27*(4), 502-505.

Stein, E. L., & Weidman, J. C. (1989). *Socialization in graduate school: A conceptual framework*. Paper presented at the annual meeting of the Association for the Study of Higher Education, Atlanta, GA. (ERIC Document Reproduction Service No. ED 339 258)

Taub, D. J., & Komives, S. R. (1998). A comprehensive graduate orientation program: Practicing what we preach. *Journal of College Student Development, 39*(4), 394-398.

Tinto, V. (1993). *Leaving college: Rethinking the causes and cures of student attrition* (2nd ed.). Chicago:University of Chicago Press.

Turner, C. S. V., & Thompson, J. R. (1993). Socializing women doctoral students: Minority and majority experiences. *The Review of Higher Education, 16*(3), 355-370.

Upcraft, M. L. & Farnsworth, W. M. (1984). Orientation programs and activities. In M. L. Upcraft (Ed.), *Orienting students to college* (New Directions for Student Services, No. 25, pp. 27-38). San Francisco: Jossey-Bass.

Vlisides, D. & Eddy, J. (1993). Graduate student orientation models. *College Student Journal, 27*(1), 96-98.

Ward-Roof, J. A., & Hatch, C. (Eds.). (2003). *Designing successful transitions: A guide for orienting students to college* (Monograph No. 13, 2nd ed.). Columbia, SC: University of South Carolina, National Resource Center for The First-Year Experience and Students in Transition.

Weidman, J. C., & Stein, E. L. (1990, October). *The professional socialization of graduate students in educational administration*. Paper presented at the Annual Meeting of the University Council for Educational Administration, Pittsburgh, PA. (ERIC Document Reproduction Service No. ED 326 945)

Weidman, J. C., Twale, D. J., & Stein, E. L. (2001). *Socialization of graduate and professional students in higher education: A perilous passage?* (ASHE-ERIC Higher Education Report Volume 28, Number 3). San Francisco: Jossey-Bass.

▼ Chapter Seven ▼

The Transition Course: Supporting Graduate Students' Adjustment

Jan Allen

Graduate students in their first year face multiple challenges (e.g., academic, social, cultural, career). In an attempt to assist students with these transition issues, institutions are responding with the introduction of a range of programs, policies, and supports (many of which are detailed in other chapters in this volume). One recent initiative is a first-year transition course,[1] which several institutions have pioneered to help students with the difficulties inherent in the transition to graduate study and their development as scholars and professionals.

This chapter will provide background and rationale for the transition course, including identifying the issues that confront new graduate students. It will also offer information regarding course content, logistics of a transition course, specific course topics and content, and sample modules that can be adapted for transition courses for a variety of purposes and needs.

It should be noted that this chapter will include practices and recommendations that apply to both master's and doctoral students. In spite of the differences between master's and doctoral education, some essential elements of graduate education—developing community, providing effective mentoring and advising, conveying expectations and requirements, and communicating with students about their progress—are critical components of graduate and professional study at all levels. Most of what follows applies, then, to both master's and doctoral education.

To determine the extent that institutions have developed and implemented transition courses, an e-mail survey, conducted in 2007, gathered information on existing or proposed courses at universities throughout the United States. Questions focused on course content, schedule, enrollment population, and course sponsorship. A listserv query was sent to the membership of Administrators in Graduate and Professional Student Services (AGAPSS) and to Professional and Organizational Development Network in Higher Education (POD), a group devoted to the development of faculty. In addition, more extensive surveys were sent to graduate deans at 22 institutions where a search of the institutions' web sites indicated a transition course currently or previously existed.

A total of 27 responses were received and follow-up e-mails and phone calls resulted in information about eight existing and proposed transition courses. Examples from these courses are described below; web sites for additional information and course syllabi are listed in the resources section at the end of the chapter.

Challenges for New Graduate Students

What are these challenges for new graduate students? As many as half of all doctoral students who begin a degree program do not complete it (Council of Graduate Schools, 2004). In the introduction to this monograph, Tokuno notes that attrition appears to be a problem at the master's level, though it is not as well documented as attrition from doctoral studies. Moreover, Lovitts (2001) has shown that a surprisingly large number of students who exhibited factors we assume to be predictive of graduate school success were, in fact, more likely to drop out. For example, students who reported being mentored, presenting papers outside the classroom, subscribing to a professional journal, and attending professional meetings as undergraduates were less likely to complete graduate school, although students who had these experiences as graduate students had lower attrition rates.

Recent research suggests that the blame for graduate student attrition does not rest solely with students' inadequate academic ability and performance. In fact, Lovitts (2001) suggests that undergraduate cumulative grade point average was not a reliable predictor of completion or attrition in graduate programs. Rather, some of the blame should be directed at the structure and process of graduate education, including inadequate advising/mentoring, financial resources, and "moral and intellectual support" (Lovitts, p. 27). Yet, many programs (and faculty as well), failing to recognize their "corporate responsibility," maintain a belief that students are singularly responsible for not completing their graduate degrees (p.25).

Compared to a decade ago, more graduate students receive multi-year funding while they take classes, conduct research, and write their theses or dissertations, yet this increased support has not comparably reduced the length of time students take to get their degree. In fact, in some disciplines, students are taking longer to finish, even in the face of evidence that longer time-to-degree correlates negatively with success on the academic job market. The failure of the job market to fulfill predictions made in the 1990s for increased demand for new faculty at the millennium has intensified pressure and frustration for those entering and persisting in graduate programs (Brodie, 1995; Gilbert, 1996).

Responses to these difficulties are coming from various places within the institution. Faculty mentors advise, encourage, and support their students (i.e., financially and otherwise). Program chairs and graduate program directors develop graduate seminars, workshops, and other academic and social activities to engage students academically and personally. They also create departmental expectations and support for effective mentoring of students by faculty. Individual schools offer courses and workshops for related clusters of graduate programs, especially for smaller programs that cannot practically or financially develop and offer sufficient programming for their own students. And, more centrally, graduate schools, offices of academic services, and teaching and professional development centers work to create and offer various kinds of support for first-year graduate students as well as use their resources and expertise to facilitate this support at the department and school level.

Rationale for Transition Course

To address the concerns and challenges associated with graduate student transition and socialization described in earlier chapters, institutions have developed transition courses to help students learn about roles, responsibilities, and strategies for success in graduate school. A transition course can contribute in multiple ways. Boyle and Boice (1998) synthesized existing research and suggested that new graduate students are more likely to succeed when they have opportunities to develop a sense of collegiality; experience effective mentoring; and are given structure related to goals, assignments, and feedback. The transition course can do this and more.

Research and other literature on successful graduate transition, persistence, and completion support the following rationales for a transition course: (a) enhanced recruitment and enrollment, (b) community building, (c) communication, and (d) socialization into the profession and discipline. Each of these points is discussed more fully below.

As students become increasingly attuned as "consumers" of graduate education, (i.e., they shop for the best experience and funding package among multiple institutions), they also have learned to inquire about student attrition and completion rates. These questions may include the following: How many students enter and then complete your program? Where do they get jobs upon completion? What percentage of your students get tenure-track faculty positions? A transition course appeals to students as institutions market their programs to recruit and enroll the best students who recognize the course as a head start to success.

A transition course builds community among an entering cohort of graduate students in a program or at an institution. Lovitts (2001), in her research on students who persist and those who leave graduate school, described the "absence of community" (p. 82) for those students who left the program. They lacked both the structures and opportunities to be engaged and integrated into the program and discipline that were experienced by students who were more likely to complete. For example, among students who received funding, those whose support came in the form of teaching and research assistantships had lower attrition rates than those who had fellowships. Those without any support—assistantships or fellowships—had the highest attrition rates. Although the funding support certainly helps address the financial reasons that cause some students to leave their graduate programs, the interaction and integration into the program provided by teaching and research responsibilities were associated with lower attrition rates. The transition course can provide a structure, in this case one of both social and intellectual engagement that helps students to integrate into the department and be more likely to persist in their graduate study.

A transition course can communicate to students the specific requirements and expectations associated with success in the degree program. What are the milestones in progress and time to degree that are required? What are the student's and the faculty's responsibilities in ensuring these milestones are met? What is different about these activities at the graduate level that contribute to persistence, integration, and success? How are students asked to think and write differently once they are in graduate school? Students benefit from knowing as soon as possible the role that analytical, conceptual, and critical thinking have in faculty assessment of students' abilities to conduct independent research and produce serious scholarship. Also, students who understand the different expectations and assessment of intellectual ability in graduate school will more quickly develop the strategies to achieve the necessary skills.

A transition course is a first step in the socialization of students into the discipline. Golde, Walker, and their associates (2006) have addressed the importance of socialization of graduate students as stewards of the discipline. Students must be knowledgeable about the problems and challenges facing both the discipline and the profession as those who will soon be asked to help transform and reform it. For example, one important issue facing many graduate programs is the overproduction and unemployment of Ph.D. graduates. A discussion of the issues (e.g., academic and non-academic job markets, funding for students in fields with decreased academic job positions) helps students make the best decisions about both an academic and post-graduate career path in the earlier stages of their graduate program by being better-informed consumers.

Content of the Transition Course

A transition course should provide the information students need to succeed in graduate school and beyond. Several common class topics include the history of the discipline/field; how to be a successful graduate student; working with mentors; developing a professional identity; departmental degree requirements; ethics; writing proposals for fellowships and grants; writing skills for dissertations, theses, and publishing; presentation skills; and balancing academic scholarship with personal responsibilities.

History of the Discipline/Field

Some transition courses introduce students to the history of the discipline. Further, discussion about the primary theories and methodologies can be included as well as the reasons and ways the discipline's predominating theories and methods have changed in response to new knowledge, political conditions, funding sources, and cultural and societal changes. Faculty address the "state of the discipline" when they entered graduate school relative to today and share how they used this information to determine their graduate and career goals and specialties.

Conrad, Duren, and Haworth (1998), from interviews with almost 800 faculty, students, and graduates of master's programs, have described the importance of this "critical dialogue anchored in a two-way interactive, or dialogical approach to teaching and learning" (p. 68). That students and faculty "conjointly question existing knowledge, challenge key assumptions in their field, and develop and critically refine new understandings of knowledge and professional practice" (p. 67-68) was one of two "meaningful" features identified by master's program students and graduates related to the rigor and effectiveness of their graduate training. Students should realize how the stewards of the disciplines have responded to challenges and demands; they also should begin to identify their role as a steward of the discipline in the coming years.

The Successful Graduate Student

Discussing the characteristics of successful students as well as programs and mentors who have persisting students offers insight into a complex mix of factors related to success and completion. To help students develop their own path to success, I use Bronfenbrenner's (1999) person-process-interaction model and ask students to consider their individual traits (i.e., strengths and weaknesses) within the context of the program requirements and support structures. Then, they write two narratives: (a) one about their goals and aspirations when applying to and entering graduate school and characteristics about them that make this graduate degree and discipline a good match and (b) one about this program and its faculty and what qualities of the program and faculty make this a good match for them.

Working with Mentors

It is valuable to discuss the role of mentoring in students' success not only in graduate school but beyond, as mentors become colleagues, collaborators, and co-authors. Here, faculty can help students learn how to find and use mentors effectively. More importantly, they can help students prioritize the characteristics they would value in a mentor. Asking students to write a personal ad seeking a mentor—"Hard-working student in history ISO [in search of] faculty mentor who...." (Allen & Johnston, 1997, p.8)—is one strategy for helping them do this. (See chapter 8 for a more detailed discussion of mentorship.)

Developing a Professional Identity and Strategic Plan for Graduate School

Several courses include a discussion about the need to plan and make important decisions at various stages of the graduate, and later professional, career. I encourage students to develop a strategic plan that includes timelines for completing degree requirements and milestones and for gaining knowledge and skills in different areas (i.e., research, teaching, publishing, writing fellowship applications and grant proposals). Students can be provided with a template based on the example in Figure 1.

Departmental Requirements for the Degree

This session helps students clearly understand specific departmental, graduate school, and university requirements in progress to the degree. Focusing on required and suggested timeline and consequences for not meeting the deadline, such as losing a fellowship or assistantship or termination from the program can help students meet these expectations or, at least, anticipate the consequences for not doing so. Several instructors mentioned including this topic as a strategy to reduce student complaints and even grievances for being "unfairly" dismissed from the program. This session also can emphasize the resources and support provided by the program, department, school, and university.

Ethics, Professional Behavior, and Responsible Conduct of Research

Almost all transition courses reviewed the role of ethical, responsible behavior in the discipline's scholarship. It is important to help students understand the rules and policies that exist and that there are guidelines that encourage and suggest appropriate behaviors. Ethics discussions for doctoral students may also include how to best search for, or develop their own, best practices consistent with the belief that all sound scholarship is based on the highest standards of integrity.

Writing Proposals for Fellowships and Grant Applications

For practical reasons, some graduate students must secure external fellowships. At Columbia University, Ph.D. students who receive five years of full fellowship funding are expected to apply for external awards, because of the prestige associated with receiving such awards (e.g., a Fulbright Scholarship or National Science Foundation grant). It also demonstrates students' grant writing skills to future employers. In this session, faculty focus on government agencies and private foundations that fund research in the discipline as well as department and campus resources that help with fellowship application writing. They could also share copies of successful applications from more advanced students.

Writing Skills for the Dissertation, Thesis, and Publishing

In this session, faculty focus on common problems that graduate student-writers experience—overcoming writing anxiety and blocks; understanding expectations for graduate-level writing and scholarship; and identifying steps to a defensible, publishable dissertation or thesis. As with other topics, faculty discuss the ethical issues associated with writing and publishing. Some courses encourage first-year students to form student-organized writing communities or support groups. Unlike writing or dissertation/thesis seminars, where a faculty member in an evaluative role has a major impact on the expectations and dynamics of the group, the writing support group provides peer evaluation, as well as support, in a safe environment.

Task/ Goal	Funding/Support	Degree Requirements	Research	Teaching	Presentations	Publications	Professional Development
Year 1	University fellowship	Fellowship	Pick advisor; seek mentor; talk with faculty with funded projects	Attend 3 teaching workshops spring semester			Attend new graduate student orientation and workshops on mentoring, time management, and writing skills
Year 2	Teaching assistantship	6 classes; complete master's paper; MA degree awarded	Collect pilot data or work with faculty data set	Attend new TA orientation in fall			Attend workshops on presentation skills and publishing
Year 3	Teaching assistantship; identify external funding sources	6 classes	Analyze/ write up pilot data or faculty data set; draft dissertation proposal	Attend 4 teaching workshops	Present pilot data paper at department symposium in fall, at local/regional conference in spring	Revise and submit a seminar paper for publication	Attend workshops on grantsmanship
Year 4	Research assistantship; begin to write fellowship applications	4 classes; comprehensive exams spring semester; M.Phil. degree awarded	Select graduate committee members; choose dissertation sponsor	Attend 2 teaching workshops	Present paper at graduate symposium conference		Attend workshops on writing and publishing
Year 5	Dissertation year fellowship; submit fellowship applications		Dissertation proposal approved; IRB approval; start research; summer travel to archives/ data collection	Attend 2 teaching workshops	Present pilot data paper at national conference	Write/submit pilot data for publication	Attend workshops on networking and preparing for discussant role at conferences
Year 6	External fellowship or teaching assistantship		Research and write; summer travel to archives/data collection	Attend 2 teaching workshops	Serve as discussant at conference	Write and submit (review or theory) paper from dissertation	Participate in PFF colloquium
Year 7	External fellowship or teaching assistantship		Analyze/ write up dissertation data	Attend teaching philosophy/ portfolio workshop			Attend academic job search, vita writing, interview workshops
Year 8	External fellowship or preceptor teaching	Defend dissertation			Present dissertation at national conference	Write and submit paper from dissertation	Attend transition-to-faculty workshop

Figure 1. A strategic plan for graduate school from start to finish for a doctoral student in a social sciences or humanities program (Allen, in press). Used by permission.

Presentation Skills: Classroom and Conference Talks

This session helps students develop skills and strategies for organizing and delivering lectures, conference presentations, and job talks. A key element is allowing students to deliver and receive faculty and peer critiques on presentations they will be expected to give in the course of their academic career and the job search, including the "elevator" talk ("Tell me about your specialty" in the length of time it takes to ride an elevator 10 floors), an interview presentation, a conference presentation, and conversation about their research at a poster session.

Emerging Issues in the Field: New Technologies, Methodologies, and Challenges

Several institutions use this session to bring in faculty to discuss new directions and issues for the future of the discipline—what graduate students this year will confront and address in the current job market. With a doctoral class, this session also includes a discussion of what the undergraduates they will teach in 10 to 30 years might be like as learners. This session also describes the tenure and promotion system, professorial hierarchy, and university governance that characterize their graduate institution and other schools where they may be employed after graduation.

Serious Scholarship in a Balanced Life

Instructors in this session discuss with students how to balance and manage time, work, passions, and commitments. They talk about maintaining energy for multiple projects and roles as a graduate student, teaching assistant, research assistant, and fun-, family-, recreation-, and leisure-loving person. Faculty can also share their experiences of entering and succeeding in graduate school. In addition, it is helpful to emphasize campus resources such as the counseling center that can help students in times of stress or crisis. However, transition course instructors can also explain that the campus counseling center is not just for crisis intervention. For example, the counseling center at Columbia University offers workshops on time management, procrastination, and dissertation writing.

The course topics suggested above cover the skill areas in which students are expected to excel—writing, taking class and comprehensive exams, presenting papers and lectures, writing fellowship applications and grant proposals, and publishing. The transition classes in this sample emphasize the ethical and responsible conduct that is critical in all these efforts. Instructors devote discussions to the obstacles that may arise and pitfalls to avoid. They focus on new skills, or skills applied at new levels, that students will need. It is helpful to include both intellectual skills such as synthesizing, evaluating, and thinking critically as well as life and work management skills such as organizing, managing multiple projects and deadlines, and managing and resolving conflict.

Logistics of the Transition Course

There are important logistical and practical issues to consider when developing a transition course, regardless of its focus (i.e., master's, doctoral, or combined graduate student groups) or administrative home (program, school, or central graduate school or teaching center).

Length and Format of the Transition Course

Transition courses extend for at least a term, either semester or quarter. Readings relevant to the topic help prompt questions and facilitate discussion. Assignments for the transition course require students to reflect, self-assess, and integrate personal and professional goals. Instructors create an environment where students feel comfortable asking questions, even if the answers lead them to determine that graduate school is not a good match with their interests or skill levels. With a safe space for challenging questions, students may express concerns and complaints about their experiences as new graduate students. Be prepared for this. One class session might include a school or university administrator to confidentially address students' concerns without the presence of program faculty.

Locating the Transition Course in the Program or Graduate School

For the most part, the suggestions thus far have reflected a transition course taught within a single department by a faculty member focusing on specific program requirements and disciplinary issues. For many reasons (e.g., resources, program size, faculty availability/interest) transition courses may be located in the school/college, graduate school, office of academic services, or campus teaching center rather than the department. Modifications can be made, such as discussing the history of the profession rather than the discipline and using examples of research ethics compliance and violations that cut across disciplinary lines. Faculty who represent different programs are invited to discuss how chemists and classicists confront research questions or ethical dilemmas in similar, and different, ways.

Instructor for the Transition Course

One faculty member typically has the faculty-of-record role for the course and is responsible for preparing the syllabus, arranging guest speakers, and responding to students' assignments. Other faculty and even advanced graduate students are invited to the course, either individually or as a panel, to discuss a topic and respond to students' questions. In one transition course, the instructor devotes a class session to advanced graduate students sharing their experiences and advice with new students. Most transition courses have avoided having each class session taught by a different faculty member to ensure continuity among the sessions. Students seem to value the course and experience if they believe faculty value it as well.

For some programs with limited resources or smaller enrollments, it is neither practical nor time- and cost-effective to offer a transition course for each new cohort of students. When the class is created for a cluster of programs, offered school-wide (e.g., University of Tennessee), or facilitated by a central unit such as the graduate school (e.g., Columbia University), it is reasonable and necessary to have different faculty or panels of faculty and advanced students address course topics in each session. In this case, the facilitator role, be it graduate school or student services staff, is critical for creating continuity, community, and communicating the importance of the information shared, albeit by a rotating set of speakers.

Syllabus for the Transition Course

Like any good syllabus, the transition course syllabus conveys important information to students about expectations and requirements, helpful readings and resources, and course content and schedule. It can also convey to students that the program faculty and staff are interested in, even committed to, helping students be as successful as possible in their graduate career. This commitment is communicated in this example from the program in criminology, law, and society at the University of California, Irvine:

> This course is designed to ensure that later in your graduate career you don't find yourself asking (or, more likely, screaming), "Why didn't someone tell me that earlier," especially if/when the "that" is consequential to your educational experience and professional career.... This course will provide you with an opportunity to learn about how to perform some of the "dos" such that you are considerably better situated to perform well in graduate school and beyond. For example, we will discuss a variety of things designed to enhance your success, including how to write like a social scientist, how to secure external funding, how to produce publishable work, how to balance your own academic interests against "what sells" and will render you marketable. To be perfectly blunt, the point of this course is to offer you a focused, sustained, and consequential opportunity to be professionally indoctrinated and socialized—in the positive sense of the words! (http://www.seweb.uci.edu/users/jenness/ProSeminar.pdf)

From the sample syllabi reviewed, specific elements of the transition course syllabus include

- ◇ Topics related to graduate student success—both essential knowledge and skill development
- ◇ Objective or description for each class session
- ◇ Assignments for session topics
- ◇ Readings relevant to the topics

The resources section includes links to sample syllabi and other information from transition courses and professional seminars at various institutions.

Sample Class Sessions for the Transition Course

Transition courses can be developed for different levels of graduate study—master's, doctoral, or for combined cohorts in a program. They can be offered either centrally by the graduate school, office of academic services, or the teaching center on campus or by field or discipline. Figure 2 shows a proposed class session on the history and development of the discipline, in this example for a seminar in a history doctoral program. Students read both classic and recent articles about the discipline, discuss how history has moved from its historical foundations to current research questions and methodologies, and consider emerging research questions and issues for historians. This session is often the first in the seminar; multiple faculty in the program can attend, introduce themselves to the students, and discuss their own entry into an academic career and development as historians. Questions to be considered in this class session include: What does it mean to be an historian in this decade? What issues are we preparing to confront in the coming decade? Are there ways we are working to transform the discipline and in response to what needs and demands do we undertake this effort?"

Figure 3 shows a class session from the School of Social Ecology at University of California, Irvine. From a two-term class, this is one of a three-session series on developing the writing and publishing skills required for graduate school. Students are asked to read a how-to article on writing research manuscripts and another article authored by one of the program faculty. Their

Class Topic: History and highlights (perhaps a few lowlights) in the development of our discipline

Description: Understanding the development of the discipline as a field of inquiry and scholarship permits us to build on the past and transform to meet current challenges

Assignments: Bring to this session a list of your expectations for this course and questions you want answered before the end of the term.

Readings:

Emerton, E. (1893). *The requirements for the historical doctorate in America*. American Historical Association. Retrieved on July 4, 2006, from http://www.historians.org/projects/cge/Related/Emerton.htm

"Trends in history Ph.D.s awarded and job openings advertised, 1970-71 to 2004-05." American Historical Association. Retrieved on August 2, 2006, from http://www.historians.org/info/Data_Jobs_Ph.D.s.pdf

Appleby, J. (2006). Historians, the historical forces they have fostered, and the doctorate in history. In C. Golde, G. Walker, & Associates. (Eds.). (2006), *Envisioning the future of doctoral education* (pp. 311-326). San Francisco: Jossey-Bass.

Stimpson, C. (2006). Words and responsibilities: Graduate education and the humanities. In C. Golde, G. Walker, & Associates (Eds.), *Envisioning the future of doctoral education* (pp. 390-416). San Francisco: Jossey-Bass.

Figure 2. Proposed class session on the history and development of the discipline in a first-year transition seminar for a Ph.D. program in history, "Professional Seminar in History: Striving, Surviving, and Succeeding in the Program, Discipline, and Profession."

Class Topic: Writing Right, Part II: The Academic Journal Article

Readings:

Bem, "Writing the Empirical Journal Article." Chapter 10 in Darley, Zanna and Roediger (Eds.), *The Compleat Academic*, 2nd edition, American Psychological Association, 2004.

Any article by a CLS faculty member that appeared in a respected journal within the last three years.

Guest Faculty: Henry Pontell

Assignment: In two-three typed, double-spaced pages, discuss one or two strengths and weaknesses of the writing style (not the substance) of the article you selected. What types of challenges do you personally face in anticipating writing in this form?

Figure 3. Class session on developing writing skills. From the course "Professional Seminar Criminology, Law, and Society," in the School of Social Ecology at the University of California, Irvine, taught by Professors Valerie Jenness and Cheryl Maxson. Used by permission. Full seminar topics and schedule available at http://www.seweb.uci.edu/users/jenness/ProSeminar.pdf.

assignment is to analyze the latter for approach and style of writing, then to consider their own readiness for producing similar scholarship.

Figure 4 is from a class, "Academic Acculturation," open to all graduate students at the University of Tennessee and taught by faculty awardees in the Chancellor's Teacher-Scholar program. The session topic is ethics, essential training across all disciplines in all graduate and professional training programs, and required for students on federally funded training and research grants. Discussion in this session addresses many issues, including plagiarism, acknowledging and citing the work and ideas of others, co-authorship practices in the discipline (and specific departmental and faculty policies), responsible conduct of research (RCR) and Institutional Review Board (IRB) and Institutional Animal Care and Use policies (IACUC), supervisory and collegial relationships, data ownership and intellectual property issues, consequences of academic misconduct and data fabrication, financial conflicts of interest in research, intellectual conflicts of interest in peer review and mentoring, and many more.

Class Topic: Ethics, Professional Behavior, and Responsible Conduct of Research

Description: Developing an ethical code of conduct for research, teaching, and collegial roles in the academy

Assignments: Read one chapter from the Allen and Moran (2006) novel. Make a list of the questions and concerns you would have as a graduate students in this scenario.

Readings:

Allen, J., & Moran, M.J. (2006). *Research ethics: A novel approach.* Retrieved September 25, 2006 from http://ori.dhhs.gov/education/products/rcr_general.shtml.

Interlandi, J. (2006, October 22). An unwelcome discovery: Walter DeNino was a young lab technician who analyzed data for his mentor, Eric Poehlman. What he found was that Poehlman was not the scientist he appeared to be. *New York Times Magazine*, pp. 98-103.

White, J. (2007). Anticipating and avoiding misperceptions of harassment. In L. Deneef & C. Goodwin, (Eds.), *The academic's handbook* (pp. 98-111). Durham, NC: Duke University Press.

Figure 4. Class session on responsible academic and research conduct in a first-year transition seminar for a cluster of master's and doctoral programs in the life sciences. Adapted and updated from a campus-wide graduate seminar, "Academic Acculturation," taught at the University of Tennessee, Knoxville, by Sky Huck and Jan Allen. Used by permission.

Conclusion

In addition to the courses cited thus far, faculty or administrators at several additional institutions responded that they are developing a transition course. These program faculty, graduate deans, and academic services directors are encouraged to create a transition course that reflects institutional, disciplinary, and students' needs. Theory, research, and recommended practices from institutions that have already created such courses can contribute to the design of a transition course that increases students' competence, confidence, and persistence to successful degree completion. Above all, the transition course should communicate to students that there are multiple, complex factors that contribute to graduate school success. And it should convey the commitment that graduate faculty and graduate administration have to each student's successful transition. As examples shared here demonstrate the course can be extremely valuable in helping graduate students reach their academic and career goals.

Notes

[1]I use the term "transition course" throughout the chapter to distinguish it from the professional seminar in which different faculty attend the course each week and present their research to new students. It is also distinguished from capstone courses in students' degree programs that aim to help students successfully transition from the role of graduate student to faculty or professional. Examples of these include the Professional Development and Community Engagement program (formerly the Intellectual Entrepreneurship program) at the University of Texas, the Developing Future Faculty as Teacher-Scholars program developed at the University of Tennessee (and now implemented at Columbia University), and most notably the Preparing Future Faculty program, begun in 1993 and now implemented at more than 45 doctoral degree granting institutions nationwide.

References

Allen, J. (in press). *The new faculty and graduate mentor: A guide for developing teacher-scholars for mentors, faculty, administrators, and graduate students*. Sterling, VA: Stylus Publishers

Allen, J., & Johnston, K. (1997, February). Mentoring, being mentored. *Context, 14*(6), 15.

Boyle, P., & Boice, B. (1998). Best practices for enculturation: Collegiality, mentoring, and structure. In M. Anderson (Ed.), *The experience of being in graduate school: An exploration* (New Directions for Higher Education, No. 101, pp. 87-94). San Francisco: Jossey-Bass

Brodie, J. (1995). Whatever happened to the job boom? *Academe, 81*(1), 12-15.

Bronfenbrenner, U. (1999). Environments in developmental perspective. In S. Friedman & T. Wachs (Eds.), *Measuring the environment across the lifespan* (pp. 3-20). Washington, DC: American Psychological Association.

Conrad, C., Duren, K., & Haworth, J. (1998). Students' perspectives on their master's degree experiences: Disturbing the conventional wisdom. In M. Anderson (Ed.), *The experience of being in graduate school: An exploration* (New Directions for Higher Education, No. 101, pp. 65-76). San Francisco: Jossey-Bass.

Council of Graduate Schools. (2004). *Ph.D. completion and attrition: Policy, numbers, leadership, and next steps*. Washington, DC: Council of Graduate Schools.

Gilbert, S. (1996). The academic job system and the economy, stupid, or should a friend let a friend get a Ph.D.? *Academe, 82*(5), 12-15.

Golde, C., Walker, G. & Associates. (Eds.). (2006), *Envisioning the future of doctoral education* (pp. 311-326). San Francisco: Jossey-Bass.

Lovitts, (2001). *Leaving the ivory tower: The causes and consequences of departure from doctoral study*. Lanham, MD: Rowman & Littlefield Publishers.

Resources for Developing a Graduate Transition Course

Course and Syllabus Information

University of California, Los Angeles, Graduate School of Education and Information Studies, Department of Education: http://www.gseis.ucla.edu/courses/rac/

University of California, Irvine, School of Social Ecology, Program in Criminology, Law, and Society: http://www.seweb.uci.edu/users/jenness/ProSeminar.pdf

University of South Florida, The Graduate School: Comparative Studies 6934 Best Practices in Teaching and 6935 Best Practices in Research (courses offered in 2006-07 currently being restructured for 2008-09)

University of Maryland, Graduate School of Management and Technology MBA Fundamentals 600: http://www.umuc.edu/departments/bus-exec/content/mba/requiredCourses/syllabus/AMBA600.pdf

Resources for Lectures and Assigned Readings

Allen, J. (in press). *The new faculty and graduate mentor: A guide for developing teacher-scholars for mentors, faculty, administrators, and graduate students*. Sterling, VA: Stylus Publishers.

Darley, J., Zanna, M., & Roediger, H. (Eds.). (2004). *The compleat academic: A career guide*. Washington, DC: American Psychological Association.

Golde, C., Walker, G., & Associates (Eds.). (2006). *Envisioning the future of doctoral education*. San Francisco: Jossey-Bass.

Goldsmith, J., Komlos, J., & Gold. P. (2001). *The Chicago guide to your academic career*. Chicago: University of Chicago Press

Gosling, P., & Noordam, B. (2006). *Mastering your Ph.D.: Survival and success in the doctoral years and beyond*. Berlin, Germany: Springer.

Peters, R. (1997). *Getting what you came for: The smart student's guide to earning a master's or Ph.D.* New York: Farrar, Straus and Giroux.

Chapter Eight

A New Context for Mentoring: Graduate Learning Communities

Richard Pratt and Kenneth A. Tokuno

The term "mentor" comes to us from Greek mythology. When Odysseus left for the Trojan War, he entrusted the care of his son Telemachus to his good friend Mentor. Today, we continue to think of a mentor as a trusted friend, counselor, or teacher. Although the terms "mentor" and "advisor" are often used synonymously and may even be the same individual, they have different official roles. Most graduate students have someone who works with them formally in the role of advisor and provides information on course selection; university, department, and subfield requirements; and progress to degree (Nettles & Millet, 2006).

A mentor is a faculty member who serves as a guide to the student's entry into graduate education, movement toward mastery of the discipline, and understanding of the norms of the profession or professions with which the discipline is associated. Good mentors go beyond fulfilling the need for periodic academic advice to personal attention in the form of social support, goal setting, and, when needed, advocacy. If, as most theorists suggest, integration into graduate-level study is critical for success, one of the best methods for ensuring success is good mentoring. The relationship between mentoring and graduate student success has theoretical support in Lovitts (2001) and Parent (2003). (See chapter 2 of this monograph for a discussion of these theories.)

Good mentoring relationships that on a regular basis provide information, feedback, opportunities for dialogue, role modeling, and support relevant to a student's specific situation have been a key aspect of graduate success. This chapter explores both traditional and new approaches to mentoring that assist students during their transition into graduate study. Specifically, the questions we address are: What role does the mentor play in graduate programs today? And how might it be improved? The first section identifies the major components of the mentoring role. This is followed by a brief review of the literature on the effectiveness of mentoring as it occurs in graduate school. The last section of this chapter presents a model, the learning community, which embeds mentoring into a new context that can strengthen the process of transitioning to graduate study.

Components of the Ideal Mentoring Relationship

There is both theoretical and empirical agreement that good mentors make a difference in the success of graduate students, but what makes a good mentor? Zeldich (1990) stated that

> Mentors are advisors, people with career experience willing to share their knowledge; supporters, people who give emotional and moral encouragement; tutors, people who give specific feedback on one's performance; masters, in the sense of employers to whom one is apprenticed; sponsors, sources of information about and aid in obtaining opportunities; models, of identity, of the kind of person one should be to be an academic. (p. 11)

Several graduate programs have developed standards for mentoring in the form of online guides. These guides are distinct from advising manuals, which provide basic information about graduate policies and procedures. In contrast, mentoring guides provide strategies for faculty to develop their interpersonal "mentoring" skills. The Rackham School of Graduate Studies at the University of Michigan (2006) has one of the most comprehensive guides. It identifies the basic mentoring strategies as (a) engaging graduate students in ongoing conversations, (b) taking the mystery out of graduate school by explaining terminology and clarifying procedures, (c) providing constructive feedback to students and being supportive and encouraging, (d) helping the student develop social networks, (e) keeping the students interest at the forefront, and (f) treating mentees with respect and personal attention. The guide offers specific suggestions as to how each of these strategies can be accomplished.

A key element of mentoring, according to the Rackham guide (University of Michigan, 2006) is to clarify expectations. Students need to know how often a mentor will be available to them, what kinds of feedback to anticipate from a mentor, what the quality of their writing should be, what their intellectual property rights are, and whether and how often they should be publishing and presenting their work. The guide also offers tips to faculty on how to assess the student in the initial meeting, as well as information about the kinds of advice that mentors should give to students, such as being responsible and committed to their studies. In addition, there is information given to departments as to how to support mentoring of their highly diverse graduate student population. For example, many students suffer from feelings of isolation, especially as they get past the euphoria of the first week or two as a graduate student. It is likely that this is even more acute for students of color, international students, and other specific populations who may feel out of place. A mentor can take an active role in introducing the student to faculty and to other students in the program or find ways to include them.

The University of Washington (2006) publishes a mentoring guide modeled after Michigan's, but also provides a companion guide for students, *How to Obtain the Mentoring You Need*. It lets students know what a mentor is, how to recognize what good mentors do, how to determine what their own mentoring needs are, and how to make the most of the advice and assistance they may get from a mentor.

Beyond support for the student's degree progress, some aspects of mentoring are important for professional development as a scholar or educator. For example, mentoring specifically for research is a critical facet of many programs, notably in the natural and social sciences. Such mentoring should begin very early, because it is an important part of the first-year transition. Indeed, the need to begin to understand how to be an independent scholar is one of the unique tasks of graduate study. Thus, where a thesis or dissertation is required, the mentor is usually the thesis advisor, i.e. a research mentor. King (2003) writes that the role of a research mentor is to show empathy for the students' anxiety, risks, problems, and special circumstances. At the same time, the mentor needs to empower the student to pursue his or her own research interests. A faculty mentor should never ask a student to pursue a line of research serving only the mentor's interests. This points to the strong ethical dimension of good mentoring, whether the student is in a research-oriented program or not.

Many graduate students, especially at the doctoral level, are appointed as teaching assistants (TA) or research assistants (RA). Each of these appointments includes supervision by a faculty member. The role of faculty supervisor for RAs is similar to that of a thesis advisor. The role of a faculty advisor for a TA is more distinct. It is important for the faculty to assist any TA in learning the role of instructor. Many of these TAs are only a few months removed from being undergraduates. While there are programs, such as one at the University of Hawai'i at Manoa, that provide some basic information about this role, the TA is best served in being guided by an experienced faculty member who regularly talks with them about teaching and discusses the nuances of grading, classroom management, and one-to-one work with students.

The Reality of Mentoring at the Graduate Level

Despite the long tradition of the mentoring role in higher education and despite institutional efforts to encourage good mentoring, the fact remains that the support of a mentor rests primarily on the good will of individual faculty. The process by which mentoring occurs as well as the quality of that mentoring is therefore subject to much variation.

The Effects of Mentoring

Expressing dissatisfaction with graduate-level mentoring, Minor (2003) argues that the relative autonomy of graduate programs leads to large variations in the quality of mentoring available to graduate students, suggesting there are ways to improve mentoring within the department context by taking advantage of existing opportunities, providing more incentives for good mentoring, and creating more social events for student-faculty interaction.

In their survey of 948 graduate students at both the master's and doctoral level, Girves and Wemmerus (1988) correlated the students' perceptions of faculty with specific outcomes. The perception of faculty included (a) quality of advising, (b) existence of a mentor, and (c) whether or not their mentor treated them as a junior colleague. Girves and Wemmerus use the terms *advisor* and *mentor* interchangeably. The quality of advising/mentoring was measured by a seven-item scale to include the students' perceptions of their mentor's concern for the student, quality as a teacher or scholar, and usefulness of information provided. The existence of a mentor and whether their mentor treated them as a junior colleague were measured by asking graduate students directly about them. The outcomes were students' grades, degree progress, satisfaction with the program, and involvement.

For master's students, the quality of advising/mentoring was slightly correlated with degree progress and grades and highly correlated with the students' satisfaction with the graduate program. Being treated as a junior colleague was slightly correlated with involvement. The mere presence of a mentor was not found to be correlated with any of the outcome measures.

For doctoral students, being treated as a junior colleague was correlated with degree progress and the students' satisfaction with the graduate program. The highest correlation was between the quality of advising/mentoring and the students' satisfaction with the graduate program. Based on whether the student believes that he or she is treated like a junior colleague, Girves and Wemmerus concluded, "The role of the advisor is critical at the doctoral level" (p. 185).

The failure to find a relationship between mentoring and grades is not surprising at the graduate level, because the variability of grades is relatively small. Most grades are A or B in graduate school. Nettles and Millet (2006) argue that research productivity is the best index of graduate student success at the doctoral level, and they found that one of the best predictors of such productivity was having a mentor.

In a survey of 189 graduate students across nine different disciplines at the University of California at Santa Cruz, Tenenbaum, Crosby, and Gilner (2001) distinguished between instrumental and psychosocial support. Instrumental support, which was related to scholarly productivity (as measured by journal publications and conference presentations), involved such things as assisting with skill development, providing helpful information, and acting as a sponsor. Psychosocial support, which correlated with higher levels of students' satisfaction, included such behaviors as role modeling, being empathic, and sharing experiences. Interestingly, gender was not found to be a significant factor, with male and female students responding similarly across most of the findings.

In her research on doctoral students, Lovitts (2001) found that students who completed the Ph.D. were three times more likely than noncompleters to note their mentor's style (e.g., ability to balance challenge with support) as a reason for their satisfaction. Lovitts notes that students need freedom to explore their ideas creatively while having someone assist them with appropriate advice. Although only a very small proportion of students were less than satisfied with their mentoring, a common perception among those who were not satisfied was that their mentors were too controlling. Accessibility was a problem with 75% of all students. These students felt that their mentors did not interact with them enough.

Green and Bauer (1995) wanted to minimize the variability of selection procedures among graduate programs, so they focused their study of mentoring on doctoral students in the "hard sciences." They considered the mentoring relationship from a cost-benefit perspective. Because mentoring takes a great deal of faculty time and, therefore, has opportunity costs associated with it, faculty seek to mentor the students with the most potential. Clearly, there are professional benefits to mentoring strong students, such as the possibility of finding someone with whom the faculty member can generate good research, but there is also a great deal of satisfaction in helping a young student develop into a successful scholar.

For that reason, Green and Bauer (1995) hypothesized that the higher the level of student potential, the more advising the mentor would provide. More advising, in turn, would result in more productivity by the student. Green and Bauer found evidence to support this hypothesis in their longitudinal study of 357 doctoral students within their first two years of study. Faculty spent more time on both instrumental and psychosocial support of students with higher potential, as measured by the student's GRE scores, grades, commitment, and previous research experience.

To check the extent to which mentoring was an expected duty of graduate faculty, Green and Bauer asked department heads whether faculty were expected to be mentors to their doctoral students and whether these students' initial advisors went on to become their dissertation advisors. Of the 24 department heads, 96% replied affirmatively that faculty were expected to be mentors and about the same number reported continuity of this role through the dissertation level. They also asked the students to state whether they had changed advisors over the two-year span of the study, and only 21 of the 357 (or 5.9%) indicated that they had. It was mentioned that many students in these fields "targeted" faculty to be mentors (i.e., they matriculated into the program specifically to study with their mentor). Finally, in agreement with Tenenbaum et al. (2001), Green and Bauer found that despite the fact that 90% of the faculty were men and 23% of students women, there were no differences in the mentoring experience across genders.

At the master's level, Conrad, Haworth, and Millar (1993) found through student interviews that the most effective types of master's degree programs included at least one person who attended to each student's personal and academic needs in the program. They noted that this kind of attention was valuable for the students, because it helped assure that their needs were met. The attention also made them believe that they had the ability to grow into the role of contributing professionals.

In summary, although the research on the effect of graduate mentors is neither deep nor broad, the existing evidence supports the value of the mentoring role and reveals that a good mentor makes an important difference. At the doctoral level, good mentoring is related to research productivity, degree progress and completion, and satisfaction with the program. At the master's level, good mentoring is related to higher grades, better progress, and more satisfaction. All of this points to the complexity of the role and its importance.

Institutional Support for Mentoring

Wunsch (1994) argues that there needs to be more institutional support for mentoring because of the resulting institutional gains. Some of the benefits Wunsch identified for the campus include improved recruitment of minority students, higher retention rates, an increase in graduate student publishing, and better placement into jobs.

The Council of Graduate Schools (King, 2003) makes the important point that support for mentoring comes from the collective faculty of a program. The responsibility for mentoring is one of a myriad of faculty duties for which they are neither compensated nor recognized. Such compensation or recognition is one way in which institutions could better support mentoring. For example, the University of Washington and the University of Hawaii provide an annual award for outstanding graduate mentoring.

Mentoring begins with the program's selection of students. Students who are not a good fit for the program will create additional burdens for the faculty who must mentor them. Recognizing that mentoring begins before the student even accepts an offer of admission, the program as a whole should provide accurate and up-to-date information on their programs to students, giving them realistic ideas about the program. Decisions based on such advice will convey to the student that they know what to expect from the program and the faculty. Finally, care should be taken not to admit so many students that the faculty cannot attend to their needs, a challenge for programs under pressure to increase their enrollments.

Mentoring by Discipline and Degree

The mentoring role is known to vary across institutional settings, especially by discipline and degree sought (i.e., master's degree or doctorate). For example, the variation is easily seen as one examines the disciplines in broad terms. In the natural sciences, it is not uncommon for students to begin to conduct research in laboratories or in the field from the very beginning of graduate study. This approach means that they are truly apprentices to faculty who model the skills students' need to develop. Similar apprenticeship occurs in the fine arts, where students in studios or workshops get direct assistance and feedback in developing their creative skills. In social sciences and humanities outside of the fine arts, such direct contact with a mentor is less likely as the early portion of graduate school involves taking courses from a number of different faculty, only one of whom is or may become the mentor.

Mentoring may also vary considerably between master's and doctoral programs. While there certainly are important exceptions, in many master's programs the degree candidates have only a passing relationship with anyone approximating the role of mentor (Conrad et al., 1993). This might be because the sheer number of students exceeds the capacity of the department or program to provide this kind of support or because the academic unit has made a decision to focus its resources on doctoral-level students. Effective mentoring is unlikely in these situations, because it might be confined to someone officially hired as the graduate advisor, or it might come on a less formal basis from more experienced graduate students. Two important exceptions might be those students who from the beginning select the master's degree thesis option or whose focused work and future graduate study ambitions might make them seem better choices for a mentoring relationship. In the first case, the need to conduct research will create an incentive for the student to have a mentor in the form of a thesis chair. In the second case, which may occur in programs with both master's and doctoral programs, promising master's students might attract the attention of a faculty member who will mentor them with the intent of encouraging them to seek the Ph.D.

Mentoring is a much more common part of the doctoral experience, because there are relatively fewer students and the academic unit as well as the individual faculty scholar have a much bigger investment in them. Because the doctoral student usually is aspiring to a future role as faculty or practitioner, whose work is closely identified with the discipline, the mentor plays a critical role in introducing the student to the profession. In their study of more than 9,000 doctoral students, Nettles and Millett (2006) found that having a mentor had a positive effect on the following outcomes across all disciplines: (a) student-faculty social interaction, (b) student-faculty academic interaction, and (c) overall research productivity. Therefore, the gains from establishing a good mentoring relationship are substantial for both students and faculty.

New Forms of Mentoring

As we have seen, good mentoring is an important factor in the success of graduate students. However, there are strengths and shortcomings in traditional approaches to it as well as variability of quality and availability of mentoring across disciplines and type of degree. Yet, there are innovations that can enhance mentoring and increase its reach and consistency.

Peer Mentoring

One of these innovations is the introduction of peer mentoring at the graduate level. In recent years, there have been efforts to make use of advanced graduate students as peer mentors to new graduate students. There appears to be strong support among graduate students to offer peer advising. A survey of graduate students on one campus showed that 88% of respondents would be willing to mentor a new or younger graduate student (Luna & Cullen, 1998).

Often, these are centralized efforts, such as the peer-mentoring program at the University of California at Berkeley (2006), which is a campus-wide effort supported by the graduate student assembly. The program's "Guide to Grad Mentoring Groups" shows graduate students how to join together to learn coping skills, develop strategies for success, and understand the politics of academia.

Many more programs are specific to fields of study. At Washington University (2006), the department of chemistry has a peer mentoring web site whose mission statement sets a goal of zero attrition by having graduate students help one another. The department of earth and environmental sciences at Columbia University (2006) has a peer-mentoring program as well. The goal of the New Graduate Student Mentoring Program is to help first-year graduate students adjust to the demands of their program and become successful members of the academic community. In this program, 25 experienced graduate students volunteer as mentors, helping new graduate students understand and meet the challenges of adjusting to graduate school and life in New York City.

Exploring Learning Communities

One step beyond peer mentoring is an innovation called cohort mentoring (Mullen, 2005). In this approach, a cohort (e.g., graduate students who enter together and take courses together, often in education) meets regularly with a faculty member, who serves as their mentor. Participants in the cohort describe it as a "safe place where we meet with our mentor to have scholarly debate and interactions on things we are learning and struggling with in our research" (Mullen, p. 73).

Combining mentorship with a peer group is an interesting innovation, borrowed from successful undergraduate learning communities. Learning communities reflect a deliberate strategy to restructure elements of an educational setting to create synergistic relationships between students and faculty that are more supportive of learning. These relationships have a number of implications on the role and nature of mentoring. The rest of this chapter explores the ways in which learning communities can provide an opportunity to expand our ideas of graduate student mentoring.

Although every graduate department has an academic program that gives students a sense of direction and relates one educational experience to another, programs vary from institution to institution. Similarly, learning communities also vary substantially. However, they all start by creating a coherent academic structure, which requires and encourages student-faculty connections. To achieve this, learning communities focus on three kinds of integration: (a) peer, (b) disciplines, and (c) faculty.

The first integration is of students with one another. To meet the most basic criteria of a learning community, the school or department brings a set of students together over an extended period of time for a significant portion of their work. Simply as a by-product of their shared involvement in meeting the challenges presented by common program of study, they are making relationships that influence learning.

The second integration is of disciplines. Here, steps are taken to see that students are regularly required to interpret the same issue or issues from more than one disciplinary perspective. This means that a graduate student in environmental studies looking at new approaches to processing urban waste, for instance, takes into account perspectives coming out of chemistry, geography, and political studies. Another student in political science would interpret a health care policy problem as an economic, cultural, and organizational issue.

The third dimension of integration is of faculty. This occurs when two or more faculty are working with one another to design coursework. This collaboration will make students view and interpret the same issue from each of their perspectives.

What learning communities do is directly relevant to the challenges and opportunities of mentoring. Graduate students, no matter how talented or responsible, are less likely to succeed if their department/program does not play a supportive role. Research tells us that designed learning environments that balance support and challenge will increase the likelihood of graduate students succeeding. Learning communities are based on the premise that "structure matters."

Their structures are used as designed environments for enhancing learning that can encourage a broader range of mentoring relationships.

Learning communities are best known in undergraduate education, where over the last 30 years they have spread across the United States to a large and growing number of community colleges and four-year colleges and universities. They are less prevalent at the graduate level, still it is common for graduate programs to incorporate some elements from the learning community concept. Many students move through graduate school in a cohort group, so it is possible to say there are many graduate programs that have one dimension of a learning community structure. The strength of the cohort experience is not known, nor is the degree of faculty collaboration in teaching individual courses—a hallmark of many undergraduate learning communities. While, as noted, benefits for graduate student success can be expected from any degree of cohort development, the greatest educational pay-off will come from a more fully developed learning community.

Educating for Public Service Leadership: A Graduate Learning Community

The Public Administration Program (PUBA) at the University of Hawai'i at Manoa provides an example of a developed learning community approach at the graduate level. This program is explicitly designed to embody key learning community elements and illustrates how these elements change our understanding of mentoring and its role in graduate student success.

The PUBA program is comparatively small, with 60 to 70 students actively working on their degree at any one time. The number partly reflects available resources and a consensus that having more students means admitting an entire second cohort if the intimacy of the cohort experience is to be protected. The program is strongly mission driven. That mission is to develop leadership in public service and to enhance the effectiveness of public institutions. This is something on which there is strong mutual agreement and the focus energizes almost everything. In contrast, the unit's mission plays a less important role in the day-to-day life of most graduate programs. When the unit mission is discussed, disagreements sometimes surface. While each cohort group is highly diversified with respect to age and experience, a substantial portion are returning to school after a number of years in the workforce. Their motivation and challenges are different from graduate students fresh from the baccalaureate. Finally, while many graduate students elect to go to school full-time, most continue to work full- or part-time. Thus, many have substantial claims on their time.

Program Design and Rationale

PUBA adopted a learning community model for several reasons including the program's mission, the desired image of its graduates, and the need for a structure that has a built-in mentoring component. Also important is the reality that today the diversity of issues and challenges facing people in public service positions requires them to draw from a variety of disciplines—political science, sociology, psychology, economics, business, and human resources law. To the greatest degree possible, those disciplines must be brought together to address the same issue, which is one of the three attributes of learning communities. In addition, once graduated, these individuals must be able to hear and understand opinions and perspectives that are different from their own, to come to their own conclusions, to act firmly on them, and to remain open to future perspectives that may require changing their minds. Learning this balance between openness and action, critical in public roles, is also well served by a learning community model.

Finally, we utilize a learning community structure because it encourages relationships between students and with faculty that enable them to remain significant resources to one another once they become working professionals.

Relevance to Mentoring

Three elements of PUBA's structure help to define it as a graduate learning community and carry significant implications for mentoring graduate students in transition. As noted above, all learning communities must find ways to integrate the student experience and use that shared experience as a resource. This process occurs at a number of places in PUBA, but the most powerful, and the one of most significance for graduate students in transition, is the Core Year. The Core Year accounts for 14 of the 30-credit-hour master's in public administration; that is, it is almost one half of the required coursework for the degree. The Core Year is essentially one long course, although for administrative reasons it is divided into two seven-credit blocks. Every new graduate student, without exception, must enter PUBA through the Core Year. During the Core Year, students, by design, come to form learning relationships with one another.

The Core Year begins with a half-day convocation in which the 30 students most recently admitted to graduate study meet one another, all of the program faculty, and a few alumni. They are introduced to the program's expectations and norms and are given a detailed schedule for the next five months and a general schedule for the next two semesters. During the convocation, they are required to participate in interactive activities that begin the process of using one another as resources and of engaging different perspectives.

Soon after the convocation, they begin their first module of the Core Year, and over the next 10 months, there are 12 or 13 additional modules they will take together. Each module represents one response to the question of what they need to know to be effective in public service work. Two faculty with different disciplinary backgrounds teach every module, sometimes with other guest speakers as well. One of these two instructors remains with the cohort group for the entire semester, and sometimes for the entire year.

The modules are sequenced to build on one another and are deliberately diverse in the kinds of graded work required. For example, in one of the modules, students must write an individual paper, in another, they make an oral presentation, in the next they turn in a group written report, and in another they provide mock testimony on legislation. This menu of evaluation tools is designed so students may perform in the different ways they will be challenged to perform as professionals, but with the explicit understanding that their ability will vary with each requirement. There is also the expectation that they will serve as resources for each other.

The second learning community feature that has important implications for mentoring is the continual involvement of faculty with students and with one another in relation to the students. The Core Year is especially important here too, particularly for new graduate students, because it is taught by two faculty at all times, and every faculty member participates in it by presenting modules that are in their areas of expertise or interest. "Participation" here refers not to simply showing up and delivering a series of lectures, but to joining another faculty member in designing a learning experience that will not duplicate other parts of the Core Year and will be appropriate for the way a particular cohort group is developing. The consequence is that each faculty member gets to know the new students in the program, assumes a sense of responsibility for their development, and regularly discusses those students with other faculty.

The third feature that identifies PUBA as a learning community and has implications for mentoring is the interconnectedness of the degree program's four components. Those components (i.e., Core Year, Individuated Concentration, practicum or internship, and Capstone) by design, lead from one to another, presenting experiences and challenges that are best met by drawing on the collective knowledge of other students, recent graduates, and the faculty.

The Core Year, just described, is the first of the components. Next is Individuated Concentration, in which each student defines a theme of special interest and then enrolls in courses, directed readings, or directed research that explore aspects of that theme. The theme, selected as late into the Core Year as possible in order to make use of what the student is exposed to in the modules, is worked out in discussions with an advisor and in formal and informal meetings with other students.

The third component is the six to eight week practicum or internship, a requirement for every student and most often undertaken in the summer or fall after the Core Year. The student meets with her or his advisor to arrange the practicum and defines learning goals that can be met by spending time in an organizational setting different from ones with which they are familiar. There are also on-going conversations, both informal and formal, with other students and recent graduates where the real-life challenges and opportunities of the practicum are discussed.

The last of the four integrated components is the two-semester, team-based Capstone,[1] which emphasizes three learning outcomes: (a) to make full and appropriate use of what has been learned in the program; (b) to operate effectively in teams; and (c) to make positive contributions to a significant public issue by working with individuals, groups, and organizations in the community. These teams work closely with faculty during both the planning and execution stages of the Capstone. Consideration of the project begins during the Core Year when recent graduates and second-year students share their perspectives and tips for success with new students.

Mentoring in a Graduate-Level Learning Community

In a traditional program, the primary mentoring-related encounters would take place between the student and the faculty or department advisor over program requirements, course and specialization choices, graduation status, and for professional guidance; between the student and course instructors over course-related work; and between the student and peers from individual classes about the merit of different classes, the reputation of instructors, and specific assignments.

Mentoring is not a fundamentally different experience in a graduate program with substantial learning community elements. However, reflecting the basic reasons for establishing a learning community structure in the first place, mentoring is more continuous and integrated, and this difference addresses issues that have been identified in research as likely to contribute to graduate student success. This is now illustrated with respect to the program at the University of Hawai'i.

Faculty mentoring. The mentoring process for faculty begins prior to admission. Because the program emphasizes individuals learning from one another, admissions are not made on an individual basis, but as a cohort. Faculty must participate in these decisions, because they influence the nature of their own future mentoring relationship with not only individual students, but also the group as a whole. While a person's academic credentials (i.e., grade point average) are important in terms of demonstrating the capacity to do the work, how they will contribute to the class's learning-related diversity is also a significant factor. This refers in part to diversity in age, disciplinary background, and work experience, but also to their capacity to learn from and teach others. This information is gathered through interviews with individual applicants.[2] In these interviews, faculty use protocol questions to try to get a sense of what the person will bring to the next cohort group. At the same time, the faculty communicate the program's norms and expectations to the prospective graduate student. Judging by the number of times that students and graduates later refer to the interview, this early norm-setting experience plays a memorable role in orientating new students to graduate work. It also serves the function of discouraging those who have expectations of graduate study that are incompatible with program norms and who are not prepared to change their views.

Once in the program, the timing and focus of mentoring activities are primarily dictated by the student's choice of individuated concentration and practicum, the Core Year evaluation narratives, and the capstone. The choices of individuated concentration and practicum are made through a discussion process between the graduate student and his or her advisor. The nature of the choices being made require pulling together prior educational experiences, current academic interests, and future goals, which means that almost inevitably the discussions will reach into many aspects of the graduate student's work, including what is not going well for them. Moreover, unlike the Core Year in which the graduate student has no choices, these conversations intentionally signal a shift in responsibility from decisions made by the program to decisions made in a consultative process between the student and the advisor.

The Core Year evaluation narratives and the capstone process include important mentoring that is done by faculty who are not the graduate student's advisor. The Core Year narrative evaluations are written at the conclusion of the first and second semester by two faculty who have been in regular attendance. The essays, which the faculty consult one another in preparing, provide each student with a summary of her or his strengths, weaknesses, and areas for improvement. Students are in turn invited to discuss the narratives with one of these faculty members or his or her advisor. This is most likely to happen with those new students who are struggling, or who find themselves to have been evaluated below their expectations, both of which are excellent opportunities for a mentoring discussion.

By the capstone stage, the relationship between graduate student and faculty member has, by design, shifted again. The faculty advisor to the capstone group project now is much more in a consultant role to a team of students who are using a largely self-determined project to demonstrate that they have met the program's learning goals. The way the faculty member fulfills the role is determined in discussion with the team he or she is advising, sometimes meeting regularly with them, and other times responding to their requests and intervening when that seems necessary.

The ways in which mentoring is woven into the faculty role in relation to admission, the individuated concentration, practicum, Core Year narrative evaluations, and capstone summarizes much about how mentoring occurs within this learning community model. There is, however, one other aspect of the process that speaks directly to mentoring as a continuous and integrated part of the process. Because all new students must complete the Core Year, and because at one point or another all of the faculty participate in it, it is possible for the faculty to talk knowledgeably about how the students as a group, and individually, are doing. Moreover, because the faculty believe that they are participating in a shared educational enterprise, as opposed to teaching their own course in relative isolation, there is interest in having this conversation. As a result, it is common in faculty meetings to discuss how a cohort group is or is not coming together as a learning community, and how specific individuals are progressing. These discussions often lead to suggestions to try something different in the class, or for either the advisor or one of the Core Year faculty to get together with a student to discuss his or her situation and help the student address any difficulties.

Student mentoring. Numerous studies have shown that one of the most significant learning resources for students is other students (Astin, 1997). Because learning communities deliberately cultivate education-relevant relationships among students, they have distinct advantages in this area.

Mentoring by other graduate students begins at the program convocation a few days before classes. On that occasion, several second-year graduate students and alumni are invited to share what they learned about how to succeed in the program's different phases. They offer their recollections of what was helpful when they were transitioning into graduate study. Typically, one presentation might focus on time management, another on coming to class ready to participate, a third on building supportive relations with each other, and another on how to work with the faculty. Their specific advice, as well as simply the experience of seeing how they work together, is meaningful to the new graduate students, many of whom at this point have doubts about their ability to succeed. The presentations also are valuable to the faculty who learn something about what has been the most, and least, helpful to these students' success.

A second designed encounter between seasoned graduate students and those just entering occurs part way into the first semester of the Core Year. It is a long-standing tradition that members of the just completed Core Year class host the new class for an evening of food and talk during the first semester. The focus here is on academic issues. The idea is to help the new students avoid being misinformed by rumors that are inevitably part of all graduate programs. To this end, one second-year student might talk about what she did to get the needed time off from her job, another might talk about the process for locating and landing the right practicum host, and a third might talk about what can go wrong. Although the focus is on providing highly relevant information about the practicum, time is always set aside for questions about any aspect of their transition into the program and what it takes to be successful.

The two student-to-student mentoring activities just described are important in helping new students adjust to and progress in graduate school. Of at least equal importance are the ways in which learning community models create a subculture in which all students in the program provide timely and consistent counsel to one another. This assistance evolves from the high levels of regular contact and shared experience that are designed into the program. The resulting trust and personal knowledge make it easer to ask for, accept, and give assistance, as well as to see when someone is struggling. There are strong incentives to seek and give assistance, because the community standard is that everyone can succeed, and that the best way to learn a topic is by teaching that topic. These beliefs are given an added boost by the collective sense that develops in the Core Year that one person's failure is inevitably a partial responsibility of the cohort.

Conclusion: Employing the Graduate Learning Community in a Mentoring Context

There is no one solution for individuals trying to adapt to the challenges of graduate school. The traditional approach to mentoring has many strengths. At the same time, it is clear that there are a number of ways to improve mentoring, including providing better institutional support in the form of incentives for individual faculty to engage in it and rewards for those who do so well.

This chapter has explored another approach that may be of special interest given changes within disciplines, the more extensive relationships between disciplines, and the less territorial and walled off institutional environments in which university graduates can be expected to operate. Learning communities require us to look at many things differently. In this case, it is to view the program's mentoring less in terms of discrete faculty and student activities and more in terms of the deliberately interrelated and reinforcing supports that make success more likely.

Clearly, there are challenges of moving toward a learning community model to enhance mentoring. (For another perspective on the benefits and challenges of cohort groups in graduate education, see Barnett and Muse, 1993). A full-blown learning community is something that would most easily be created within a graduate program just being established. It would be very difficult to completely transform an existing, traditional program to such a model. The point of this chapter is to provide perspective on the elements of a learning community model that will enable modifications of the current mentoring structure into something that is, at the same time, more collaborative and mutually supportive of the student. If some of these elements are so used by a traditional program, it will improve mentoring.

First, introducing elements of a learning community inevitably means individual faculty members will be asked to collaborate in ways to which they are not accustomed. While there might be initial enthusiasm for this, it can devolve into empty ritual if the graduate faculty see it as something they have to endure that takes them away from their real work doing research and conducting seminars.

Next, adopting elements of a learning community may create issues within the program by changing the curriculum that connects specific courses to department requirements. It also may create external issues for the graduate program with administrative support units because the courses are no longer organized as three- or four-credit packages.

Third, this may create challenges in evaluating graduate student performance. Traditional graduate programs focus heavily on individual performance as a mark of success or failure. Learning communities encourage collaborative efforts and this requires that they develop evaluative tools appropriate to them. Finally, a learning community approach may simply run afoul of faculty and student images of how graduate-level work is supposed to be done.

Given the above challenges, the question becomes, how might we access the significant benefits of mentoring and increase graduate student success? Any changes, however small, to the first year of graduate study that intentionally create shared learning experiences by a cohort are a good place to start. Fortunately, the flexibility of design that learning communities have adds to their attractiveness. Sequencing existing requirements so that new students know they will be sharing the same classroom experiences for the first two semesters is one example of this. If this kind of cohort model is not possible, another option is to create a special integrating seminar that pulls together perspectives from various courses. Bringing in diverse faculty to interact with the cohort so that students and faculty become familiar with one another can also enhance the benefit of these cohort arrangements. Incorporating into the cohort group experience exposure to seasoned, successful graduate students and alumni can further enhance this.

Today, there is increased emphasis on faculty collaboration in research across disciplines and subdisciplines, especially within the natural and hard sciences. Because of this, many contemporary faculty are more predisposed to and skillful in establishing and maintaining the relationships that learning communities encourage and that enhance mentoring. Finally, graduate programs can encourage, or at least permit, more collaborative student research. It is possible that, given changes in the last several decades in the environment in which research is done, the natural sciences may understand the value of collaboration better than their colleagues in other areas. Whether or not this is the case, jointly undertaken graduate student research, accompanied by appropriate forms of evaluation, offers an opportunity to increase the quality of work and at the same time contributes to the recasting of the mentoring relationships within the program.

Notes

[1]One semester is for planning.

[2]Most, but not all, applicants are interviewed. Those with strong academic records, letters of reference, records of public service, personal goal statements that clearly fit with the program's educational goals and learning format are admitted without interview.

References

Astin, A. W. (1997). *What matters in college: Four critical years revisited.* San Francisco: Jossey-Bass.

Barnett, B. G., & Muse, E. D. (1993). Cohort groups in educational administration; Promises and challenges, *Journal of School Leadership, 3*(4), 400-415.

Columbia University. (2006). *DEES graduate students committee launches new graduate peer mentor program.* Retrieved August 15, 2006, from http://www.earthinstitute.columbia.edu/news/story9_4_01.html

Conrad, C. F., Haworth, J. G., & Millar, S. B. (1993). *A silent success: Master's education in the United States.* Baltimore, MD: Johns Hopkins University Press.

Girves, J. E., & Wemmerus, V. (1988). Developing models of graduate student progress. *Journal of Higher Education, 59*(2), 163-189.

Green, S. G., & Bauer, T. N. (1995). Supervisory mentoring by advisers: Relationships with doctoral student potential, productivity, and commitment. *Personnel Psychology, 48,* 537–561.

King, M. (2003). *On the right track: A manual for research mentors.* Washington, DC: Council of Graduate Schools.

Lovitts, B. (2001). *Leaving the ivory tower.* Lanham, MD: Rowman & Littlefield Publishers.

Luna, G., & Cullen, D. (1998). Do graduate students need mentoring? *College Student Journal, 32*(3), 322-330.

Minor, J. T. (2003). For better or worse: Improving advising relationships between faculty and graduate students. In A. L. Green & L. V. Scott (Eds.), *Journey to the Ph.D.: How to navigate the process as African Americans* (pp. 239-253). Sterling, VA: Stylus Publishing.

Mullen, C. A. (2005). *Fire and ice: Igniting and channeling passion in new qualitative researchers.* New York: Peter Lang.

Nettles, M. T., & Millet, C. M. (2006). *Three magic letters: Getting to Ph.D..* Baltimore: Johns Hopkins University Press.

Parent, E. (2003). *A systems model for doctoral student development and retention.* Retrieved February 16, 2006 from http://weber.ucsd.edu/~eparent/part1/Final_description_model.html

Tenenbaum, H., Crosby, F., & Gilmer, M. (2001) Mentoring relationships in graduate school. *Journal of Vocational Behavior, 59,* 326-341.

University of California at Berkeley. (2006). *Peer mentoring @ UC Berkley.* Retrieved August 15 from: http://ga.berkeley.edu/academics/peer.html

University of Michigan. (2006). *How to mentor graduate students.* Retrieved September 8, 2006 from http://www.rackham.umich.edu/StudentInfo/Publications/FacultyMentoring/Fmentor.pdf

University of Washington. (2006). *How to mentor graduate students.* Retrieved September 7, 2006 from: http://www.grad.washington.edu/mentoring/GradFacultyMentor.pdf

Washington University. (2006). *Chemistry peer mentoring program.* Retrieved August 15, 2006, from http://peermentor.chemistry.wustl.edu/

Wunsch, M. (1994). New directions for mentoring: An organizational developmental perspective. In M. Wunsch (Ed.), *Mentoring revisited: Making an impact on individuals and institutions* (pp. 9-13). San Francisco: Jossey-Bass.

Zeldich, M. (1990, March 16-18). Mentor roles. *Proceedings of the 32nd Annual Meeting of the Western Association of Graduate Schools,* Tempe, AZ, p. 11.

Chapter Nine

Graduate Student Centers: Locus for Services and Community

Lydia Soleil

First-year undergraduates have many opportunities to integrate into the campus community. After participating in the general orientation with students from various disciplines, entering undergraduates are able to meet students from all different majors in their courses, their residential life experience (in the case of residential students), and through participation in campus organizations and activities. In addition, there are typically many institutional efforts designed to inform undergraduates of the multitude of resources available to support them through campus-wide orientation programs, residential life programs, and through direct marketing to them by various offices and programs. These programs are run by student affairs staff who understand the developmental needs of undergraduates and consider those needs in the creation of their programs.

Graduate students often have a very different experience when they first arrive on campus. They are usually introduced and exposed only to their department and do not participate in sports teams, clubs, fraternities/sororities, or other extracurricular activities. There are often few, if any, formal or informal opportunities to meet graduate students in other departments. Often, graduate students are unaware of the many campus-wide resources available to support them during their matriculation, primarily because these offices and programs focus their attention on undergraduates (Gansemer-Topf, Ross, & Johnson, 2006; Pontis & Harper, 2006). As a result, although both undergraduate and graduate students are entering a new and unfamiliar world, first-year graduate students may not receive adequate support (Gansemer-Topf, Ross, & Johnson et al.; Pontis & Harper).

Many educators are beginning to realize that additional resources are needed to support both the transition and overall experience of graduate students. They have recognized that providing opportunities for community building and promoting the knowledge of and access to resources, which are common for first-year students, would also benefit graduate students (Brandes, 2006; Guentzel & Nesheim, 2006; Pontis & Harper, 2006). As a result, a number of institutions have created graduate student centers that provide both master's and doctoral students a central place where they can build community outside their departments and receive support services designed with their needs in mind (Brandes).

Because attrition in graduate school (which is well documented elsewhere in this monograph) is of critical concern, it is important to determine what interventions might increase persistence, particularly in the first year. In Brandes' (2006) discussion of graduate student centers, she references Lovitts (2001) findings, which indicate that graduate student persistence increased with opportunities for integration. Others have also argued that a connection to the campus community may be important to persistence (Cooke, Sims, & Peyrefitte, 1995; Stringfellow, Dahlstron, & Kwinn, 2005; UMBC, 2002-3). Pontis and Harper (2006) reviewed evidence that student engagement and socialization impact persistence and argued that "student affairs divisions should offer timely information and relevant campus services, and collaborate with departments to create supportive communities for graduate and professional students" (p. 5). Graduate student centers may be one incarnation of an intervention universities can implement to increase engagement and persistence by providing graduate students opportunities to build community and access programs and services that support their transition to graduate school and their overall experience.

This chapter begins with a discussion of the common principles in the missions of existing graduate student centers and how those principles align with many of the transition theories covered in chapter 2. Next, there is a brief description of the two precursors of graduate student centers: (a) dedicated space and (b) a graduate student life office. A more detailed discussion of the two major types of centers, full-service and hybrid, as well as examples of each follows. Finally, this chapter explores the potential advantages of graduate student centers and how assessment efforts might be a catalyst for increasing the number of centers at universities and colleges with significant graduate populations.

In order to explore this topic, a Google search was conducted to find existing graduate student centers. The web sites of identified centers were examined. In some cases, the director of the center was interviewed by e-mail or phone in order to gather information not available on the center's web site and to identify other centers that were not found via the Internet search. Officials at seven centers were interviewed during May and June 2006. Four of the interviews were conducted via phone (i.e., University of Pennsylvania, Yale, University of North Carolina at Chapel Hill, and University of Michigan), one was conducted in person (UCLA) and included a tour, and two were conducted via e-mail (i.e., University of Maine, Harvard University). In addition, the limited literature on graduate student centers was reviewed (Brandes, 2006) for inclusion in this chapter.

Missions of Graduate Student Centers

The graduate student center is a relatively new concept, first defined in the literature by Brandes (2006) as "graduate student space, [offering] specialized graduate student services and programs, [operated by] graduate student affairs staff, and professionals or involved graduate students" (p. 87). For the purpose of this chapter, a graduate student center is defined as a space on campus sponsored by the university and designated for and used primarily by graduate students. It should be noted that some centers, regardless of the type, also serve professional students and post-doctoral scholars either formally or informally. Each institution's center will undoubtedly have unique elements, but most can be categorized as full-service or hybrid (described in greater detail below). Others have only the basic elements of a center: dedicated physical location on campus for graduate students or a graduate student life office.

The mission, either stated or implied, of most graduate student centers addresses the inadequacies of the current graduate student experience as described above. Most center missions have two principles in common: (a) the understanding that graduate students need opportunities to build community outside their department and (b) the recognition that there are resources graduate students need to know about and have access to in order to support their transition to graduate school and their overall experience (Brandes, 2006). These two principles are supported by the current theories of graduate student development, which will be discussed below, along with examples of centers' missions. The theories of development discussed here have already been dealt with in some depth in chapter 2 of this monograph. The reader is referred to chapter 2 and to the original sources for a fuller treatment of these theories.

Community Building

A common element in the mission of most graduate student centers is the focus on graduate students' building community (Brandes, 2006); however, the focus and purpose of this idea of community varies among centers. Some centers focus on graduate students creating community with other graduate students, such as the center at the University of Pennsylvania, which strives to "empower graduate and professional students to create and participate in a graduate community at Penn" (University of Pennsylvania, n.d.). Other centers expand the notion of community to encompass the entire campus community. Boston College (2007) is one such example as their graduate student center's mission states that its "primary purpose is to build a sense of community among the entire graduate student population and cultivate a sense of belonging to the University as a whole." Similarly, Cornell's graduate student center web site boasts that it is "a center to meet students from other fields and schools" that provides "a setting for student, faculty, and staff interaction" (Cornell University, 2008).

In terms of the focus of community interaction, some graduate student centers deliberately mention a desire for intellectual interaction. Virginia Tech's graduate student center "provides an intellectually stimulating and rich learning environment that builds a strong graduate community" (Virginia Polytechnic Insititute and State University, 2007) while the University of Pennsylvania's (n.d.) graduate student center also mentions a social aspect in stating that it "creates intellectual, social, and professional development programs to bring together the wide range of graduate and professional students at Penn for cross-disciplinary, cross-cultural exchanges."

Tinto (1993) discusses the importance of community for doctoral student persistence. He argues that doctoral students need to make the transition into the departmental community, both academically and socially with no mention of the need to transition into the larger community of the university. However, graduate students have indicated that having a larger community is valuable and important. Brandes (2006) argues that a graduate student center creates a space for graduate students to build a social and academic community and references surveys on the doctoral experience in which graduate students report a lack of community and a desire for it (Golde & Dore, 2001; Lovitts, 2001). Institutions that have built graduate student centers have found that graduate students use them regularly as opposed to staying solely within their departments, evidence that graduate students value the opportunity to use centers to build community (Brandes).

Resources

The most recent theory that relates to centers providing graduate student-specific resources is Parent's model (2005). Parent argues that in order to make a successful transition to and persist in graduate school, graduate students must learn about the four R's—roles, rules, responsibilities, and resources—as they pertain to three realms: themselves, their departments, and their disciplines. Graduate students need to understand the four R's in relation to the university as well as the other three realms. For example, if graduate students only learn about themselves, their departments, and their disciplines, they might not learn about the roles and responsibilities of the graduate studies office in the final dissertation filing, the rules of the university as they pertain to leaves of absence, or that psychological and career counseling are resources available to them.

A graduate student center can play a very important role in helping graduate students learn about the four R's for all realms. As a central entity with access to all graduate students, graduate student centers often make deliberate efforts to educate students (via graduate student orientations or other efforts) about the four R's as they relate to the overall institution. They also may serve as a central location that provides resources, such as career counseling, help with writing, and so forth. Many of these university-wide resources can be critical to students' transition and overall success.

Connections Between Community Building and Resources

Erikson's psychosocial theory (1950, 1959) is a useful framework for describing how a graduate student center provides explicit resources for the student to succeed. The John Courtney Murray graduate student center at Boston College indicates in its mission statement that building community requires more than space, it also requires resources, described specifically in the mission as programming. Their mission illustrates one way community and resources can be related:

> Founded in 1997, The John Courtney Murray, S.J. Graduate Student center is dedicated to the support and enrichment of graduate student life at Boston College. Its primary purpose is to build a sense of community among the entire graduate student population, and cultivate a sense of belonging to the University as a whole.
>
> The Murray Graduate Student center strives to fulfill its mission by providing a welcoming space set aside exclusively for graduate students, as well as through a wide range of programming developed, implemented, and promoted specifically for and by graduate students. (Boston College, 2007)

Baird's (1997) integrated model provides another lens for investigating how community can support graduate students. Both the graduate program (internal agent) and forces outside of the institution (external agents) are important elements supporting graduate students in the dissertation (or thesis) process. Baird's model can be expanded to consider the role that those outside the graduate program yet inside the institution can play in supporting graduate student success. The center acts as an agent that, beyond family or friends, supports the graduate student by providing needed resources. The University of Michigan provides an example of an institution that understands its ability to assist graduate students. According to the center's web site, it "is dedicated to providing students with the support they need at each stage of their graduate experience" and that it can "provide individual support and advocate for policies and programs that best help students meet their educational goals" (University of Michigan, n.d.) This illustrates an important point that Brandes (2006) makes about graduate student centers being "a visible sign that the institution values and cares about its graduate and professional students" (p. 89).

Types of Graduate Centers

Building Blocks for a Graduate Student Center

When a campus has a dedicated space for graduate students or a graduate student life office, they have important building blocks for a graduate student center as defined in this chapter. Some institutions (e.g., Arizona State University; Brown University; Rutgers University; University of California, Santa Cruz) already have designated space for graduate students, operated by either the university's graduate student government or a governance board composed of graduate students. Yet, these spaces often do not have professional staff with overarching graduate student development responsibilities connected to them. If there is staff, it is graduate student or non-student staff with facilities/administrative responsibilities such as scheduling and facility maintenance. These spaces are often financed by the graduate student government's budget, student fees, revenue from food and drink sales, and/or room reservation fees. So although these spaces provide a location that is dedicated to graduate students, they are not considered graduate student centers as they are not sponsored or financed by the university and nor is an affiliated office offering significant resources designed to meet graduate students needs.

Other institutions (e.g., George Washington University; Princeton University; New York University; Brandies University; University of Maryland College Park; University of California, San Francisco; Duke University; and Massachusetts Institute of Technology) have a graduate student life office, which offers resources and may organize programming. However, these offices typically do not have public space dedicated for related activities and services (unless they are affiliated with one of the hybrid centers described below). The lack of programming, dedicated space, or both is what differentiates graduate student life offices from both full-service or hybrid graduate student centers. However, by creating and supporting such an office, the university administration has shown commitment to meeting some of their graduate students' needs, an important first step toward the greater commitment that would be represented by creating a hybrid or full-service graduate student center.

Full-Service Centers

The term "full-service" is used to describe a graduate student center that is self-contained, meaning the space, staff, and budget are dedicated solely to running the center and supporting the dual mission of creating community and providing resources. Examples can be found in Appendix A.

Space and staff. The current full-service centers range from about 1,000 sq. ft. (plus additional shared programming space) at the University of California, Los Angeles to 36,000 sq. ft. at Virginia Polytechnic Institute and State University (2005). A "full-service" center typically has professional staff, and in some cases, student staff. Some full-service centers have a part or full-time director, one or more support staff, and Graduate Student Fellows (e.g., Harvard University, Yale University, University of Pennsylvania, and Cornell University) who are directly responsible for developing and implementing programming. The staff is responsible for maintaining the operation of the center, providing resources that support graduate student development, and supporting graduate student community building in various ways.

Relationship with graduate student government. Some full-service centers have a working relationship with the graduate student government, a governance board of graduate students, or both. For example, at UCLA and the University of Pennsylvania, the graduate student government provides some financial support (decided on a yearly basis) for the center's functioning and/or for special projects.

Reporting structure and budget. It is difficult to generalize about center budgets because (a) salary figures may not be included in the operating budgets, (b) funding may come from several sources including graduate student government and rental fees or concessions, and (c) those figures may fluctuate widely each year. In general, graduate student centers receive their funding from the University via the unit to which they report, which can vary. Often, centers report to the graduate school (e.g., Harvard University, Yale University, and Cornell University), student affairs (e.g., University of California, Los Angeles), the provost (e.g., University of Pennsylvania), or they may be a collaboration between various units (e.g., Virginia Polytechnic Institute).

Hybrid Centers

Like full-service centers, "hybrid" centers also fulfill the dual mission of creating community and providing resources but are more fragmented in nature. These centers have a dedicated space that is designated as a graduate student center, but usually there is a relationship with another office that provides staff, budget, and or programming that is associated with the center but not considered part of the center. Examples can be found in Appendix B.

Space and staff. It is difficult to estimate actual square footages of hybrid centers, because they typically have a relationship with another office. Staff with the graduate student life office or the graduate school who are concerned with graduate student life usually operate hybrid centers (among other responsibilities). The related offices' staffs are not considered part of the graduate student center; however, similar to staff in a full-service center, they provide resources that meet graduate student needs and support graduate student community building in various ways. If hybrid centers have dedicated staff, they tend to be graduate student or non-student staff with facilities/administrative responsibilities such as scheduling, facility maintenance, and so forth.

Relationship with graduate student government. Some hybrid centers contain office space for the graduate student government. Also, the office associated with the center may seek input from the graduate student government on how to best meet graduate student needs.

Reporting structure and budget. In general, hybrid graduate student centers are financed in part or completely by the affiliated office and often by other sources as well. Most centers do not have significant staff so the center can only be said to "report to" the affiliated office.

Common Elements of Full-service and Hybrid Centers

The type of programming offered and the facilities available vary greatly from center to center, be it hybrid or full-service. Table 1 offers a list of programs and types of facilities organized by dominant purpose (i.e., community building or providing resources). Specific examples of both programs and facilities can be found in the center profiles below.

Table 1
Programs and Facilities in Graduate Student Centers

	Programming	Facilities
Community Building	◇ Art, film, cultural events, shows, and receptions ◇ Guest lecture/colloquia series ◇ Student research symposiums ◇ Social events/outings ◇ Community service drives/events	◇ Kitchen, dining area, café, and/or cafeteria ◇ Meeting rooms that can be reserved (e.g., small study rooms, conference rooms, and large multi-purpose rooms.) ◇ Offices for staff (e.g., professional, student, or both), student groups, and/or student government ◇ Student lounge ◇ Entertainment-related amenities (e.g., video rentals, game room, multi-media equipment) ◇ Outdoor space (e.g., lawn, patio)
Resource Delivery	◇ New student orientation for graduate students ◇ Teaching assistant orientation and/or workshops ◇ Career development and job search workshops ◇ Personal effectiveness/wellness workshops (e.g., time management, conflict resolution, depression, mental illness, maintaining healthy habits) ◇ Professional development workshops (e.g., grant and dissertation writing, public speaking, ethical research, using the library, mentoring, information organization) ◇ Workshops for special populations (e.g., women, international students, minorities, families) ◇ Retreats for academic or personal development (e.g., dissertation boot camp) ◇ Drop-in or scheduled appointments with relevant professionals (e.g., topics relating to career and teaching)	◇ Business center with computers, printers, and other amenities ◇ Library (e.g., resources on funding, teaching, career development, and periodicals) ◇ Reading room ◇ Information desk, may include ticket sales for campus or community events ◇ Bulletin boards (e.g., resource information, educational messages, event listings) ◇ Web site (e.g., calendar of events, newsletter, resources)
Miscellaneous		◇ Lockers ◇ Short-term childcare, play room/corner, or both

Profile of a Full-Service Graduate Student Center: University of Pennsylvania

The graduate student center at The University of Pennsylvania (Penn) is an example a full-service center.[1] Penn's graduate student center evolved out of a grassroots student effort and opened in 2001. The university administration was also strongly committed to this effort as evidenced by the organizational and reporting structure in place. The center reports to the Provost's Office and receives its yearly budget of $300,000 (which includes salaries) from that office. In 2004-5, an additional $60,000 was donated by the graduate student government for projects, including adding wireless access and creating a terrace.

The center is intended to serve the 2,376 graduate and 6,842 professional students at Penn. While they do not advertise their services to post-doctoral fellows, they do not turn them away. The director estimates that about one third of all graduate and professional students used the center in 2004-2005. The mission and vision statement are provided in Figure 1 below.

The University of Pennsylvania
Graduate Student Center

Mission Statement

The graduate student center was established in 2001 to meet the unique needs of graduate and professional students at Penn. The center:

- Empowers graduate and professional students to create and participate in a graduate community at Penn
- Creates intellectual, social, and professional development programs to bring together the wide range of graduate and professional students at Penn for cross-disciplinary, cross-cultural exchanges
- Provides services such as new student orientation, resource referrals, notary services, promoting activities, general information, and so forth
- Provides graduate and professional students with a centrally located home that includes a lounge, computer lab, and meeting and event space.

Vision Statement

The Graduate Student Center's Core Purpose: To encourage the development of Penn's graduate and professional student community through academic and social initiatives

The Graduate Student Center's Core Values: receptivity, adventurous and fun spirit, reliability, and support of the entire graduate student experience

Figure 1. Mission and vision statements of the Graduate Student Center at University of Pennsylvania. Source: University of Pennsylvania (n.d.).

The graduate student center is about 8,500 sq. ft. and houses a lounge, study areas, computer lab, and meeting/event space. Wireless access is available throughout the building and one room has built-in audiovisual capabilities. Some space can be reserved by students.

Two full-time professional staff, a director and an assistant director, run the center. In addition, there is a 20 - 30 student volunteer advisory board and 15 paid fellows. Fellows assume responsibility for a number of programming and resource areas including arts and culture, career/life skills, giving lectures, mentoring, Ph.D./teaching assistant support, recreational outings/community service, new student orientation, web site development, and publicity. The number of fellow positions and their responsibilities vary based on their different programming specializations. Any graduate student can apply to be a fellow, and the director and assistant director interview selected applicants. Fellows are hired based on relevant skills and experience needed to fulfill the different program and resource responsibilities. Each full-time staff member supervises seven or eight fellows and provides a structured development opportunity for them. Fellows are given a budget for the year and standards (e.g., numbers and type of programs) that they must meet. The experience of being a fellow provides graduate students the chance to develop many useful skills, such as budgeting, working with a supervisor, and event planning. In addition, fellows get feedback on a regular basis so that they can modify their work performance, as needed, and the supervisors can give more autonomy, as appropriate, based on the student's maturity and performance.

As noted above, the center provides programming on a variety of topics. For example, the fellow for arts and culture may coordinate a group trip to a local attraction, arrange for discounted tickets to a local cultural event, or plan a student art exhibition in the center. The center may host a seminar on home buying as part of its personal development workshop series. The fellow responsible for community service may organize donations for various causes and/or advertise local volunteer opportunities.

In order to support graduate students' academic success and professional development, the center offers three distinct programs, known as the "Navigating" programs, for the classroom, the dissertation, and the grant. Each program consists of several workshops and other resources on the topic (i.e., an online discussion board or web site links). The center may also sponsor an interdisciplinary academic conference or a guest speaker on an academic topic with broad appeal. In addition, the center sponsors a mentoring program where graduate students mentor undergraduates interested in attending graduate school, which gives graduate students valuable mentoring experience.

Several programs address both academic and non-academic concerns. The center offers three new student orientation sessions each fall. Two of the orientation sessions are four-days long and designed to accommodate the graduate students who arrive on campus at different times during the summer before the fall term begins. The third session is a one-day orientation for last-minute arrivals. In addition to the new student orientation, the center also sponsors several film series throughout the year. For example, they offered a series during Black History Month that focused on films featuring a specific black actor. Annual programming also includes language chats, which give students the chance to both practice language skills and socialize.

Many of the programs the center offers are co-sponsored by student groups, university offices, and/or outside organizations. The center deliberately has two to three events each year that will appeal to any graduate student. Most programs attract 20 to 30 students, but some have attracted as many as 300 students. In 2004 – 2005, the center offered 500 programs attended by approximately 3,100 students. The center's director estimates that 200 to 300 of the attendees participated in more than one event.

The center also provides a variety of services to graduate students such as selling tickets for large-scale campus and graduate student events, providing students with complimentary coffee and tea, managing room reservations for meetings and events, providing wireless access, and offering notary and printing services. In 2004 – 2005, space in the center was reserved for 806 events by graduate students or graduate student groups. In addition, 300 documents were notarized. The center also provides an online Graduate and Professional Student Resource Guide;

a list of graduate student organizations; a list of other departments on campus that graduate students might use (e.g., the Career Center); and links to announcements and information about funding, health insurance, and so forth. In 2004 – 2005, 2,500 students subscribed to the center's electronic mailing list, and there were 180,000 hits on the web site.

Evidence of strategic planning and thoughtful organizational development can be seen in the mission statement and annual reports that are published and archived on the web. The center also shows a formal consideration of longevity and sustainability through the staff's deliberate attempts to stay connected with alumni. They have a strong alumni network maintained through a database, an alumni web site, and alumni events. Penn's graduate student center represents a mature unit that is thinking broadly about ways to better serve graduate students through day-to-day operations and post-graduation.

Profile of a Hybrid Graduate Student Center: University of North Carolina, Chapel Hill

The graduate student center at the University of North Carolina, Chapel Hill (Carolina) is an example of a hybrid center.[2] With the support of campus administrators, the center was developed in 2002-2003 by an external funding advisory board. In 2005, the center opened in a temporary space on the edge of campus. The center's mission is in Figure 2.

The University of North Carolina, Chapel Hill
Graduate Student Center

The Graduate Student Center (GSC) is designed to be a central space where graduate and professional students from all disciplines and departments on campus can come together. Shared research ideas, interdisciplinary seminars, professional development activities and meetings are all encouraged. The centralized meeting space will create a stronger sense of community among all graduate and professional students and provide a well-rounded Carolina experience.

Figure 1. Mission statement for the Graduate Student Center at the University of North Carolina, Chapel Hill. Source: UNC, Chapel Hill (n.d.).

The center is available for use by 8,008 graduate students and 2,345 professional students enrolled at Carolina. The 1,200 sq. ft. center houses one meeting room that seats approximately 40 people and two smaller meetings room that seat approximately 8-10 people and 12-15 people, respectively. Another small room houses two computer stations. In general, the center is used for two to three events per week. Users include departments who are having seminars geared for only graduate students, groups that include graduate students, faculty, and fellowships groups (i.e., students receiving fellowships who have required professional development meetings).

The biggest and ongoing challenge facing the institution has been finding appropriate permanent space that is convenient and accessible to all students. The current space is off campus and is not wheelchair accessible. As a result of ADA (Americans with Disabilities Act) compliance issues, events open to all graduate students (e.g., academic interviewing workshops) cannot be scheduled there. The center provides assistance to groups who have members with disabilities in reserving alternate, accessible space.

As mentioned previously, most hybrid centers have an affiliation with a related office. Carolina's center is under the auspices of the Graduate School and is funded through that office. After renovations of the space were complete, the center had a kick-off event that cost about $15,000. Annual expenses for rent, phone, and materials (e.g., computer paper) total approximately $12,000.

Currently, the center has no dedicated staffing, in part, because the center is in temporary space and can be used by reservation only. In the future, it is anticipated that the staff from the Graduate School would be responsible for ongoing management of the center since this office already does significant professional development programming for graduate students. Currently, the staff involved in professional development programming includes one assistant dean for academic initiatives, who spends up to 25% of her time on programming and a graduate student assistant, who works full-time in the summer and 15 to 20 hours per week during the school year. In addition to a stipend, the graduate assistant receives remission of tuition and fees. The Graduate School also had a graduate student professional development advisory council that is composed of four to five graduate students, staff (e.g., Career center, Leadership center, staff graduate counselor in departments), and faculty who are graduate advisors of departments. Other staff include a person who handles reservations and an information technology person who maintains the two computers in the center. The graduate student government has also been very involved in the development of the center.

The annual programming budget is about $5000, and program topics in 2005-2006 included the role of graduate students in service-learning; dissertation tips; research and library skills; interviewing skills; transferable skills and the post-academic career; mentoring; identifying, analyzing, and adapting to academic and professional cultures; and effective presentations. The Graduate School also provides professional development for students receiving specific fellowships. Because the center is not ADA accessible, these events were held outside the center.

With funding provided by the Office of the Provost, The Graduate School and the Center for Teaching and Learning coordinate a one-week seminar for students about to embark on careers as faculty members in higher education. The course agenda addresses a wide range of concepts related to teaching, learning, and professional life at the college level. Sessions are held twice a year in May and August, with approximately 40 students participating. Each participant receives a certificate noting their advanced training in preparation for their role as future faculty.

Needs assessment surveys and focus groups are a very important part of Carolina's assessment efforts to date. All programs are assessed to determine whether they were effective. Poorly attended programs are not necessarily an indication of lack of interest; the time of the program or the marketing strategy may have been the issue. Thus assessments also attempt to account for factors that contributed to a program's success or failure. In the future, the center plans to survey alumni, both five and 10 years after graduation, on broader issues (i.e., professional development).

Carolina presents a case where the administration of the institution is very supportive of efforts to provide resources to graduate students and programming that encourages community. However, to realize both of these principles fully, a more appropriate space will be necessary, one that is accessible to all students and has some of the programs and facilities that explicitly support community building. There are plans to move to an ADA accessible space in the near future, although this space will also be temporary and continue to be available only by reservation.

Assessment of Graduate Student Centers

As described earlier, there are two principles common in the missions of the existing centers, the understanding that graduate students need opportunities to build community outside their department and the recognition that there are resources graduate students need to support their transition to graduate school and their overall success. Although theories of graduate student development support these principles, no one has yet studied whether or how graduate student centers are impacting the transition experience and overall success of these students. Although programmatic assessment is common, assessment of a center's effectiveness in meeting its mission has been limited at best. Some qualitative data from Harvard's Dudley House provides insight into the graduate student experience and the center's positive impact in the lives of two graduate students.

> My decision to attend Harvard over Berkeley or Yale, my other top graduate school choices, was due to the presence of a visible social life for graduate students at Harvard. I had attended a liberal arts school as an undergraduate, and I intend to return to teach at such a school after graduation. I consider my participation in Dudley House activities to be a part of this training. The best years of my graduate school career were those in which I was most active in Dudley House. (Mendelsohn & Anderson, 1999, p. 11)

> Looking back over my years at Harvard, it is impossible to imagine what my graduate life would have been like without Dudley House. It goes without saying that Harvard is infinitely capable of feeding the mind. Graduate school, as anyone who has experienced it knows, can be rather taxing on the soul. Dudley House is soul food. It's a meeting ground for interesting people, a melting pot of ideas and opinions. All of the scientists, philosophers, and literary critics I know at Harvard, I met at Dudley. I have learned a great deal about the University and the universe of ideas through my association with the House. More importantly, Dudley House has been a home-away-from-home for me, a place where I can relax, forget the stresses of academia, stop taking myself too seriously, and remember that there really is a world outside the library walls. (Mendelsohn & Anderson, 1999, p. 11)

The most obvious barrier to outcomes assessment for most graduate student centers is the lack of clearly identified outcomes. Recently, several graduate schools such as Michigan State University (Stoddart & Campa, 2006), University of North Carolina, n.d.), and the University of Texas, Austin (2006) have begun to develop objectives for graduate education. Such objectives provide a powerful guide for the work of graduate student centers and can be used to develop or refine outcomes specific to the center. Given the types of programs and facilities frequently offered by graduate student centers and the theories discussed in chapter 2, potential outcomes for students using these centers include:

- ◇ Increased use of campus and community resources
- ◇ Ability to manage conflict
- ◇ Use of exercise or other tools to manage stress
- ◇ Improved confidence
- ◇ Stable mental health (University of California at Berkeley, 2004)
- ◇ Student achievement in the areas of resources, rules, roles, and responsibilities (Parent, 2005)
- ◇ Increased motivation

- ◇ Higher self-esteem
- ◇ Improved intellectual development
- ◇ Positive attitudes about department and institution
- ◇ Increased number and quality of personal and professional interactions (support systems)
- ◇ Increased retention, persistence
- ◇ Decreased time to degree
- ◇ Increased satisfaction with career choice
- ◇ Improved job placement rates

Outcomes assessment planning and implementation could provide valuable data that may show that graduate student centers are having significant impacts on graduate student transitions and success, which could greatly help transform the innovation of the graduate student center into an integral part of graduate education. In addition, information such as this could provide the many schools considering graduate student centers concrete data to support the creation of such a center at their institution. This additional information may spur a tipping point (Gladwell, 2002) in graduate education leading to a sharp increase in the number of graduate student centers at U.S. institutions and an overall improvement in the graduate student experience.

Conclusion

Even though graduate student centers are a relatively new phenomenon, it is interesting to note that the concept is increasing in popularity. Many of the centers reviewed for this chapter have opened since 2000. In addition, it is estimated that 25 other institutions are interested in creating a graduate student center, have proposals or recommendations for a graduate student center, or are currently undertaking the implementation of such a center (Brandes, 2006). As noted above, some institutions have not created centers but have an important building block for a center, a graduate student life office, which is a visible sign of the institution's commitment to serving graduate students' needs. Other campuses have dedicated space but thus far lack administrative support for serving graduate student needs by providing programs, services, and the development of community via an official university-sponsored center. These are important first steps, but more needs to be done.

An assessment of the common principles found in the missions of graduate student centers helps make clear why many centers exist and are supported by their university. Those institutions believe that the center will support graduate student success by providing a sense of community and access to resources graduate students need. Considering the large number of graduate students who leave after the first year, graduate student centers may be an important tool in reducing attrition.

Notes

[1] The profile was created by information gathered from the center's web site (http://www.gsc.upenn.edu/index.html) and via an interview with the Director, Anita Mastroieni, in May of 2006.

[2] This profile was created by reviewing the center's web site (http://gradschool.unc.edu/gsc/index.html) and via an interview with the Associate Dean of Academics in the Graduate School, Stephanie Schmitt, in May of 2006.

References

Baird, L. (1997). Completing the dissertation: Theory, research, and practice. In L. F. Goodchild, K. E. Green, E. Kluever, & R. C. Katz (Eds.), *Rethinking the dissertation process: Tackling personal and institutional obstacles* (pp. 99-105). San Francisco: Jossey Bass.

Boston College. (2007). *Mission of the John Courtney Murray, S.J. Graduate Student Center.* Retrieved March 13, 2008 from, http://www.bc.edu/offices/gsc/mgc/mission.html

Brandes, L.C.O. (2006). Graduate Student centers: Building community and involving students. In M. J. Guentzel & B. E. Nesheim (Eds.), *Supporting graduate and professional students: The role of student affairs* (New Directions for Student Services, No. 115, pp 85 – 99). San Francisco: Jossey-Bass.

Cooke, D. K., Sims, R. L., & Peyrefitte, J. (1995). The relationship between graduate student attitudes and attrition. *The Journal of Psychology, 129*(6), 677-688.

Cornell University. (2008). *Welcome to the Big Red Barn!* Retrieved March 13, 2008, from http://brb.gradschool.cornell.edu/index.php?p=1

Erikson, E. H. (1950). *Childhood and society.* New York: W. W. Norton & Co.

Erikson, E. H. (1959). *Identity: Youth and crisis.* New York: W. W. Norton & Co.

Gansemer-Topf, A. M., Ross, L.E., & Johnson, R.M. (2006). Graduate and professional student development and student affairs. In M. J. Guentzel & B. E. Nesheim (Eds.), *Supporting graduate and professional students: The role of student affairs* (New Directions for Student Services, No. 115, pp 19 – 30). San Francisco: Jossey-Bass.

Gladwell, M. (20002). *The tipping point.* Boston: Back Bay Books.

Golde, C. M., & Dore, T. M. (2001). *At cross purposes: What the experiences of doctoral students reveal about doctoral education.* Philadelphia, PA: The Pew Charitable Trusts. Retrieved February 11, 2008, from http:// www.Ph.D.-survey.org

Guentzel, M. J., & Nesheim, B. E. (2006). Throwing pebbles at Stonehenge: Advocating for graduate and professional students. In M. J. Guentzel & B.E. Nesheim (Eds.), *Supporting graduate and professional students: The role of student affairs* (New Directions for Student Services, No. 115, pp 101 – 106). San Francisco: Jossey-Bass.

Lovitts, B. E. (2001). *Leaving the ivory tower: The causes and consequences of departure from doctoral study.* Lanham, MD: Rowman & Littlefield.

Mendelsohn, E., & Anderson, M. B. (1999). *Dudley House report.* Boston: Graduate School of Arts and Sciences, Harvard University.

Parent, E. (2005). *The academic game: Psychological strategies for successfully completing the doctorate.* West Conshohocken, PA: Infinity Publishing.

Pontis, J. L. & Harper, S. R. (2006). Principles for good practice in graduate and professional student engagement. In M. J. Guentzel & B.E. Nesheim (Eds.), *Supporting graduate and professional students: The role of student affairs* (New Directions for Student Services, No. 115, pp 101 – 106). San Francisco: Jossey-Bass.

Stoddart, J., & Campa, III, H. (2006). PREP: A model for career and professional development. In *The Graduate Post.* Michigan State University, Graduate School. Retrieved May 31, 2006 from, http://grad.msu.edu/all/gps06.pdf

Stringfellow, A., Dahlstrom, D., & Kwinn, L. (2005). *Graduate and Professional Student Experience Survey 2005: General report.* Retrieved March 14, 2008 from, http://gsa.ucsd.edu/files/gsa/GPSES_general_report_COLOR.pdf

Tinto, V. (1993). Toward a theory of doctoral persistence. In *Leaving College: Rethinking the causes and cures of student attrition* (2nd ed., pp. 230-243). Chicago: University of Chicago Press.

University of California at Berkeley. (2004). *Berkeley Graduate Student Mental Health Survey.* Berkeley Graduate and Professional Schools Mental Health Task Force Retrieved September 16, 2006 from, http://www.ocf.berkeley.edu/~gmhealth/reports/gradmentalhealth_report2004.html

University of Maryland Baltimore County (UMBC). (2002-3). *Ph.D. student persistence & attrition study.* Office of Institutional Research. Retrieved on August 1, 2007 from, http://www.umbc.edu/oir/Reports/Ph.D.Attrition/Ph.D.Attrition.pdf

University of Michigan. (n.d.). *Graduate student affairs.* Retrieved March 13, 2008 from, www.rackham.umich.edu/student_life/gsa/.

University of North Carolina. (n.d.). *Conceptual framework.* Retrieved September 16, 2006 from, http://gradschool.unc.edu/profdev/framework.html

University of North Carolina, Chapel Hill. (n.d.). *The graduate student center.* Retrieved March 14, 2008, from http://gradschool.unc.edu/student/gsc/index.html

University of Pennsylvania. (n.d.). *Graduate student center mission statement.* Retrieved March 13, 2008, from http://www.gsc.upenn.edu/general/mission.htm

University of Texas at Austin. (n.d.). *PDCE objectives.* Graduate School. Retrieved on October 21, 2006 from, http://www.utexas.edu/ogs/pdce/objectives.html

Virginia Polytechnic Institute and State University. (2005). *2004 - 2005 Annual Report.* Administrative and Business Services & University Unions. Retrieved on October 21, 2006 from, http://www.uusa.vt.edu/aboutUs/AnnualReports/2004_05/2004_05ABS_UUar.pdf

Virginia Polytechnic Institute and State University. (2007). *About the graduate life center.* Retrieved March 13, 2008 from, http://www.glc.vt.edu/about.html

Appendix A

List of Known Full-Service Graduate Student Centers

Institution	Center Name	Web Site (if available)
Cornell University	Big Red Barn Graduate and Professional Student Center	http://brb.gradschool.cornell.edu/index.php?p=1
Harvard University	Dudley House[a]	http://www.fas.harvard.edu/~dudley/
University of California, Los Angeles (UCLA)	Graduate Student Center	http://gsa.asucla.ucla.edu/gsrc/index.htm
University of Pennsylvania (Penn)	Graduate Student Center	http://www.gsc.upenn.edu/index.html

table continued on pg. 150

Institution	Center Name	Web Site (if available)
Virginia Polytechnic Institute and State University (Virginia Tech)	Graduate Life Center at Donaldson Brown	http://www.glc.vt.edu//index.html
Yale University	McDougal Graduate Student Center[b]	http://www.yale.edu/graduateschool/mcdougal/welcome.html

[a] Harvard Dudley House also services a small number of undergraduate commuter students and has some unique staff and programming for that population. It is also unique in that it only serves graduate students in one of the schools, the Graduate School of Arts and Sciences.
[b] Has Graduate Student Life Office but is not considered a hybrid due to unique (and planned) configuration of three Directors who share responsibility for the center.

Appendix B

List of Known Hybrid Graduate Student Centers

Institution	Center Name	Web Site (if available)
Boston College	John C. Murray, S.J. Graduate Student Center	http://www.bc.edu/offices/gsc/mgc.htlm
Columbia University	Graduate Student Lounge	http://www.columbia.edu/cu/gsas/pages/cstudents/std-ser/grad-lng/index.html
Lehigh University	Graduate Student Center	http://www.lehigh.edu/gradlife/gsc.html http://www.lehigh.edu/%7Eingrador/index.html
Savannah College of Art & Design	Graduate Studies Center at Smithfield Cottage	
Stanford University	Graduate Community Center	http://www.stanford.edu/group/glo
University of Maine	Graduate Center	http://www.glc.vt.edu//index.html
University of Michigan	Rackham Graduate School	http://www.rackham.umich.edu/Building/ http://www.rackham.umich.edu/StudentInfo/apsl.html
University of North Carolina-Chapel Hill (UNC-CH),	Graduate Student Center	http://www.gradschool.unc.edu/gsc/index.html

Chapter Ten

An Expanded Perspective on the Graduate Transition: Strategies for Supporting Students From Application to Completion of the First Year

Leslie B. Sims

The transition to graduate study begins before the student even applies to a graduate program. Students contemplating graduate study usually seek out prospective graduate programs where there is a "fit" between program objectives, structures, and outcomes and their own educational, personal, and professional goals. Research has shown that the better the fit, including the extent to and ease with which new students are integrated into the intellectual culture and social structure of the program, the more likely there will be a smooth first-year transition and completion of the degree program (Lovitts, 2001). Even with a good fit between student and program, the first year of graduate study can be a challenging transition for students. This challenge may be attributed to the significant differences between graduate or professional education programs and undergraduate education for those continuing directly into graduate programs or between the world of work and graduate study for the increasing number of adults returning to higher education after an extended absence.

Earlier chapters have made the case for the need for interventions, strategies, or formal programs that address the first-year transition of graduate students. However, the transition to graduate education may be viewed as a continuum that begins when the student first explores opportunities for graduate study through the application and admission stages and into the first year of a graduate program. With this broader concept of the transition experience in mind, this chapter will discuss additional transition strategies and expand upon some of those mentioned in earlier chapters.

Rationale for Transition Programs

Collectively, transition strategies and programs, as well as those designed to enhance degree completion and career preparation, represent responses to recommendations for change in graduate education as a whole (AAU, 1998) and in the graduate and postdoctoral education of scientists and engineers in particular (National Academies Committee, 1995; 2000). Among the first and most visible of the responses are several programs initiated by the National Science Foundation (e.g., Alliances for Graduate Education and the Professoriate, AGEP; Integrative

Graduate Education and Research Training, IGERT; Vertical Integration of Graduate Research and Education, VIGRE), which integrate many of the transition strategies described elsewhere in this volume.

As noted previously, low completion rates in doctoral programs are a primary concern for entering graduate students, as well as for business and industry leaders, public policy analysts, and government agencies. Yet, completion rates in professional doctoral programs (e.g., M.D., J.D.) are generally 90% or higher as compared to 50% to 75% for academic doctoral programs (Denecke & Slimowitz, 2004). One possible explanation for the difference in completion rates is that professional doctoral programs provide detailed information about program structure and requirements and, more particularly, about student expectations, assessments, and the nature of the profession and job market. Ph.D. programs, on the other hand, seldom provide this type or level of information even to students admitted to their programs. Thus, information provided in professional degree programs may contribute to a successful first-year transition to graduate study and to degree completion. The uncertainty of new graduate students, especially doctoral candidates, about many aspects of their program—especially the rate of and time to completion and subsequent employment opportunities—may be a significant factor affecting their performance during the first year. Providing such information on a departmental and institutional level can help mitigate concerns among entering students and allow them to concentrate on issues more relevant to the first-year transition experience (e.g., advising, mentoring, funding, developing clear program expectations, and obtaining timely feedback on progress.)

Less is known about the completion rates of master's students, but one institutional study found a 20% attrition rate among first-year master's students (K. Tokuno, personal communication, July 3, 2007). However, since master's degrees represent more than 90% of all graduate degrees awarded (Sims, 2006) and are highly valued credentials by business, government, and nonprofit agencies, any significant dropout among master's students is a serious problem in that it represents a genuine workforce problem and threatens the massive national investment in master's programs to help sustain the US's global economic competitiveness. Although different in magnitude and in some details than doctoral completion, the issues affecting completion of master's degrees are similar and can be addressed by programs similar to those in doctoral education.

Transition Strategies, Programs, and Projects

Graduate Program Information for Prospective Students

The first encounter a prospective student often has with a graduate program is the general information available about the program (i.e., catalog descriptions, recruiting materials, personal references from current students or graduates, and especially program web sites). These resources represent early opportunities for a program to provide information that may not only attract prospective students, but also help potential students assess the fit between the program and their goals, entice promising students to apply, and help entering graduate students make a successful first-year transition into the program. One way to encourage prospective students to consider issues of fit is to include information about first-year student activities and program expectations in program brochures and web sites. For example, the University of Hawaii at Manoa (www.hawaii.edu/gradstudies/university/html/aboutuh.htm) provides a prospective student a sense of what it might be like to attend UHIM by describing the campus environment, setting, and history as well as information about housing, transportation, dining, and culture. The web site of the Department of Mathematics at Rutgers (www.math.rutgers.edu/grad/grad.html) includes information on the application process for both domestic and international students, program environment, and degree requirements, with a link to a new introductory course for new graduate students. Appalachian State University (www.graduate.appstate.edu/gradstudies/current/newadmit/html) provides specific information for newly admitted students that will help them prepare for matriculation and entry into the community.

Application and Admissions Processes and Materials

Prospective graduate students face an application and admissions process that is generally quite different from their previous experiences. Thus, these processes and materials offer another opportunity to inform prospective students on how to prepare for a successful transition into the graduate program. If departmental representatives create an inviting atmosphere to discuss how to prepare application materials, then prospective students may feel comfortable exploring other questions and concerns regarding the program. In addition, it is helpful for all application materials to reference first-year transition activities. Getting this information early can be particularly effective in converting initial student interest into completed applications by those who perceive the program as being a good fit for them. This strategy can also improve yield (i.e., the number of acceptances among students offered admission) of a cohort of qualified entering students whose interests and goals closely match the strengths and opportunities offered by the program. The web site for the American Studies program at the University of Iowa is especially useful to prospective students (http://uiowaledu/~amstud/application_process.html), because it includes information about the structure and requirements of the program and a checklist of items needed to apply. It also guides the student through the application process.

New Graduate Student Handbooks

A comprehensive graduate program student handbook is a particularly effective way of providing a wealth of information that can be immensely helpful to prospective students in their decision to apply to the program and, more particularly, to students entering the program. Current students and recent graduates of a program are ideal authors or co-authors (with a program or graduate college advisor) of handbooks that contain information about the first-year experience, academic advising, progression through the program, faculty expectations, mentorship, assistantships, and other forms of support. Separate versions of the handbook might be appropriate and useful for prospective, matriculating, and enrolled students.

In an effort to ensure that all entering graduate students have access to the same kinds of information, The Michigan State University (MSU) Graduate School has developed a template for creating a departmental graduate handbook (http://msu.edu/~gradschl/staff/handbook.pdf). The template includes a rationale for using a standard format and describes each section to be included in any graduate handbook. Most MSU departments and programs have used this template to create program-specific handbooks (See http://msu.edu/~gradschl/staff/ght.htm for an index of departments who have created graduate handbooks, with links to each). The American Studies program at the University of Iowa has an excellent graduate handbook (http://uiowa.edu/~amstud/guidelines2005.pdf) that includes information about the program appropriate for applicants and new students with a preview of the graduate experience that is especially useful for new students beginning their first-year transition to graduate school.

Contact with Admitted Graduate Students

A frequent complaint of new graduate students is that they received virtually no contact from their department or program after they accepted the offer of admission (e.g., typically between early to late spring) until they arrive on campus in late summer or fall. Regular contact with admitted students during this period, who can offer program updates, can make new students feel included as members of the program and significantly aid in a smooth transition. Other useful information that can be conveyed during this period includes: new faculty appointments, the makeup of the entering graduate student cohort, a "progress report" on continuing students, degrees awarded the previous academic year, post-graduation plans of students who recently completed the program, and campus news that may affect new students. Contact can easily be done by e-mail, with attachments or links to such things as a checklist for new graduate students, such as the one provided by Florida State University (http://www.gradstudies.fsu.edu/forms/newgradchecklist.pdf).

It may also be helpful to offer or recommend a subscription to the local newspaper, which is an inexpensive way to inform admitted students of opportunities for housing, employment, education, and community events. A free Chamber of Commerce information packet is another example of outreach to admitted students. These information programs have been initiated for new faculty at the University of Arkansas, North Carolina State University, and the University of Iowa. The University of Iowa program was first extended to fellowship students and later, based upon uniformly positive responses, extended to all entering graduate students. Hosting visits of admitted students who seek housing and employment is another way to help students make a smooth transition to the graduate community; costs can be minimized by organizing currently enrolled students or faculty to host visits and/or provide lodging and some meals.

Transition Programs and Services for Entering Graduate Students

First-Year Graduate Residential Programs

In recent years, there has been a significant shift in graduate student housing options available on university campuses, which reflects the growth and success of living-learning initiatives. While most campuses have special housing options for international and married students (i.e., undergraduate, graduate, and professional students), until recently, few universities had explored the extension of successful living-learning concepts to graduate students. Separate graduate residence halls are designed to recognize the common characteristics of graduate students and the advantages of promoting interaction among these students with distinct interests and needs. However, few of these represent serious efforts to build living-learning programs that support the transition of students into graduate programs.

A recent example of an exemplary program is the University of California at Irvine's (UCI) Graduate First Year Initiative (GFYI), whose goal is to serve as a national model of "exceptional opportunities for graduate research, housing, and cocurricular activities." The GFYI program is designed to enhance and support the academic and cocurricular experiences of first-year UCI graduate students and to specifically address their transitional and developmental needs through coordinated resources and services within residential communities. The program focuses on expansion of housing for graduate students, a guarantee of on-campus housing for all Ph.D. and M.F.A. first-year students, and programmatic efforts to support these students. Implemented in fall 2006, the program accommodates approximately 80% of incoming graduate students, thus making these student-housing communities the connection point between the University and the new graduate student cohort.

The GFYI program, the result of comprehensive assessments with UCI students and national graduate reform studies, provides specialized programs and services that address the needs of specific target populations (i.e., graduate students with partners, 41%; families with children, 16%; and international students, 32%). Specific elements of the program include:

- An orientation to campus and community resources for students, spouses, and families, including walking tours offered in several languages
- A series of workshops designed to help international students with their adjustment to the campus and U.S. culture
- A series of programs on financial planning and related stress factors
- A campus-wide welcome event and reception for students and families
- A mentoring program using emeriti faculty on panels, dinners, and social events dealing with issues related to faculty careers, interdisciplinary research, and graduate student and professional development issues

Future plans include expansion of career planning activities, a comprehensive assessment of the GFYI program, a possible PFF[1]-based living-learning program and similar "professional interest group"-focused programs. Additional information concerning the UCI-GFYI program is available at http://www.housing.uci.edu/graduate.

Workshops for First-Year Graduate Students

New graduate students face many issues. Some are particular to the program of study, while others transcend disciplines and are shared issues by most new graduate students. Students often seek out peers with whom they can discuss these issues. Such discussions may involve senior graduate students or those with teaching assistant appointments, who informally serve as mentors to their newer colleagues. However, these informal discussions may provide incomplete or inaccurate information. A formal arrangement for discussions among students with common interests and needs that includes successful, experienced senior graduate students, faculty, and perhaps staff, can provide complete and accurate information and promote useful interchange, common understanding, and self-assurance among new graduate students. A wide variety of discussion venues among graduate students exist (e.g., weekly student seminars; introduction to departmental faculty research/scholarship areas; Friday afternoon socials).

Workshops for new graduate students that explore a variety of first-year issues and concerns are particularly effective in developing a sense of community and helping new students successfully negotiate the first-year transition. Workshops differ from the courses described in chapter 7 because sessions may extend beyond the typical one-hour classroom format and may consist of one session or, preferably, several regularly scheduled sessions (i.e., weekly or monthly) that extend over a few months, the first semester, or throughout the first year of graduate study. First-year graduate workshops may occur within a department or program, across a college, or at the campus level. Workshops that include some departmental, college-wide, and campus-level sessions may be especially useful. Topics may range from time management, milestones toward degree progress, and skills-building components (e.g., communications, writing for publication, oral presentations), to interviewing and job search techniques. In general, workshops provide greater opportunities for meaningful personal interchange among students and between students and presenter, which promotes the development of personal relationships.

"The Introduction to Mathematics" at Rutgers (IMR) provides an example of a weeklong departmental workshop that includes information and activities related to the program, the college, and the university (http://www.math.rutgers.edu/grad/IMR/IMR_2006.html). A first semester-long program entitled "A Little Practice, Help, and Advice" (ALPHA) is presented for students entering the Statistics and Actuarial Science graduate program at the University of Iowa (http://www.stat.uiowa.edu/~jblang/ALPHA). The site includes a list of topics covered in the program, with links to other resources that first-year students can access. Other examples include workshops offered for special groups of new graduate students, such as several for international students at the University of Iowa that focus on the life in Iowa, the U.S. classroom experience, employment options, tax assistance, and so forth (http://intl-programs.uiowa.edu/oiss/oissprogramsguide.htm).

Due, in part, to the popularity of workshops for first-year graduate students, many departments have developed additional workshops that include all graduate students. In some cases, workshops for all students may be interspersed with the first-year workshops, so that new graduate students interact with and form relationships with both cohort peers and senior graduate students. Florida State University offers professional development workshops geared to first-year students, such as "Navigating Graduate School;" and others for both first-year and advanced graduate students, such as "Research Resources and the University Library." Others are geared primarily to senior graduate students, although open to all, such as "Writing Research Articles" (http://www.gradstudies.fsu.edu/worksops.html). Michigan State University has an extensive array of graduate workshops (http://msu.edu/~gradschl/stuwork.htm) including "Setting Expectations and Resolving Conflict Between Graduate Students and Faculty" and "Responsible Conduct of Research."

First-year graduate workshops typically include presentations by departmental faculty and staff on policies and processes and invite discussions with students on the obligations and requirements for moving forward successfully through the first year in the program. Testimonials from senior graduate students are common presentations that are especially meaningful to first-year students. Involving senior graduate students in the planning and subsequent delivery of first-year graduate workshops or assigning senior students as TAs in first-year graduate courses can be especially valuable strategies for developing a sense of community and common purpose among all those involved in the program.

Departmental Advising and Service Programs

Many universities have centralized undergraduate advising, supplementing the efforts of a professional advising staff with self-assessment tools (often online) for students to monitor their progress toward university and major requirements. Undergraduate student service programs (e.g., counseling, career planning) also tend to consist of campus-wide centers that serve all students, although some professional colleges (e.g., business, education) have additional service centers that serve their own majors. Traditionally, most campus student advising and service centers have provided little if any support for the distinct and particular needs of graduate students. Within the past decade, several campus programs have extended some services to graduate students and a few universities have developed separate and complementary graduate student service centers and programs, as discussed in chapter 9.

Many departments supplement these campus efforts by providing discipline- and program-specific advising for their graduate students. In addition to the common practice of assigning new students or allowing them to choose an initial academic advisor, some programs have advising programs that assist students with such issues as choosing coherent programs of course work, developing thesis/dissertation topics, preparing for and delivering presentations at professional meetings and conferences, and professional networking. Some topics are of particular relevance to first-year students (e.g., advising on course work); others serve primarily advanced students, but they also provide a useful perspective for first-year students that can help them during their transition. Additionally, first-year students view such programs as assurance of departmental support beyond their first year of graduate study, which can positively affect their chances of success.

The mathematics department at the University of Iowa, for example, expanded its successful workshops for new international students to a series of workshops on topics ranging from those primarily focusing on the first-year experience (e.g., familiarization with the range of research in both mathematics and applied mathematical and computational sciences, choosing a research topic and mentor) issues relating to progress beyond the first year (e.g., preparing for comprehensive exams—a summer seminar run by senior graduate students for those having just completed the first year), to issues dealing with career preparation and placement. These efforts have significantly increased retention beyond the first year of graduate study.

Self-Assessment of the Transition Experience

Most students would welcome some means to assess their own progress toward program objectives, goals, and deadlines. A degree audit or progress checklist is available at many universities (some online) that allows undergraduate students to monitor their progress in completing degree requirements. Progress in graduate programs is a more complex issue, but a prominent feature of reports and initiatives to improve graduate education (Carnegie Foundation for the Advancement of Teaching, 2002; University of Washington, 2000; Woodrow Wilson National Fellowship Foundation, 2001) include recommendations for better and more timely feedback of students' performance. Many graduate schools have created requirements to provide graduate student evaluation and feedback. For example, Michigan State University has developed a web site (http://www.msu.edu/~gradschl/progress.htm), which includes the rationale for annual progress evaluations and a template for departments to develop program-specific progress evaluation instruments for both master's and doctoral-level graduate students.

A simple extension of these ideas suggests the possibility of creating an online graduate program self-assessment tool that would allow students to monitor and understand their transition experience. The desirability of such a tool is suggested by the reluctance of many graduate students to approach faculty about their performance and progress toward meeting requirements. Thus, a recommendation for the future includes the development of a self-assessment tool of graduate student performance by graduate school or departmental graduate administrators. The list in Figure 1 includes items that might serve as a template for development of an online instrument that students could use to assess their progress in acclimating to the graduate program during their first-year. Not all items are necessarily applicable to all students or programs, but a choice among those listed with items added that reflect the concerns or needs of individuals students or programs can result in a useful checklist. In addition to standard items, students should be encouraged to add their own "benchmarks" for socialization and professionalization within the department, the university, and the profession.

Graduate programs usually provide information and assistance concerning most of the items on this list, although students should be informed that it is their obligation to seek additional information or help as needed to assess their performance and progress. In using the list, it is suggested that students check an item once it has been completed, when they understand the role it will play and their responsibility in meeting the department's and their own expectations, or as they regularly attend to an item (i.e., seminars).

Pre-Entrance Activities

_____ Familiarize yourself with departmental/ program literature and other information.

_____ Process all forms and paperwork required by the program and the university.

_____ Seek information on or secure housing (e.g., department, local paper).

Academic Advising and Mentoring

_____ Understand the requirements for the degree you are pursuing (list each requirement and deadline and check off when met).

_____ Meet with an academic advisor (assigned or one you choose) to develop a tailored program (e.g., courses, activities) that meets your goals and interests.

_____ Obtain information on funding possibilities (e.g., TA, RA, other assignments).

_____ Become acquainted with areas of faculty research/scholarship.

_____ Choose a faculty mentor for your area of specialization (if not assigned to you).

Integration Into the Program

_____ Attend orientation session and any opening social events.

_____ Become acquainted with other students in the entering cohort.

_____ Become acquainted with advanced students in the program.

_____ Meet all program faculty members.

_____ Introduce yourself to program staff members.

_____ Attend functions that allow social interaction with faculty, students, staff.

_____ Develop first-name or appropriate personal relationships with a sizeable fraction of program faculty, students, and staff.

_____ Initiate discussions or social activities involving other program members.

_____ Attend departmental seminars and post-seminar events.

Figure 1. Checklist for self-assessment of graduate transition experience.

Transforming Transition Strategies Into Sustainable Strategies for Success

As suggested earlier, successful first-year transition programs occupy an important and distinct position in graduate education, and successful programs position the student along a favorable trajectory toward successfully completing his/her graduate degree. The transition to graduate school may be significantly influenced, however, by providing early information to new graduate students concerning later stages of the program. The differences between undergraduate and graduate education become amplified as a student moves beyond the first year into the later stages of their graduate programs. Many graduate schools and departments have thus developed programs to assist students at this later point in their graduate careers. For those programs that have done so, it is helpful to provide information about such programs to new graduate students early in their first year. If first-year students are able to affiliate with these programs in some way, participation becomes an evolutionary experience that begins during the transition period and extends through all stages of the program. Moreover, the presence of these programs may give first-year students an added sense of security about their future endeavors in the program and can be a positive factor in realizing a successful transition to graduate study. The following programs are some notable examples that have yielded positive transition outcomes for first-year graduate students.

Jobs Skills Programs

Skills needed in most employment sectors are substantially different than those required for success in graduate education. Often, graduate programs do not include opportunities for students to acquire job-related skills during their graduate career. The notable exceptions include some business, education, and health-related professional programs, which are mostly master's programs. Calls for changes in graduate education have highlighted the need to include career planning and preparation and development of jobs skills in graduate programs (AAU, 1998; The Carnegie Foundation for the Advancement of Teaching, 2002; National Academies Committee, 1995; University of Washington, 2000). Programs that have responded to these recommendations include the Preparing Future Faculty (PFF) program for doctoral students aspiring for academic careers and the Professional Science Master's (PSM) and Professional Master's (PMA) initiatives for students desiring non-academic employment. If students are convinced before entering a graduate program or during the first year of the program that they will acquire skills they need to obtain a job and pursue a successful career, it is more likely that they will have a successful first year of graduate study and subsequently persevere and complete the degree.

A common lesson from the PFF, PSM, PMA, and other formal programs to change or enhance graduate education is that graduate students should be exposed to career-related issues during their first year and that career planning and development should be integral aspects throughout the graduate experience. Specifically, graduate students should have opportunities within their graduate program to acquire the skills they need to begin the job search process, negotiate terms of employment, and be prepared to successfully commence their career.

Following is a list of topics that various graduate programs have included in program components intended to acquaint students with facets of the world of work and to better prepare them for the jobs likely to be available following completion of their degree:

- ◇ Summary of placement and employment history of recent program graduates
- ◇ Survey of current and projected job market for program graduates
- ◇ Resumé and portfolio development
- ◇ Writing and presentation skills development for appropriate workplaces
- ◇ Interviewing skills, including mock and taped interviews
- ◇ Social and personal interaction skills (including even such seemingly basic skills as dining etiquette and social conversation)
- ◇ Negotiation skills for employment conditions, salary, and support
- ◇ Basic ethics issues for research/scholarship and for business and government
- ◇ Team-work projects—often solicited from the employment sector—typical of problems that new employees experience
- ◇ Internship or externship opportunities in appropriate employment sectors

Many programs have found that alumni or other persons from the employment sector are excellent resources and often better presenters of these topics than are faculty. Abundant anecdotal information points to unexpected results of graduate programs engaging with the world of work: Alumni and other employees are excellent resources for program advisory boards, external members of students' thesis/dissertation committees, and external support (i.e., financial and in-kind) for graduate programs. Such persons also frequently serve as presenters of work-related components of graduate programs and, as their involvement with the program evolves, as adjunct faculty who teach or team-teach graduate courses with other faculty members. Those who interact with graduate students can be important resources for students as they enter the job market. Additionally, such persons often help create internship opportunities for graduate students and/or placement opportunities for program graduates.

Career Preparation Programs

Aside from the centralized or campus-based graduate support programs discussed in earlier chapters (e.g., university career counseling and placement centers), there is an array of programs that address various aspects of jobs skills and career preparation that can serve as resources for introducing job-related components into a graduate program. Both applicants and graduate students report that knowledge of these programs provides a perspective that positively affects the first-year transition experience; this is especially true of programs that allow affiliation or participation of first-year students. There are two programs that have become national movements with many participating institutions, both of which usually allow involvement by first-year students, and both of which have been shown to be positive factors in helping students make a successful first-year transition to graduate study—Preparing Future Faculty and professional master's programs. Personal contacts and web sites of departments or professional societies are excellent sources of additional information on these and other programs.

Preparing Future Faculty Programs: Career preparation for doctoral students. Faculty positions at research, doctoral, comprehensive, liberal arts universities, and community colleges represent the largest segment of employment for recipients of doctoral (Ph.D.) degrees. Research and doctoral universities have traditionally emphasized and rewarded faculty devotion to research/scholarship that expands the boundaries of knowledge in the field. Traditional models of doctoral education have excelled in preparing graduates to assume a research role within the types of universities from which they received their degrees. Today, nearly all hiring institutions, including many research and doctoral institutions, expect faculty to be active in research/scholarship and to be effective teachers and good academic citizens able to work effectively with an increasingly diverse group of college students. Yet, preparation for these varied faculty roles has not been a prominent feature of traditional models of doctoral education. Preparing Future Faculty programs were developed to supplement doctoral education by adding components that address preparation for these various faculty roles, while preserving the historical pre-eminence of developing skills in research/scholarship that are the hallmark of the Ph.D. degree.

Programs to better prepare students who aspire to college and university academic careers have existed for some time within colleges of education with isolated examples elsewhere. The broadening of this concept by the Council of Graduate Schools' (CGS) Preparing Future Faculty (PFF) initiative began in 1993 at research universities, in collaboration with several partners representing different types of hiring institutions, to introduce explicit elements into doctoral education that better prepare graduates across the disciplines for academic careers. Several professional societies[2] also received grants from CGS to promote development of PFF programs among disciplinary departments. Many other institutions have since begun similar programs, so that PFF today represents a prominent national movement that has become an integral aspect of doctoral education at a significant number of major universities. The need for preparation recognizing these various faculty roles is especially critical at this time, when more than two thirds of undergraduate students indicate their intention of pursuing graduate education (Sax et al., 2003) and the large number of faculty expected to retire early in this century, foreshadowing the need to hire many new faculty members.

PFF enhances doctoral training through integrated components that include:

- ◇ Research that may include not only the traditional scholarship of discovery, but also that of integration, application, and teaching/learning (Boyer, 1990)
- ◇ Introduction to the academic profession and the diversity of faculty roles among various types of institutions that hire doctoral graduates
- ◇ Teaching assignments that are varied and increasingly independent
- ◇ Mentoring in all areas of professional development by research faculty as well as by faculty at partner PFF institutions
- ◇ Exposure to and experience with the service roles and responsibilities of faculty
- ◇ Experience of faculty life at different types of institutions (including in many cases, supervised or team teaching or internships at partner institutions)

A history of PFF, details of established PFF programs, recommendations for creating PFF-like programs, and information on publications specific to the sciences and mathematics and to humanities and social sciences is available from the CGS web site (www.preparing-faculty.org).

Professional Master's Programs: Career preparation for master's students. As discussed in chapter 1, master's education is the largest and most varied segment of graduate education. The issues students face in transitioning to master's programs are generally quite different from those related to doctoral programs. Students who enter master's programs are more likely to make a successful transition to graduate study if they perceive the program to be a departmental priority and if there is a clear connection between the goals, course work, other requirements of the program, and the student's educational and personal goals—whether entry into doctoral study or an entry-level professional position related to the master's degree.

The master's degree in business, education, public administration, practice-oriented health sciences, and a few other professional fields constitutes the common requirement for entry into professional practice. Yet, the Ph.D. has been considered the desired and, in many instances, required credential for professional advancement. Thus, most master's programs in these areas have been regarded either as a degree awarded to those who were unable to complete the doctorate or as a degree that prepares graduates to enter a doctoral program. These trends occur at a time when many national studies indicate that the future workforce will require many more people with graduate-level training, especially in the sciences and social sciences, specifically at the master's level. These same studies stipulate that the focus of the master's degree must be to prepare students for entry into professional work in the business, government, and nonprofit sectors.

Within the past decade, new options have developed within master's education for students pursuing these areas. These include the Professional Science Master's (PSM) degree in the sciences and mathematics and the Professional Master's (PMA) degree in the humanities and social sciences. Such programs should attract greater numbers of undergraduate arts and sciences majors who otherwise would not pursue graduate education in their chosen field of specialization.

The PSM and PMA degrees include advanced core courses in the discipline comparable to the traditional M.S. and M.A. degrees and supplement this with professional components (e.g., principles of business or public policy, ethics in the workplace), activities to gain workplace-related skills (e.g., communications, presentation, personal interaction skills), and experience that is directly related to work cultures (e.g., group projects, internships). Students in the first year of such professional masters' programs are provided with an overview of professional opportunities awaiting graduates. During their program, students also get work experience, usually as interns, within a workplace related to their interests. Thus, students from the beginning of their program can see a clear relation between the requirements of their master's program and entry into the world of professional work. This clarity of purpose and program structure mimics that of the M.B.A. (or M.S.W., M.P.A., and other established professional master's degrees) and should contribute to a successful first-year transition experience and enhanced degree completion. These expectations are being realized among the first group of these PSM and PMA programs established since 1997. Additional information on PSM programs can be obtained from the national web site, www.sciencemasters.com. Information on PSM and PMA programs is also available from the Council of Graduate Schools' web site, www.cgsnet.org, and from a recent CGS publication on establishing professional master's programs (Sims, 2006).

Placement: Career Preparation for All Graduate Students

Students entering graduate programs have a significant interest in employment opportunities for graduates and assistance seeking a first position. First-year transition programs need to touch on these issues and instill confidence among new students about employment prospects, assistance in the job search process, and initial placement at the end of their graduate degree program. University placement programs have primarily served undergraduate students, particularly those from professional colleges/schools such as business, education, and the health professions, although some centralized placement offices have recently begun to offer some services for graduate students. Departments have often delegated to faculty mentors the responsibility of assisting graduates with placement, which is especially true for doctoral students seeking academic employment and for master's students seeking entry into doctoral programs. Few examples exist of formal programs to assist graduate students with placement or to better prepare them to navigate the job search terrain and to negotiate job offers. Such assistance is recommended in many reports on improving U.S. graduate education, as a "capstone" to professional and career development programs that begin early in the graduate career (i.e., during the first-year transition period) and continue and expand (see above section on jobs skills programs) as students proceed through their program toward degree completion and the often parallel processes of exploring employment opportunities and seeking job offers. Professional master's programs, especially PSM and PMA programs, generally have incorporated placement as an integral program component, as have some PFF and other doctoral-level programs.

The American Studies program at the University of Iowa offers an example of a comprehensive placement guide relating to academic employment that is provided to entering graduate students. This guide includes information such as:

- ◇ Where to look for notices of open positions
- ◇ When to apply
- ◇ What to include in a letter of application
- ◇ How to construct an appropriate curriculum vita or resumé
- ◇ What to include in a placement file

- What to submit as writing samples for various types of positions
- How to prepare a teaching packet
- What to expect after you have applied
- How to prepare for and participate in a successful job interview
- Convention interviews
- Campus interviews
- What to expect as a job offer
- What to expect from offers of temporary positions

Other graduate programs establish workshops that allow students to create and refine their job-related documents (e.g., application letters, resumés, portfolios), undergo mock interviews (which may be taped to provide feedback), and develop statements on goals (i.e., teaching/research/scholarship) for those aspiring to academic careers. Although advanced graduate students are most directly affected by placement concerns, the anxiety of new students surrounding these issues is reduced by early information on how the program addresses the issues. When programs provide this information early, students are more likely to successfully negotiate other issues that more directly affect the process of transitioning to graduate study during their first year.

Conclusion

In addition to the many transitioning strategies and programs described in earlier chapters, a number of opportunities exist for graduate programs to affect the first-year transition experience positively and to increase persistence to later stages of graduate study. These opportunities exist through every stage of students' exploration, application, admission, curriculum, and first-year program activities. Collectively, all transitioning strategies and programs are part of a larger continuum of graduate professional development services that extend throughout the formal curriculum and degree requirements and include areas of career planning, job skills development, job search processes, placement, and career development assistance. First-year graduate transitioning programs are an essential first step in helping graduate students acclimate to graduate study, succeed in completing their degrees, and preparing for a rewarding and successful career.

Notes

[1] Preparing Future Faculty, a national set of programs designed for doctoral students aspiring to academic careers.

[2] American Association of Physics Teachers, American Chemical Society, American Historical Association, American Mathematical Society, Mathematical Association of America; American Political Science Association, American Psychological Association, American Sociological Association, National Communication Association, National Council of Teachers of English, and the Special Interest Group on Computer Science Education of the Association for Computing Machinery

References

Association of American Universities (AAU). (1998). *Report and recommendations on graduate education.* Washington, DC: Author.

Boyer, E. (1990). *Scholarship reconsidered: Priorities of the professoriate.* Baltimore, MD: The Carnegie Foundation.

Denecke, D. D., & Slimowitz, J. (2004). *Ph.D. completion and attrition: Policy, numbers, leadership, and next steps.* Washington, DC: Council of Graduate Schools.

The Carnegie Foundation for the Advancement of Teaching. (2002). *Carnegie initiative on the doctorate.* Retrieved from March 26, 2008, from http://www.carnegiefoundation.org/programs/sub.asp?key=29

Lovitts, B. E. (2001). *Leaving the ivory tower: The causes and consequences of departure from doctoral study.* New York, Rowman & Littlefield.

National Academies Committee on Science, Engineering, and Public Policy. (1995). *Reshaping the education of scientists and engineers.* Washington, DC: National Academy Press.

National Academies Committee on Science, Engineering, and Public Policy. (2000). *Enhancing the postdoctoral experience for scientists and engineers.* Washington, DC: National Academy Press.

Sax, L. J., Lindholm, J. A., Astin, A. W., Korn, W. S., Saenz, V. B., & Mahoney, K. M. (2003). *The American freshman: National norms for fall 2003,* Los Angeles: Higher Education Research Institute, UCLA.

Sims, L. B. (2006). *Professional master's education: A CGS guide to establishing programs.* Washington, DC: The Council of Graduate Schools.

University of Washington. (2000). *Re-envisioning the Ph.D.* Retrieved March 26, 2008 from, http://www.grad.washington.edu/envision

Woodrow Wilson National Fellowship Foundation. (2001). *The responsive Ph.D.* Retrieved March 26, 2008, from http://www.woodrow.org/responsivephd

Chapter Eleven

Conclusion: Recommendations for Practice

Kenneth A. Tokuno

This monograph introduces the idea that students experience a critical transition during the first year of graduate study. Yet, given the fragmented nature of this population, can we assume graduate students share a common need for assistance in adjusting to programs for advanced degrees? As a whole, the chapters confirm that more support is needed for students no matter whether they are fresh from their undergraduate study or returning after 20 years in the work force; whether they are from New York or New Zealand; whether they work full time, part-time, or not at all; and whether they are located on campus or a thousand miles away.

A secondary focus of this monograph is an emphasis on the need for support for master's students. With more than 90% of all graduate students pursuing a master's degree and a large number of institutions granting master's degrees only, this attention is long overdue. Those institutions will benefit from this volume, but it is hoped that universities whose emphasis has been on doctoral education will also benefit from the ideas offered here. Chapter 3, by Josh Alexander and Michelle Maher plays a key role in this regard, but the needs of master's students should be apparent throughout the monograph. Given the short time that most master's students have to navigate the path toward degree, a successful transition is even more critical for them than for doctoral students.

Anyone who is concerned about methods to improve retention and completion rates among graduate students would be well advised to consider the beginning point of the transition as the moment the prospective student makes initial contact with the institution, whether via the Internet, a phone call, or a visit to the campus. These initial contacts lay the groundwork for the more intense transition challenges to follow. The monograph makes the case that what occurs at the beginning of the student's term in the program is likely to have a profound effect on him or her for some time, determining eventual success or failure.

Although it is less apparent, an important point to connect across the chapters is the idea that graduate students must make a transition from being competitive with other students to being cooperative with their peers. At the undergraduate level, students tend to study as individuals competing for the highest grades and academic honors. At the graduate level, there is no less stress on grades, but there is a need to become part of a community of scholars. Students need to become skilled at working in conjunction with their faculty, peers, and other scholars if they are to be successful.

What steps should institutions take, then, to develop or improve programs and initiatives designed to facilitate graduate students success?

- *Gain the cooperation of the principal players.* Enlisting partners to create change is not so much a matter of funds or space or personnel as it is about wanting to create change. For example, the learning communities concept discussed in chapter 8 can be adapted for use across a variety of programs. Similarly, the principles underlying graduate student centers or orientations can be used to design programs in a variety of contexts.
- *Research the needs of your own students.* While this monograph did not address the specific needs of all sub-populations of graduate students, it should be readily apparent that the ideas presented can be applied to almost any group if it is carefully combined with an awareness of the specific needs of those groups. While it is beyond the scope of this monograph to explain how a needs assessment is done, it is always a good idea to do regular assessments to see what are the current needs the graduate student population on an individual campus or in an individual department.

  Students should be involved not only in conducting such an assessment but also in designing and implementing any efforts to address the needs identified by the assessment. For example, Michael Poock, in chapter 6, specifically points out the need to provide an orientation experience for part-time graduate students. He goes on to suggest the importance of involving students in planning and building a sense of community through orientation. Such principles can be applied to any group whether they are students with disabilities, military veterans, married students, or students studying at a distance.
- *Communicate actively.* It does no good to provide services and resources if students do not know about them. An overriding principle that can be derived from these chapters is that students need to be kept informed of their role as graduate students and the resources available to them to help them make progress toward their degrees. Accessible locations, be they virtual or real, should be made intentionally available to students. Too often, information is posted on web sites with the expectation that students will see it and read it, but more active delivery methods are necessary for effective communication.

  Lydia Soleil presents the most ambitious concept for intentionally supporting graduate students in transition in her chapter on graduate centers. To be fully institutionalized, graduate centers would require the support of the Graduate Dean or the Chief Student Affairs Office or both. Institutions with the vision to create such centers will be able to engage in active communication more readily. Given the increased number of distance learning programs, as well as part-time graduate students, the idea of incorporating some of the elements of a graduate center into a virtual online center should also be a consideration.

  Chapters 6 and 7 also suggest outstanding vehicles for providing important information to new graduate students and an opportunity to meet other graduate students, staff, and faculty. At the program level, a fair question is to ask whether it is better to have a brief orientation or a course introducing students to graduate study? A course provides more time for students to become acquainted with the degree program, its faculty, and each other. Yet, it also displaces course time needed for substantive subject matter and requires a lot of faculty time. Though a program-level orientation cannot cover all the topics required, it is brief and less-labor intensive for faculty. If the time and expense of a course are too great, departments may opt to combine an orientation with a thorough graduate student handbook or ongoing workshops as described in chapter 10.

◇ *Create a sense of community.* Some combination of the programs and practices discussed in this monograph will send the clear message to transitioning students that they are part of an academic community. Of course, nothing creates a sense of community like a true learning community as discussed by Dick Pratt and myself in chapter 8. It bears repeating, however, that even if the learning community idea cannot be fully implemented, its underlying principles can be extracted to good effect. The idea of matriculating students through cohorts is one of the simpler ones.

It is still early in the 21st century, but it is late to be realizing the growing importance of advanced degrees for the future of our country and, indeed, the world. As more nations provide higher levels of education, they will continue to look to the United States as the model for graduate education. If they find that we are no longer providing quality education, we will begin to lose ground as the century rolls forward. Such quality should be advanced not only in the classrooms, seminars, and labs of our colleges but also in the way we help our students enter, adjust, and advance toward their educational objectives. This monograph introduces readers to various ways we can do that. It is up to us as members of the educational community to see that it happens.

About the Authors

JOSHUA ALEXANDER is a community director at the University of North Carolina at Chapel Hill. Prior to UNC, Josh worked for two years as a resident director at Pacific Lutheran University in Tacoma, Washington. Alexander graduated with a M.Ed. in Higher Education and Student Affairs from the University of South Carolina in May of 2006 where he researched the transitional needs of masters degree candidates. Prior to USC, Josh studied music (vocal) at the University of North Carolina at Greensboro, where he received a B.A. in Music.

JAN ALLEN is associate dean for Ph.D. Programs at Columbia University in the Graduate School of Arts and Sciences. She was a faculty member at the University of Tennessee (1982-2002), where she served as assistant dean in the Graduate School. She also was associate dean of the Graduate School at Northwestern University (2002-2005). Her current research focuses on research ethics and mentoring of graduate students. She has taught transition and professional skills courses and seminars for graduate students, including Academic Acculturation and Developing Future Faculty as Teacher-Scholars (at Tennessee) and Preparing Future Faculty (at Northwestern and Columbia). Her Ph.D. is in child development from Purdue University.

MAUREEN SNOW ANDRADE is associate dean at Utah Valley University. Prior to this, she was associate professor at Brigham Young University Hawai'i (BYUH), where she taught ESL and TESOL courses. She was the director of the ESL program at BYUH for nine years and served as chair of the English Language Teaching and Learning Department and editor of the *TESL Reporter*. She has an Ed.D. in higher education leadership from the University of Southern California, an M.A. in English from Brigham Young University, and a graduate certificate in TESL from Brigham Young University. Her professional interests include teaching English for academic purposes, content-B.A.sed language instruction, program assessment, and adjustment and retention issues for international students.

CHRIS M. GOLDE is associate vice provost for graduate education at Stanford University. From 2001 to 2006 she was a senior scholar at the Carnegie Foundation for the Advancement of Teaching, serving as research director for the Carnegie Initiative on the Doctorate (CID). Prior to Carnegie, she was an assistant professor in the department of educational administration at the University of Wisconsin-Madison. Golde writes and presents extensively about graduate education. Publications include co-author of *The Formation of Scholars: Rethinking Doctoral Education for the 21st-Century* (2008), co-editor of *Envisioning the Future of Doctoral Education: Preparing Stewards of the Discipline* (2006), and co-author of *At Cross Purposes* (2001). She has published research articles on doctoral student attrition, doctoral pedagogy, and disciplinary differences in doctoral student experiences. Her Ph.D. is in education from Stanford University.

MICHELLE MAHER is an associate professor of higher education administration and associate director for graduate teaching excellence with the Center for Teaching Excellence at the University of South Carolina. In this capacity, she serves as the doctoral program coordinator and teaches classes on institutional assessment and college teaching. Her research is focused on areas of adult and postsecondary learning.

MICHAEL C. POOCK is an associate professor in the doctoral program in educational leadership/higher education at East Carolina University in Greenville, North Carolina. He holds a Ph.D. in higher education administration and master's degrees in public administration and mass communication. His research interests are graduate education, enrollment management, and the application of Web technologies.

RICHARD PRATT is the director of the Public Administration Program at the University of Hawai'i at Manoa in Honolulu. He received a master's degree in educational administration from the University of Denver and a doctorate in political science from the University of Hawai'i. He has been interested in higher education reform. That interest has led him to work with schools in the US and Asia on reform projects. His other endeavors focus on organizational change, the political environment of public institutions, and leadership in public service.

KIM RAPP is the associate director of the Center for African Studies at Stanford University. Before arriving at Stanford, Rapp was a research assistant for the Carnegie Initiative on the Doctorate (CID) project at the Carnegie Foundation for the Advancement Teaching. She earned her Ph.D. in higher education leadership and policy analysis from the University of Wisconsin-Madison. Her dissertation examined the effects of student participation in non-degree granting interdisciplinary programs on doctoral student retention. Her writing and research projects focus on the administration of academic programs in higher education.

LYDIA SOLEIL is the assistant director of Teaching Assistant Programs and Graduate Student Development at the Georgia Institute of Technology. Soleil earned her Ph.D. in physiology at the University of California, Davis, where she became very interested in graduate student development through her role as a teaching assistant consultant. Soleil has a passion for working to improve the quality of the graduate student experience and spent six years at the University of California, Irvine, where she held three different positions focused on graduate student development: associate director of the Teaching, Learning and Technology Center, first-year initiatives coordinator for Student Housing, and graduate student career consultant for the Career Center.

LESLIE B. SIMS was chair in the Department of Chemistry at University of Arkansas, dean of the College of Physical and Mathematical Sciences, and associate vice chancellor for research at North Carolina State University and associate provost for graduate education and graduate dean at the University of Iowa. From 2001-2005, he was Senior Scholar in Residence at the Council of Graduate Schools in Washington, DC. Since 2005, he has been a consultant to several institutions and agencies in his areas of expertise across the spectrum of graduate education and research.

MIYA T. SIMPSON is director of Academic Program Review at Virginia Tech, where she also earned her Ph.D. in educational leadership and policy studies. Her research interests include issues of access, retention, and educational attainment among underrepresented populations. Simpson's dissertation research examined the transition experiences of ethnic minority graduate students.

VINCENT TINTO received his Ph.D. in education and sociology from The University of Chicago and is a Distinguished University Professor at Syracuse University. He has carried out research and has written extensively on higher education, particularly on student retention and the impact of learning communities on student growth and attainment. His current research, funded by grants from the Lumina Foundation for Education and the William and Flora Hewlett Foundation focuses on the impact of learning communities on the academic achievements of underprepared, low-income college students in urB.A.n two-year and four-year colleges.

KENNETH A. TOKUNO is the associate dean for Graduate Education at the University of Hawai'i at Manoa. He served on the advisory board of the National Resource Center for The First-Year Experience and Students in Transition. Prior to taking his position at the University of Hawai'i, he was instrumental in the development of first-year transition programs in the form of the Freshman Interest Group program at the University of Washington. He received his Ph.D. from the University of Hawai'i at Manoa.